The Vision Obscured

The Vision Obscured

Perceptions of Some Twentieth-Century Catholic Novelists

edited by

MELVIN J. FRIEDMAN

FORDHAM UNIVERSITY PRESS
New York   1970

© Copyright FORDHAM UNIVERSITY PRESS 1970
Library of Congress Catalog Card Number: 72-126130
ISBN 0-8232-0890-7

Printed in the United States of America

In memory of FREDERICK J. HOFFMAN (1909–1967)

CONTENTS

Introduction

MELVIN J. FRIEDMAN

> Beckett does not believe in God, though he seems to imply
> that God has committed an unforgivable sin by not
> existing.
>
> ANTHONY BURGESS, *The Novel Now*

THERE ARE FEW EVENTS in modern literary history which
have had quite the symbolic impact of Paul Claudel's religious
"illumination" on Christmas day, 1886, in Notre-Dame Cathedral. The event served as a useful paradigm for what
Martin Turnell has called in his *Modern Literature and
Christian Faith* "a radically Christian standpoint." Claudel's
urgency about his newly discovered Catholicism had much to
say about certain literary tensions peculiar to the twentieth
century. He offered, Turnell tells us, a point of view steeped
in the "disregard" for "the changes which have taken place
during the past four hundred years" and committed himself
"resolutely against the grain of his age." Much Roman Catholic literature has come out of Claudel's religious experience
of Christmas day 1886 and out of his literary solution as a
poet in the *Cinq grandes odes* and as a playwright in *Tête
d'or* and *L'Annonce faite à Marie*—but usually in a negative
way. Many writers, especially in France, underwent "conversions" at the feet of Claudel but soon abandoned their

1

early Claudelian *chants de renoncement* (Henri Peyre's expression) in favor of a less wearying literary orthodoxy.

Conor Cruise O'Brien, in the 1963 edition of *Maria Cross,* speaks of Paul Claudel as a "Counter-reformation Catholic," as "an old heretic-fighter, a man not of the thirteenth but of the seventeenth century." He means that Claudel lacks the benignity of the medieval Church and more clearly favors a verbal militancy which we associate clerically with Bossuet and in a more literary sense with Boileau. Most twentieth-century Catholic literature has taken a more generous and modest direction, ultimately away from the grimness and severity of the Claudelian model.

A typical case is Jacques Rivière, who started his career in the shadow of Claudel and French Symbolism and finally found himself (in Martin Turnell's words) "on the side of the Catholic modernists." When Claudel connected his experience in Notre-Dame Cathedral with his reading of Rimbaud's poetry and spoke of Rimbaud as being a mystic in the savage state, he started an interesting fusion which was to affect other Catholics. Thus Jacques Rivière seemed to echo Claudel when he spoke of Rimbaud as someone exempt from "original sin" and also as an inspired precursor of Christianity. Rivière seems implicitly to reject his early Rimbaud–Claudel passion in the anti-Symbolist remarks made in his essay on "le roman d'aventure" and in his dedication of his first novel, *Aimée,* to "Marcel Proust, grand peintre de l'amour." Martin Turnell ends his brilliant little book on Rivière (part of the "Studies in Modern European Literature and Thought" series) by calling him a "professional *tourmenté.*" In other words, Rivière came to wear his Catholicism more easily and gracefully than did Claudel, but not without having suffered the penalties of avoiding "a radically Christian standpoint" in favor of a more compromising middle road.

We see Rivière moving away from Claudel in the years following his World War I internment. An easy formula, accepted by many of Rivière's critics, is that he was moving in the direction of Proust. His series of essays on him, collected in *Marcel Proust* (1924); his long exchange of letters with him between 1911 and 1922; his dedication to him of *Aimée*; and his indefatigable efforts to convince Gide and others connected with the *Nouvelle Revue Française* circle of the worth of *A la recherche du temps perdu*—all offer proof of Rivière's new literary stand. There is no doubt that there is an increasing secularization in Rivière's attitude from the time of *Aimée* (written during the war but not published till 1922) and the Proust essays. *Aimée*, the only novel Rivière completed, is a Catholic novel in much the way that Mauriac's *Le Désert de l'amour* is a Catholic novel. Martin Turnell has explained the relationship between Rivière's three characters in an interesting way: "The triangle François–Marthe–Aimée stands very clearly for Weakness–Normality–Perversity." The triangular relationship involving Raymond, Dr. Courrèges, and Maria Cross in Mauriac's novel might suggest another set of "humours" to us. It is curious that both Rivière and Mauriac should have given their heroines such blatantly allegorical names: Aimée and Maria Cross. And "torment" is such an important word for both novels. The title Mauriac gave his study of Rivière underscores this condition of art which they held in common, *Le Tourment de Jacques Rivière*.

The moderate, toned-down Catholicism of *Aimée* and of the unfinished novel *Florence,* of the essays on Proust, and of the posthumous collection *A la Trace de Dieu* is an essential part of the "professional *tourmenté*" Martin Turnell aptly described. The one aspect of Rivière's life which is not easily accounted for under this useful rubric is the friendship and deeply moving exchange of letters with Alain-Fournier. The details of their meeting, the terms of their Montaignean friendship, Rivière's marriage with Fournier's sister Isabelle are now a secure part of literary history. An interesting contrast would come out of a parallel reading of the Rivière–Claudel correspondence and the Rivière–Fournier correspondence—which cover approximately the same years. The letters to Claudel have an austere, tormented quality; the letters to Fournier are more relaxed and assured. One might explain the difference by borrowing a well-known image from Henry Adams: when Rivière wrote to Claudel one can imagine the Archangel Michael of Mont-Saint-Michel in the background; the Virgin of Chartres more appropriately sets the tone for the letters to Alain-Fournier.

The latter correspondence was cut off abruptly with Fournier's death in the early months of the First World War. Like Rivière he was the author of a single finished novel. *Le Grand Meaulnes (The Wanderer* in its American translation) has enjoyed a secure place in the history of the modern novel; Stanley Edgar Hyman's recent statement about it in *The New Yorker* is fairly typical: ". . . how seminal 'The Wanderer' now seems, influencing everyone from Graham Greene to Günter Grass." There is something of the magic-lantern-of-childhood atmosphere about Fournier's novel with its elaborate itineraries into the unknown. It is easy enough to see the Rimbaud who caught Claudel's and Rivière's fancy in *Le Grand Meaulnes.* When Augustin Meaulnes, the seventeen-year-old hero, asks the narrator of the novel "But how could a man, who had once leapt at one bound into Paradise, get used to living like everybody else?" we are in the world of Rimbaud's "Le Bateau ivre" and *Illuminations. Le Grand Meaulnes,* much like Rimbaud's poetry, might be said to offer that interesting paradox of the Christian vision of life before the coming of Christ.

"Passion" is probably the word that best explains the clerical innocence of Alain-Fournier's novel. (I am using the word much as Isabelle Rivière did in her volume of memoirs of her brother, *Vie et passion d'Alain-Fournier.*) The strange "passion" Meaulnes displays for Yvonne de Galais—who bears an uncanny relationship to the "princesse lointaine" of French fable—has a mystical turn to it; in a sense it resembles a religious experience. Meaulnes' language on several occasions give us this sense; for example: "I was at the height of what stands for perfection and pure motive in anyone's heart, a height I shall never reach again."

Alain-Fournier went through much the same literary baptism as Rivière, except that their choice of models was different. While Rivière looked to his salvation as a Catholic by reading and exchanging letters with Claudel, Alain-Fournier was reading Jules Laforgue (like his Anglo-American contemporary T. S. Eliot). Each had an early, heady dose of Symbolism—but from a different source. In a sense Fournier got Symbolism out of his system by writing the purest "adventure" novel since *Robinson Crusoe* (one of his early loves). He was killed in the 1914–18 War a year after *Le Grand Meaulnes* was published. Rivière, during this time, was publishing essays on Rimbaud in the *Nouvelle Revue Française*—which seemed to be his way of getting Symbolism out of his system.

The French Symbolist movement and youthful experiences of Catholicism seemed to go hand-in-hand with these two representative figures of French literature in the second decade (the war years) of the twentieth century. Martin Turnell's judgment of Rivière as mainly a literary critic is a reliable one. Alain-Fournier will always be known pre-eminently as the author of *Le Grand Meaulnes*. The Rivière–Fournier correspondence, covering the years 1905–1914, is as fine an example of the genre *initiation du poète* as we have: initiation in both the literary and the spiritual sense.

There is another experience with the Roman Catholic Church which offered literary expression during the same years. I am thinking of James Joyce's systematic attempt to turn his back on his Catholicism and reject it out-of-hand—with quite mixed results. The matter has been studied by some of Joyce's most articulate commentators and we already have a quite impressive shelf of criticism devoted to it: William T. Noon, s.j.'s *Joyce and Aquinas*, J. Mitchell Morse's *The Sympathetic Alien: James Joyce and Catholicism*, and Kevin Sullivan's *Joyce Among the Jesuits* are perhaps the sturdiest examples. *A Portrait of the Artist as a Young Man* is a fictive working-out of a young-artist-in-progress's spiritual and aesthetic dilemmas. The third chapter offers a terrifying view of the Church through a linking together of several hell-fire sermons with their Jesuit source in St. Ignatius Loyola. The

fifth chapter, liberally borrowing its vocabulary from St.
Thomas Aquinas, presents an aesthetics which has the same
rigidity as the religious doctrines of the third chapter. Just
as Alain-Fournier and Rivière seemed to get their religion
through a literary source, so Joyce's Stephen Dedalus seems
to get his literature through a religious source. Joyce, in *A
Portrait,* seemed to be trying to get Aquinas out of his system
just as Rivière during the same years was trying to rid himself of Claudel's "radically Christian standpoint."

The Catholic Church becomes increasingly a subject of
mockery in Joyce's later work, especially in *Ulysses* with its
spirited anti-clerical beginning:

Stately, plump Buck Mulligan came from the stairhead, bearing a bowl
of lather on which a mirror and a razor lay crossed. A yellow dress-
inggown, ungirdled, was sustained gently behind him by the mild
morning air. He held the bowl aloft and intoned:
    —*Introibo ad altare Dei.*

The passage has a hymnal quality about it. Such devices as
alliteration, telescoping of words, and syntactical rearrange-
ments make us think more of poetry than of prose. As Anthony
Burgess remarked in his book on Joyce, *Re Joyce,* Gerard
Manley Hopkins' poetry offers an effective gloss for Joyce's
prose. If one were to delete the articles and prepositions from
the second sentence there would be little difference between
it and a line of Hopkins. (We can share Burgess' enjoyment
in bringing these two together, "the renegade Catholic and
the Catholic convert, the Jesuit-taught and the Jesuit
teacher.") The broad mockery of the passage, with its references to the cross, the priest, and the opening of the Mass,
is clearly the subterfuge of a writer who lives with the uncomfortable feeling that the Church is too much with us.

In a recent book, *The Conscience of James Joyce,* Darcy
O'Brien is very persuasive in showing us Joyce's "Irish Catholic fear of lust." O'Brien feels that the one lingering aspect
of his Catholicism is his distrust of sex and his horror at the
sexual act: "To Joyce, sex was the great proof of man's Fall

or original sin: hence the centrality of sex in his writings." A convincing case is finally made for Joyce's salving his moral conscience by walking the tightrope of sensuality and carnal sin. Joyce gains a peculiar "connivance with sin" much as Conor Cruise O'Brien accused Mauriac of doing.

The main difference between Joyce's Catholicism and that of Fournier and Rivière is that Joyce had to engage in an elaborate literary gesture to rid his system of it. His novels are more explicitly Catholic than theirs because the worrying process never ceases, even in the dream of H. C. Earwicker; the Luciferian *non serviam* and the *confiteor* both survive intact from *A Portrait*. Joyce's is a long, noisy rejection of Catholicism—stifled by its rhetoric—while Rivière's and Fournier's is a quiet, if sometimes nervous, acceptance.

In his discussion of Mauriac and Greene in *Modern Literature and Christian Faith,* Martin Turnell makes a statement which I find revealing about Joyce: "I think it can be expressed by saying that their outlook is theological rather than religious. There is a certain lack of spontaneity. We feel that they have been browsing too much over theological treatises. . . ." The comment seems also pertinent to Anthony Burgess, who not only has written a book on Joyce and edited *A Shorter Finnegans Wake* but is himself a most Joycean novelist. He invented (in good Joyce style) what he called the Nadsat language, with many of its words of Russian origin, for *A Clockwork Orange*. He is fond of neologisms and every variety of word-play; he coined the word *palimpcestuous,* for example, to describe *Finnegans Wake*. He uses musical references and analogies in much of his fiction. He suggests in the introduction of his first novel, *A Vision of Battlements,* that he is using a running parallel with *The Aeneid* in much the way Joyce used *The Odyssey* as a scaffolding for *Ulysses*. (One of the two epigraphs for the novel, by the way, is taken from *Ulysses*.) He not only raids Joyce, with full acknowledgment, in matters of technique and form but also enjoys an occasional Joyce in-joke, such as this one from *The Doctor is Sick*: "Edwin picked up the telephone, dialled— remembering his James Joyce—EDENville 0000, and asked for Adam." *The Wanting Seed,* his most Joycean novel, has almost as much to do with *Finnegans Wake* as Thornton Wilder's *Skin of our Teeth.*

Burgess' reluctant Catholicism escapes the pains of Joyce's pleadings against the Church. It is almost as if Burgess, through his painstaking reading of Joyce, had suffered the tortures of his kind of lapsed Catholicism but had gotten them out of his system before he started writing his own novels. Burgess' is more a light and flippant "browsing too much over theological treatises" than was Joyce's. He enjoys positing in his novels renegade Catholics, with very little conscience about their lapsed Catholicism but with a great deal of theological sophistication. They have a kind of off-handedness about their religion which one never finds in Joyce.

Thus Richard Ennis, the Aeneas of *A Vision of Battlements,* can coolly assure his Spanish girlfriend Concepción, *"yo tambien soy católico."* This causes the following outburst from the girl:

"That's what I hate!" she raged. "You'll do this, and this is a sin, we're both damned for it. And you don't go to mass, you haven't been to confession for sixteen years—you told me so—and yet you argue so smooth to those others about God. It's all lies. How can you expect me to believe you when you talk about love?"

Ennis, in his conversation, delights in such expressions as "gangster-God." He is accused, amusingly, on one occasion of having "a Catholic sort of face." The Army and the Church are several times brought into interesting juxtaposition: "The Army was rather like the Church, conditioning one to sweat with wholly irrational fears: Army crimes were like sins." "Ennis paused for a moment, his Church and Army training battling against Prometheus and Satan." Ennis' lapsed Catholicism is indeed a frequent source of amusement to his military colleagues as well as to himself.

Catholicism enters through the same kind of back-door-of-the-church in *Tremor of Intent.* Burgess' interest in phonetics merges with his religious "concerns" in this passage from the first chapter:

And, of course, you have Catholic Liverpool, a kind of debased Dublin. There we were then, two Southern exiles among Old Catholics, transplanted Irish, the odd foreigner with a father in the consular service. We were Catholics, but we sounded Protestants with our long-aaaaa'd English; our tones were not those of pure-vowelled orthodoxy.

It is suggested, at one point in the novel, that lapsed Catholics "go back to it [the Church] in retirement. A sort of hobby, I suppose." The novel ends on a note of mock-conversion; the principal character is referred to as "Father Hillier," in the final words of the book, as he pronounces "Amen."

There is much of the same thing in most of Burgess' other fiction. There is a costume ball aboard ship in *Honey for the Bears* where "the motif of the costumes seemed to be anti-clerical—sheets for soutanes, blankets for monk's habits, back-to-front collars above nightshirts and dirty pyjamas." In the fantastic world depicted in *The Wanting Seed* we discover that "God is the enemy. We have conquered God and tamed him into a comic cartoon character for children to laugh at. Mr Livedog. God was a dangerous idea in people's minds. We have rid the civilized world of that idea." Rome is referred to in the same novel as "that popeless city." I could go on almost indefinitely multiplying examples.

In an article which Anthony Burgess wrote in the London *Times Literary Supplement* for March 3, 1966, on the subject of religion and the arts, he fell back on a series of paradoxes and evasive statements, such as, "I suppose that the very concept of a 'Religious Novel' could exist only in an age of unbelief." and "The novel cannot serve religion, so religion may serve the novel." He did, however, seemingly with some reluctance admit: "For, ultimately, it is very doubtful whether any novel, however trivial, can possess any vitality without an implied set of values derived from religion." Burgess is, of course, of a later generation than Rivière, Fournier, and Joyce (all of whom were born in the 1880s), and his concerns

are much closer to the ambience of the "new theology" of
Bishop Robinson, Dietrich Bonhoeffer, Rudolf Bultmann, and
Paul Tillich. The radical theology of Bishop Robinson's
famous article in the London *Observer,* "Our Image of God
Must Go," seems very close to the tone Burgess assumes in
his fiction and in his literary journalism. An autobiographical
statement which he made in the third volume of *Contemporary Authors* is the kind of thing I have in mind: "I was
brought up a Catholic, became an agnostic, flirted with Islam,
and now hold a position which may be termed Manichee—I
believe the wrong God is temporarily ruling the world and
that the true God has gone under."

Returning to Martin Turnell's distinction between a "religious" and a "theological" outlook, we can say that Rivière
and Fournier belong to the first category, Joyce and Burgess
to the second—although with the shades of difference I have
already suggested. These writers illustrate two sets of principles which are often ignored by critics who write on the
twentieth-century Roman Catholic novel—which is why I
have treated them at some length in this introduction. The
rest of the book will proceed along more orthodox lines, at
least in the choice of writers.

The present collection of essays was conceived as a way of
reassessing the roles of a distinguished group of twentieth-
century Catholic writers, of American, English, French, Spanish, Italian, and German origin. Four of the writers—Evelyn
Waugh, François Mauriac, Graham Greene, and Georges
Bernanos—were already dealt with in an earlier and quite
remarkable book on twentieth-century Catholic literature:
Conor Cruise O'Brien's *Maria Cross.* A glance at the first section of the checklist of criticism at the end of this book reveals
other intriguing groupings of Catholic writers, by some of the
most gifted critics of twentieth-century literature, like Nathan
A. Scott, Jr., Wallace Fowlie, Germaine Brée, and Albert Sonnenfeld. *The Vision Obscured* is offered as a supplement to
their valuable work.

The long, general essay by George Panichas offers an *entrée* to a certain literary climate which is familiar to students of the relationship between literature and religion but is practically unknown to other professional critics. Professor Panichas amply convinces us that it deserves to be better known. The essays on the individual writers which follow proceed with no special critical bias. Some, like Jean Alter's essay on Julien Green, examine only a single novel. Others, like William Sessions' piece on Giovanni Papini, are more in the nature of overviews. Pierre Ullman offers a good deal of plot-summary in his treatment of Carmen Laforet because her work, with the possible exception of *Nada,* is little known outside the Spanish-speaking world. Germaine Brée's brilliant short piece on Mauriac has a fine sense of anticlimax; most of us have come to feel, with Miss Brée, that too much has already been written on Charles de Gaulle's most fervent Catholic apologist and that he has been placed too high among contemporary French novelists.

Each of the contributions, then, was conceived with something very different in mind. The subject, in each instance, dictated the length and critical direction of the essay. We have tried for variety and versatility rather than a singleness of point of view. The essays, when taken together, represent useful and agreeable differences of approach, ranging from close study of the text to more detached wanderings in literary history and biography.

A Metaphysics of Art

GEORGE A. PANICHAS · *University of Maryland*

> In vain do our modern positivists go about slashing the
> flowers of immortality and metaphysics; the selfsame
> flowers spring up under their passing feet.
>
> M. C. D'ARCY

THE ROMAN CATHOLIC PHILOSOPHER ÉTIENNE GILSON defines metaphysics as "the science of existence beyond the sciences of the ways of existing." He goes on to say that metaphysics requires its own principle of explanation; that by its very nature it is "distinct from the other sciences"; that, in fact, it "dominates them because its object is the problem without which there would be no other problems." [1] This definition is not unusual, or revolutionary. But it is eminently concise, almost a miracle of brevity in a domain of philosophy that for the past 2500 years has variously preoccupied such luminaries as Parmenides, Plato, and Aristotle in the classical period; St. Thomas Aquinas and William of Ockham in the Middle Ages; Descartes, Locke, Hume, and Kant in the Age of Enlightenment; and Josiah Royce, F. H. Bradley, and Henri Bergson in the modern period.

Gilson's words are especially relevant to the condition of "man in the modern age." And they are especially relevant

13

because one of the central and pervasive problems of modern man has been the "conceptual conflicts" emanating from his attempts to find "a way of speaking which will enable us to express the true nature of the universe." [2] Modern literature, more than theology or philosophy, has dramatized the intensity of these conflicts, whether they relate to general problems of "the true nature of the world," or to particular "problems of the human conscience in our time." Gilson's words, it will be seen, help not only to define metaphysics but also to characterize the tenor and the aspirations of some of the major works of literature since 1859.

Few would deny that modern literature has consistently demonstrated astonishing imaginative genius in responding to crucial metaphysical problems: to a view of the universe and of man's place in it, his relationship to what lies beyond it, to the transcending and transcendent. In short, modern literature has reflected a view "concerned, in one way or another, with the *ultimate* nature of the *whole* of Reality, with the *first* cause, the *final* explanation, the *complete* account." [3] When art ignores or rejects a concern with "final things" and an awareness of the "accursed questions," to use a favorite nineteenth-century Russian phrase, it diminishes itself and its communicated value, thus falling short of its vision and controverting the meaning of existence and the discovering creatively of the values of culture. Literature is but life in imagination and life in dialogue; and life as a total human experience comprises the seen and the unseen. Thus literature, as a continual creative process, within time and beyond time, discloses the seen and the unseen.

When Boris Pasternak declares that "art has two constant, two unending concerns: it always meditates on death and thus always creates life. All great, genuine art resembles and continues the Revelation of St. John," [4] he is not necessarily Christianizing art and the creative conception. Rather, he is seeking to establish the highest function and responsibility of the "creative act" and the "creative work." That is to say, he is focusing on literature as "revelation," the apocalyptic portrayal of existential and experiential truths. At the same time he is pointing to the imaginative artist's burden of vision, which must be seen as seminally metaphysical in inspiration and import.

The implicit point being made here is that "great, genuine art" is "revelation." This is true of the works of some of the greatest artists through the centuries—Aeschylus, Sophocles, Virgil, Dante, Milton, Goethe, Dostoevsky, Tolstoy, D. H. Lawrence, T. S. Eliot. Great artists, furthermore, are rarely metaphysically neutral. Nor can they be neutral if their revelation is to be an authentic contribution, "a gift to the future," as Albert Camus would have it. This does not mean that a great artist dramatizes a particular doctrine, that he gives us "philosophy in action," as it has been phrased. A great artist, after all, does not "state." He helps us to see and to understand by giving us "a presentation of human reality in a dramatically organized manner." His presentation, "ordered aesthetically," is what constitutes the criterion of true art as opposed to false art. Nevertheless, his presentation, to be fully effective, to achieve a shared vision and a sympathy of response, must give creative expression to the problematic aspects of "the true nature of the world." It is in a conjoined seeing and articulating that the meaning of metaphysics in art assumes inestimable value—and principle. "Your form is your meaning," to recall Joyce Cary, "and your meaning dictates the form." [5]

In his essay on William Faulkner's *The Sound and the Fury,* Jean-Paul Sartre declares that "the technique of the novel always refers us back to the metaphysics of the artist." He suggests also that before "evaluating" his technique, the critic must "define" the artist's metaphysics.[6] This statement may sound paradoxical, coming as it does from one who admits to being a representative of "atheistic existentialism" and who asserts unreservedly that the God Who once "spoke to us . . . now is silent, [and] all that we touch now is his corpse." Still, his statement is not incongruous or surprising, for it brings out one aspect of the struggle of modern man to comprehend "the universe of human subjectivity" in the face of the "silence of the transcendent."

If Sartre replaces "religious need" with "creative freedom" and "the sincerity which aims at itself in present immanence," he accentuates at the same time the abiding place of metaphysics in the sphere of human experience. For Sartre metaphysics can signalize nothing but the constancy of the need for a metaphysics of values—with those values that require the invention of values, or as Sartre himself says: "Life has no meaning a priori . . . ; it is up to you to give it a meaning, and value is nothing else than this meaning which you choose." [7] Sartre's words here help to explain much of Sartre, in particular his demand that one be "faithful to the earth" and show a defiant integrity, in the face of human tragedy and absurdity. His words also help to explain much of modern literature. If there is one thing that is constant among great modern artists, it is the place of values in direct relation to human experience.

Daily life, observes E. M. Forster, is "composed of two lives—the life in time and the life by values. . . . And what the story does is to narrate the life in time. And what the entire novel does—if it is a good novel—is to include the life by values as well." [8] By values we mean man's quest for a way of life, for an ethic that, though aware of and grounded in the material everyday world, must also transcend it. Value is what embodies the full range of man's attempt, through the intercommunication of thought and action, to weigh the worth of himself and of others and to judge continually, existentially, the importance of qualities, the presence or the absence of which affects the meaning and the direction of life. Value, as Sartre indicates, gives meaning to life: it is what saves life from nothingness. It is the means for perception and for discrimination which must clarify and assess meaning.

Literature is the recreation of the life of man and the life of values in a ceaseless struggle for synthesis. For some persons, as for Sartre, this struggle is one in which "man exists, encounters himself, surges up in the world—and defines himself afterwards." For others, like the religiously committed, this struggle is the struggle for grace, for salvation, when "old things are passed away; behold, all things are becom-[ing] new." [9] The first is a metaphysics of self-value, often occurring, as Martin Buber notes, during "the historic hour through which the world is passing"—the "eclipse of the light of heaven, [the] eclipse of God." The second is a metaphysics of faith, when "something is taking place between heaven and earth" and when one "submit[s] himself to the effective reality of the transcendence." [10] Literature can render for us the experience of these two metaphysics, within the world and beyond the world, in a finite act of courage and in the boundless mystery of faith. When Sartre speaks of the need to define the artist's metaphysics before evaluating his technique, he is pointing to the artist's inner experience of the metaphysics of his encounter with values and his reaction to the encounter. The artist's technique is the aesthetic, sensitizing expression of the encounter and the epiphanizing of the metaphysics.

Sartre's statement concerning the relationship between technique and metaphysics brings to mind Jacques Maritain's emphasis on the comparable relationship between Art and Poetry: Art as "the creative or producing, work-making activity of the human mind," Poetry as "that intercommunication between the inner being of things and the inner being of the human Self which is a kind of divination." [11] In this "age of criticism" Sartre has pointed out the essential task of a critic. No matter how hard he tries to assess literature objectively, scientifically, no matter how diligently he *wants* to be concerned with "the black marks on the page"—the "Art"—a critic can hardly deny, though he may ignore, a novelist's metaphysics—the "Poetry." Clearly, he cannot deny the indwelling essences either in the artist's creative process or in the subject matter of his art which relate to metaphysical elements. An artist cannot write in a void, and a work of art, to have any human pertinence, to be something more than an autonomous and autotelic object, can escape neither the pain and the wonder of existence nor the problematic nature of existence. Indeed, the beginning and the end of life are the

major preoccupations rendered in art. They constitute the
passions and the visions which give birth to the creative act
and which ultimately inhere in literary achievement.

II

Undoubtedly, as Professor Eliseo Vivas warns, it is dangerous
for a critic to look on literature as social, political, historical,
moralistic, or theological documents. Art, he maintains, "reveals"; "it tears the veil" and discloses meanings and values:
"But at the moment of revelation if the transaction is successful," Vivas asserts, "we make no comment. We behold. The
comment, the digestion of the meanings and values, their critical, which is to say, their transitive appreciation or assess-
ment, comes later." The product of the creative imagination
is not a patchwork of bare facts or a recitation of causal relationships, of axioms, of formulas within a suprahistorical
or supraobjective framework. Creative art transcends, must
transcend, the particularities, the esotericisms, the specialisms
of social prognosis and diagnosis and therapy. Obviously,
Vivas' belief that "poetry uniquely reveals a world which is
self-sufficient" contains in it much that is valuable and that
can help a critic avoid equating literature with epistemological
endeavors and nonimaginative writings.[12]

It should be said that Vivas, carefully avoiding the dead-
ends of formalism, allows for critical "comment" when one
is evaluating a work of art. Without this comment, this "dis-
ciplined speculation," as G. Wilson Knight calls it, the full
understanding and meaning of art suffer and become an incomplete experience. If, with Vivas, we recognize the power
and the potency of art, at the "moment of [our] rapt and
intransitive grasp of it," we must also recognize the long-range
need to contemplate and to comment on its meaning in sequence. In this connection, we must be willing and brave enough
to return to "the old criticism," recalling us, as George
Steiner has brilliantly shown, "to the remembrance of our
great lineage," to "the old definitions, the long-founded cate-

gories of meaning," to a sense of love and admiration, to
something philosophic in range and temper: above all, to the
belief that the great writers "have been men impelled either to
acquiescence or [to] rebellion by the mystery of God," and
that "there is at the heart of the creative process a religious
paradox." [13] (Nor must we allow ourselves to be discouraged
by those who today advise "against interpretation"; by the
babblings of a Susan Sontag, for instance, who claims that "In
place of a hermeneutics we need an erotics of art." [14])

A great work of art has more than one life and, to be great,
must continue its "grasp" in the unconscious and in the conscious, in the realm of aesthetic wonder (*technē*) and in that
of thought, which ensues (*theōria*). Thus, whether a work
of art consists in a structure of meanings, or forms, or sounds,
or ideas, it has, as Denis de Rougemont declares, the transcending function of "the bribing of the attention, the mag-
netizing of the sensibility, the fascinating of the meditation."
A work of art, he concludes, is *"a calculated trap for meditation"* which "must orient existence toward something which
transcends sounds and forms, or the words so assembled."
What de Rougemont is getting at here is that the experience
of and the reaction to the aesthetic act, its composition, its
craft, its technique, its "rhetoric," requires an extension in
time, a spatial enlargement, if the artist's vision is to be more
than a *tour de force*. In fact, de Rougemont insists that "criticism ought to be at one and the same time *technical,* on the
one hand, and on the other metaphysical or ethical—which is
to say, in the end, *theological*." [15]

His statement takes us directly back to Sartre. It stresses
the ever-emerging fact that an artist's metaphysics, in its
relation to technique, requires a special critical approach, a
"meditation." Meditative criticism, as it might be called, seeks
to achieve a break-through to the life beneath and beyond the
artist's technical skill and to reach into the recesses of his
cosmos which are not immediately observable or definable "at
the moment of the presentation," when a work holds us, to
employ Vivas' image, "as a snake is said to hold the bird,
quiveringly alive and so intent on the fascinating eyes that it

does not know it is in rigid panic." The aesthetic experience in form exerts spontaneous power, at the instant moment. The technical expertise of the artist aids in securing this power and in tightening this grasp.

But this power must wane and the grasp must weaken as the powers of cognition begin their work. Precisely at this point, however, meditative criticism can penetrate the "ironies," the "tensions," the "paradoxes," the "controlling metaphor," the "thematic structure," and the "symbolic action" with which technique is identified. In his break-through to the ground of the artist's metaphysics, the meditative critic helps to release a part of the artist's energy of vision, to approach perilously close to the center of the creative impulse, the now exposed origin of his vision that ultimately attains the organic wholeness of artistic design and the "rage for order."

Criticism that is at once technical and metaphysical and that is willing to define an artist's metaphysics before evaluating his technique is not solely meditative. It is "sapiential," as Thomas Merton would have it, approaching what can be said to be the first estate of criticism: *sapientia,* or wisdom. To quote Merton's astute observation:

It [*sapientia*] goes beyond *scientia,* which is systematic knowledge, beyond *intellectus,* which is intuitive understanding. It has deeper penetration and wider range than either of these. It embraces the entire scope of man's life and all his meaning. It grasps the ultimate truths to which science and intuition only point. In ancient terms, it seeks the "ultimate causes," not simply efficient causes, but the ultimate reasons why they happen and the ultimate values which their happening reveals to us.[16]

Both imaginative writing and criticism, Merton adds, "provide a privileged area for wisdom in the modern world." His words heighten the importance, if not the challenge, of Sartre's observation. A critic who sees through technique to metaphysics, through form to insight, thus seeks and sees and searches the "ultimate causes." He helps capture that "wisdom" in the writer which has meaning beyond aesthetic fact.

Such a critic is not merely sapiential or meditative; but, more, he is a critic who encourages great art. "Great art," John Masefield reminds us, "does not proceed from a great criticism, but from great encouragement. The great mind being given his opportunity, does great things, and it is from these that criticism derives such principles as it has. The great times of art are those when power has the intelligence to encourage it." [17]

We must ask ourselves, too, what constitutes art and what makes an artist great. Greatness implies a certain excellence and, in the final analysis, an ultimate. This ultimate coexists with intense and piercing vision, a peculiar seeing that includes not only the here but the beyond. The totality and the steadfastness of an artist's vision, if we read Sartre correctly, cannot be limited to the immediate (the technical, the seen, the achieved) but must be followed to the hidden (or metaphysical) sources of his experience, which in time becomes converted, hypostatized, into expression, when, to use Erich Auerbach's apt phrase, "style is vision." The metaphysics embodies the rage and conduces in the artist a fermentation, which, if the creative imagination's experience is as genuine as it is intense, spills over the frontier of the unconscious into the conscious. "The experience itself," I. A. Richards tells us, "the tide of impulses sweeping through the mind, is the source and the sanction of the words." [18]

The creative act, the attendant technique, the form, is a direct response to this ferment, a response to "ultimate concerns" which vibrate in the metaphysics. These words perhaps give a picture of the artist as a seer, one who may see more than he should see: who sees startlingly, sees ultimately. A large part of this "seeing" is closely tied to the artist's metaphysics. His metaphysics epitomizes not only a crisis—that is, the decisive stage in the artist's thought-adventure, his confrontation of the great universal questions—but also a peril, when the larger dangers and tensions are subsequent to the confrontation and crystallize the power of the metaphysics in the inspiration of creative insight, of communication.

An artist lives and creates in a state of crisis and in a con-

dition of peril. He sees and expresses the semblances of the
outer life, and he suffers the desperate secrets and questionings
of the inner life. As a result of his metaphysical journeys and
discoveries, his responsiveness and sensitivity to metaphysic-
crisis and metaphysic-peril, his vision has explosive clarity and
miraculous power—power that is even theurgic in its reaches.
An artist is both a creator, *homo faber,* and a traveler, *homo
viator.* His art, his craft, arises out of his vision: a vision, to
repeat, which travels back to the metaphysics, to its crisis and
peril, in time and outside time, in history and outside history.

For a critic to appraise the technique (the style) and not
the metaphysics (the vision) is to miss completely the ceaseless rhythm of life in the flesh and in the spirit: to miss, in a
word, the totality of being and becoming—*physis* and *meta-
physis*; beginning and end—*archē* and *telos.* A great artist,
in short, dwells totally in a total existence. It is total existence,
with all its known and unknown potencies, which surges in his
inspiration. To maintain that the need to define the artist's
metaphysics before evaluating his technique is to judge the
creative act as superior to the terrible process of breaking-
down to thingness. It is to maintain, provided we are willing
to take the necessary "leap" with Gabriel Marcel and provided we are to gauge the immeasurable significance of metaphysics,

that in so far as we are not things, in so far as we refuse to allow ourselves to be reduced to the condition of things, we belong to an entirely
different world-dimension, and it is this dimension which can and must
be called supratemporal.[19]

To relate the artist to metaphysics is to see his form and style
in an integral relationship to the "search for truth," the
"search for identity," the "search for meaning," the "search
for harmony," the "search for transcendence," the "search for
the divine," the "search for values." Metaphysics, as such, pre-
supposes the principle of reality and the ultimate constituents
of the universe. It also points out an inevitable interpenetra-
tion of the human and the divine. The key word here is search,

for metaphysics entails the quintessential need to return to, to find supratemporal values of existence. A metaphysical writer renders these values in his art. He dramatizes the generic interworkings of search and values, moving from existential and experiential modes of being, from a secular dynamics, to the conceptual effort to think about and to express what transcends him.

Here I use the word "effort" in the context of William Blake's supposition that "If the doors of perception were cleansed everything would appear to man as it is, infinite." [20] It is this "infinite" that tantalizes artists who are at the same time religious seekers—religious in the metaphysical sense I have been noting: in the sense of a perception of a "religious need" and search. Many modern writers disclose in their art exactly this process. Their technique is the measure and the medium of the desideratum to comprehend and approach the transcendent. The technique is the artist creating in the present world, whereas the metaphysics is the transcendent and infinite world in which the artist contemplates. The creative imagination achieves discipline in the present but is nourished and inspired by the inexhaustible infinite. This metaphysical world defies circumscription, computerization, to use a popular word of these days, and in this defiance we view a metaphysics of art—in short, the miracle of a deathless artistic imagination.

More than anything else, a metaphysics of art (in a synthesis of form and insight), hinting at a sacred view of man, helps to save man from his thingness, from that part of a meaningless existence, of a mechanical universe, identifiable on the basis of its technic authenticity or, as Alain Robbe-Grillet believes, its "contamination," its dehumanization, its objectification, its reduction to a " 'black box' of cybernetics, where only the relations of input and output matter." [21] A metaphysics of art leads to some experience of the transcendent, whereas its technique instances the evaluative dimensions and nuances of the experience. In the end, the experience of the transcendent embodies for the artist the burden of vision; the technique of his art embodies the proof of the vision—in other words, "the instrument of a recognition." The first is tantamount to a more or less mystic revelation; the second is a mode of apprehension and external evidence, the visibilizing determinants of the process of creation and the discovery "of ourselves and of our origins." [22]

"Of ourselves and of our origins": these words crystallize what for the metaphysical artist must be an immutable longing for and truth of universals, and what, in the function of criticism, purveys the need to define a writer's metaphysics. Art which gets away from "ourselves" and from "origins," gets away from the metaphysics—what in a theological texture Paul Tillich speaks of as man's ultimate concern for the ground and abyss of all finite being and the receptory of meaning, or what in an artistic texture D. H. Lawrence speaks of as the necessity for men "to know how to go out and meet one another upon the third ground, the holy ground." (His great novels are configurations of this dictum.) It gets away from language that is memory and metaphor, from "the experience of the race." A demanding truth of transcendence, once separated from self and origin, must disintegrate into antivision and antilife.

By a metaphysics of art we also mean a metaphysics that is an implicit part of the creative vision and, hence, a natural and animistic facet of an artist's "seeing" which occupies its ordered place in "a presentation of human reality in a dramatically organized manner," to use Vivas' words. A metaphysics of art must not be confused with the superimposition of "concept" or "doctrine" or "idea." (T. S. Eliot, it is interesting to note here, once said that Henry James "had a mind so fine that no idea could violate it.") The metaphysics is to be seen as working within the artist's creative imagination, the point at which the artist is immersed in a refining activity, during which he achieves a discipline of aesthetic direction in his view of and dramatization of human experience in relation to the metaphysics of values already noted.

A metaphysics of art is just that: a metaphysics belonging to the internal world of the creative imagination and not to the outer world of a philosophy or an ideology, in which, to quote Martin Heidegger, "Metaphysics thinks about beings as beings." [23] These words summarize a ratiocinative process that must be antithetical to a metaphysics of art which does not "think" its way but, altering Heidegger's words, renders beings as beings and values as values. "Never trust the artist," D. H. Lawrence emphasizes. "Trust the tale. The proper function of a critic is to save the tale from the artist who created it." [24] A metaphysics of art does not begin with some metaphysical proposition, for this would distort "the meaning of the creative act" and transform a work of art into a prosaic document or an abstract treatise.

III

In a metaphysics of art we discern the artist's insights into the life of man, into the "human condition." Art not only portrays life but also functions as a dramatic medium for attaining and then transmitting sudden flashes of understanding. An artist fuses in his imaginative achievement the creative and the metaphysical—that is, a rendering of the human element and scene which complements the eternal questions of life. What an artist sees constitutes a response to the metaphysics of the human situation. How he expresses what he sees constitutes his technique. His function, Theodore M. Greene aptly observes, is "not only to delight his fellows with new decorative patterns but to revitalize them, resensitize them, rehumanize them, respiritualize them, within the limits of possibility of his times and culture." [25]

A metaphysics of art is closely tied to the multidimensional patterns of life that the artist first recreates. The greatness of his art is in the end judged by the integrity and the purity of his transcendent imaginative vision. For it is in the power of his artistic creativeness that an artist's success must be measured, and that, in addition, tells us to what extent the act of his art has won over "the heaviness of the 'world' " and achieved "the liberation" that Nicolas Berdyaev speaks about.[26] The failure of art results from an artist's "adaptation" to the "world," specifically to some peculiar part of a metaphysics.

The triumph of art comes from the artist's "fulness of imaginative responsibility" (the phrase is Dr. F. R. Leavis') which permits him, aesthetically, to possess a metaphysics without being possessed by it.

The metaphysics of the artist, as opposed to that of the philosopher, contains modalities of and insights into human experience, disclosed, presented, in dramatic contexts, furiously and intensely (like the creative and destructive rhythms of life itself), rather than systematically, in the form of premise and documentation, of what Wordsworth speaks of as "the spiritless shape of fact." "In the novel," Sartre declares, "the dice are not loaded, for fictional man is free. He develops before our eyes; our impatience, our ignorance, our expectancy are the same as the hero's. . . . The fictional event is a nameless presence; there is nothing one can say about it, for it develops." [27] In this observation by Sartre, and in that by Berdyaev, the stress falls on "freedom," on "liberation." Art is the supreme imaginative activity and, consubstantially, the act of freedom itself.

Indeed, it is initially a metaphysics of freedom that inheres in the creative process. This freedom is of vast importance in the artist's craft, in the way in which he gives expression to "poetic intuitions," to his imaginative vision. It is a freedom no less intense and no less liberating than the creative process, which can be imaged as "a little like looking into a microscope and attempting to bring an unknown object into focus." [28] In art, the act of freedom is gradually transposed into an act of order—that is, the craft. Yet, a work of art, to achieve authentic communication with the reader, functions as a "transaction": "Our relationship or 'inter-course' with art is a 'transaction,' in which each term affects the other." [29] The act and the communication of art demand freedom and in the end synthesize into a condition of freedom—a metaphysics of freedom.

This metaphysics of freedom plays a role both in the creative process and in the creative substance, specifically in the words which "reveal" a vision of experience. Any discussion of the use and the function of words can hardly ignore the relevancy of one writer's contention that "words themselves do not convey meaning . . . ; they are but a gesture we make, a dumb show like any other." [30] Nevertheless, with all their limitations, words must give tangible, structural form to the artist's imagination. They are used to "create beauty" and to "tell the truth," and they become a "trans-acting" medium for relationship and communication between a work of art and the reader. Words are the vehicle for revelation, when, as it were, *logos* becomes *apocalypsis*. In a word, we can "behold" a whole world: It signifies value. It catches expression. It discourses. It sings. It reveals, as it makes mystery "intelligible." A word is at once a weighted measure of something it discloses and a miracle and a wonder. Although it contains a world in itself, it also belongs to different worlds and becomes, as in the famous case of James Joyce, a "wonderful vocable." Words are to the artist the tools for rendering "life in time" and "life by values." They enable the artist to "withdraw" into himself and "look," as Plotinus puts it, and then give concretization to his special vision. Thus, they render a creative process that is a testament to the endurance of faith, a concentrated visionary experience born in *ecstasis* and consummated in *askēsis*.

Virginia Woolf, in the exquisite essay "Craftsmanship" in her book *The Death of the Moth and Other Essays,* discusses the power of words and shows that they have a metaphysics of their own: transcendent powers soaring beyond boundaries of absolute meaning and coinage.[31] Words, she says, "live in the mind," and we can merely "peer at them over the edge of that deep, dark and only fitfully illuminated cavern in which they live." To the creative artist words are never a prison, or confined to a prison; they are a means of revelation, "many-sided, flashing this way, then that." What she is stressing is the metaphysics of freedom which is vital to the creative imagination—a reverence for the tradition of craft achieved through the power and the freedom of the words used by an artist who attempts to capture reality's "luminous halo."

Words can convey meaning and can help us achieve a dialogue; but it is, it must be, a dialogue in freedom. As such,

according to Mrs. Woolf, we should be wary about pinning a
word down to one meaning, for "when words are pinned down
they fold their wings and die." It is for this reason, too, that
meditative criticism (almost a religious act in itself—that is,
a literary appreciation that intuits the mystery of creative art
at the same time that it conveys its meaning) is necessary.
Nowhere else in the consideration of art is there more need
for this meditativeness than in an awareness of the combined
freedom and mystery that actualize the experience of the
artist's words and that relate to the metaphysics of the artist's
logos. She concludes:

Finally and most emphatically, words like ourselves, in order to live
at their ease, need privacy. Undoubtedly they like us to think, and
they like us to feel, before we use them; but they also like us to pause;
to become unconscious. Our unconsciousness is their privacy; our darkness is their light. . . .

These remarks by Mrs. Woolf should be helpful here as
we turn to two modern novelists: James Joyce and D. H.
Lawrence. The uses to which they put language illustrate some
of the metaphysical elements which appear creatively in and
inform their art. Joyce's accomplishment becomes clear only
by our realizing that his metaphysics is primarily a metaphysics of nihilism, of negation, but one that, according to Carl
Gustav Jung, becomes "a creative destruction." (Joyce, it is
interesting to note, once spoke of Jung as "the Swiss Tweedle-
dum who is not to be confused with the Viennese Tweedledee,
Dr. Freud.") When Jung further observes that in *Ulysses*—
a work, he adds, that "has the character of a worm cut in
half, that can grow a new head or a new tail as required"—
Joyce seeks "an almost universal 'restratification' of modern
man, who is in the process of shaking off a world that has become absolute"; or when he writes that Joyce seeks a "detachment of consciousness" as the "goal that shimmers through
the fog of this book," his comments help us to comprehend the
metaphysics of an artist that inspirits his technique.[32] Joyce's

technique, it is clear from *A Portrait of the Artist as a Young Man* and from *Ulysses,* inevitably relates back to his metaphysics, to his view of the world in which the "dominant note is the melancholy of abstract objectivity" (Jung).

E. M. Forster goes so far as to declare that in *Ulysses* the aim "is to degrade all things and more particularly civilization and art, by turning them inside out and upside down." [33] And Lawrence calls Joyce "a clumsy *olla putrida.* . . . Nothing but old fags and cabbage-stumps . . . stewed in the juice of deliberate, journalistic dirty-mindedness. . . ." [34] Such conclusions are harsh and angry and not entirely fair. They come from two writers whose metaphysics are antithetical to Joyce's: Forster with his emphasis on wisdom, eclectic and distilled, Lawrence with his emphasis on the blood and on life as an unending "adventure in consciousness." It is evident that Joyce is seeking for something entirely different. He is not interested in being merely "wise" or "alive." "Restratification"—this word captures what he demands and inheres in his metaphysics and in the technique of his language. Joyce's metaphysics of "creative destruction," his supreme attempt to overcome "the tyranny of tradition," his "restratification" above all: these are ever-present in his "way of controlling, of ordering, of giving a shape and a significance to the immense panorama of futility and panorama which is contemporary history," to quote Eliot.[35] Hence, when Joyce remarks, "I'd like a language which is above all language, a language to which all will do service," [36] he indicates the far limits of what he desires to "restratify" in art and life. Throughout the process of his "restratifying," he is fervently seeking for an "epiphany," a sudden, even divine revelation about the true nature of the universe.

Joyce's metaphysics ends in a call to the mystery of the priesthood—the priesthood of the artist. "He [Stephen Dedalus] would never swing the thurible before the tabernacle as priest," Joyce writes in *A Portrait.* "The wisdom of the priest's appeal did not touch him to the quick. He was destined to learn his own wisdom apart from others or to learn the wisdom of others

himself wandering among the snares of the world." The fact
is that Joyce is the priest as artist who vows, "I shall express
myself as I am." And it is, Joyce contends, "in the virgin womb
of the imagination [that] the word was made flesh." His technique, an uncompromising vindication of this belief, is achieved
by "a priest of eternal imagination" transmuting "the daily
bread of experience into the radiant body of everliving life."
His technique is continually colored, on the one hand, by an
elemental religionism, a pious Catholicism, to be more exact,
and, on the other, by a ferocious independence of creative
effort, which Joyce sums up in the words, ". . . I will try to
express myself in some mode of life or art as freely and as
wholly as I can, using for my defense the only arms I allow
myself to use—silence, exile, and cunning." [37]

Moreover, Joyce's art reveals a double process in an artistic
imagination that is mythically and symbolically churched, or,
as Joyce himself says, "supersaturated with the religion in
which you say you disbelieve," and of an ideational dissent
that proceeds from an epiphanic view of the life of man as "a
Vast Human Tragedy . . . in which a profound anthropo-
logical sense of the mystery and power of death takes the place
of the Christian's traditional faith in union with God and
the life everlasting." [38] This process evidences the objective
substances and the measure of an artist's technique, in Joyce's
case the levels of language and structure through which he
finds the means of exploring his vision, of conveying its meaning, and of appraising it. For Joyce it is the self-centered word
that achieves precisely the transcendence which he denies in
the universe. For him, then, the word assumes hierophantic
powers and truths and signifies the metaphysical quest for the
final restoration.

Like Joyce, Lawrence searches for new life-values, and for
him the novel is a means of achieving these in a world which
has gone "dead." "The novel," he writes, "is a perfect medium
for revealing to us the changing rainbow of our living relationships. The novel can help us to live, as nothing else can.
. . ." [39] In contrast to Joyce's, Lawrence's metaphysical quest

is nonintellectual. He is not interested in stratifying or re-stratifying, in dividing, in forming, in ordering the universe. His vision of the universe is invariably characterized by an irreversible belief that "Culture and civilisation are tested by vital consciousness." And his concern is with the elemental problems of "revitalization": How can we overcome the "old, dead things" of the cosmos? How can we fathom "the unknown modes of being" by traveling beyond "the long mean marginal stretches of our existence"? How can we achieve, in a final, transcendent sense, "the new unknown," "the sensuous flame of life"? These are questions which pervade Lawrence's art and thought.

Blake's memorable words "Awake! awake O Sleeper of the land of shadows, wake! expand!" [40] capture Lawrence's view of his art and its meaning and function in relationship to his vision of the universe and of man's role and possibilities in life. What Lawrence is doing in his art is reminding man of his real possibilities, of the need for him to "awake" and to "expand," to seek for the kind of revitalization, of "resurrection" to be more exact, which the Christ figure experiences in Lawrence's famous story "The Man Who Died." That man is capable of "moving back to consciousness" and of experiencing "the everlasting wonder in things" is what Lawrence insists upon and what conveys the nonintrospective metaphysical orientation of his art and message. ("Spunk is what one wants," Lawrence castigated Middleton Murry, "not introspective sentiment." [41])

In his Foreword to *Women in Love* he views man "in a period of crisis." This crisis is enacted between people who struggle or must struggle to "speak out to one another." There are those who "fix themselves in the old idea" and who will consequently "perish with the new life strangled unborn within them." But there are also those who "can bring forth the new passion, the new idea." For Lawrence there is always an enduring "remnant" in the world that has "the courage of ultimate truth." His art at its best renders the metaphysics of a "life-courage" as opposed to a "death-courage." The follow-

ing passage from his Foreword contains in essence Lawrence's
view of the world as it informs the whole of his art, its themes,
its meaning:

> Man struggles with unborn needs and fulfilment. New unfoldings
> struggle up in torment in him, as buds struggle forth from the midst
> of a plant. Any man of real individuality tries to know and to under-
> stand what is happening, even in himself as he goes along. This strug-
> gle for verbal consciousness should not be left out in art. It is a very
> great part of life. It is not superimposition of a theory. It is the pas-
> sionate struggle into conscious being.

Lawrence discloses a profound awareness of the mystery of
life. No examination of his cosmos, in which, as Elizabeth
Bowen has observed, "every bush burns," can escape the
"numinous awe" which Lawrence communicates. No aspect of
life fails to excite his wonder: "Awe," "awefulness," "over-
poweringness," to use Rudolf Otto's touchstones,[42] inhere in
Lawrence's recreation of life, in his striving to touch the "emotional soul" and to come closer to the primordial truths which
he associates with the "intuitional consciousness." If Joyce
can be likened to the priest of the word, Lawrence can be
likened to the priest of the passions. His novels become fervent
sermons exhorting man to move closer to the numinous essences of life, there to "touch and wonder and ponder" the
very meaning of existence. "What ails us," Lawrence com-
plains, "is that our sense of beauty is so bruised and blunted,
we miss all the best." [43]
  With its spontaneous, rhythmic flow of words and emotions,
"its pulsing, frictional to-and-fro which works up to culmina-
tion," his sermonic art feverishly strives to save the numen
from the forces of antilife, from technology, from industrialism, from intellectualism, from scientism. The numen, as Lawrence sees and reveals it—for his art is an ever-unfolding
revelation of the numen, of "divine otherness," to use a
favorite Lawrentian expression—is found ultimately not in
the *logos* (as in Joyce's work) but in the flesh. Or as Lawrence
writes in his unpublished Foreword to *Sons and Lovers*:

". . . not the Word made Flesh, but the Flesh made Word. Out of the Flesh cometh the Word, and the Word is finite, as a piece of carpentry, and hath an end. But the Flesh is infinite and has no end." [44]

In his view of the universe Lawrence attempts to help man understand that "the vast marvel is to be alive." [45] The metaphysics of this Lawrentian world view is constantly expressed in the nature of his language and technique. His claim that "work is produced by passion with me" is not difficult to comprehend when we consider that Lawrence, from first to last, employed a technique of art that had as its source of inspiration the need of teaching man that "the magnificent here and now of life in the flesh is ours, and ours alone, and ours only for a time." Lawrence preaches the sermon of the flesh in a language and a form which continually echo his nonconformist Protestant teachings, and which at the same time achieve liberation from eschatological limitations of doctrine.[46] His final position, as effected in his art and his message, is a metamorphosed religionism of the instant, the living moment when man is "alive and in the flesh, and part of the living, incarnate cosmos."

Contrary to Joyce's conception of man's isolatedness—of his being, as Joyce asserts at the end of *A Portrait*, "Alone, quite alone. You have no fear of that. And you know what the word means? Not only to be separate from all others but to have not even one friend."—Lawrence's conception of man emphasizes a communal and dialogic relationship. Man, he says again and again, fails himself and the world around him by asserting his separateness, physically or spiritually. Only when man accepts the fact of his relationship to the world about him will he understand his true meaning and the nature of his destiny.

My soul [we read in Lawrence's last prose work, *Apocalypse*] knows that I am part of the human race, my soul is an organic part of the great human soul, as my spirit is part of my nation. In my own very self, I am part of my family. There is nothing of me that is alone and absolute except my mind, and we shall find that the mind has no existence by itself, it is only the glitter of the sun on the surface of the waters.

No words better stress the sharp differences between the metaphysics of Lawrence and that of Joyce. (One recalls here Dr. Leavis' contention that "if you took Joyce for a major creative writer, then . . . you had no use for Lawrence, and if you judged Lawrence a great writer, then you could hardly take a sustained interest in Joyce." [47]) When we compare the metaphysics and the techniques of the two artists, we can appreciate the truth of J. I. M. Stewart's observation that Joyce's achievement "is the work of a man who has lived too much alone with his own daemon." [48] In Lawrence's art, on the other hand, we are always in the presence of a creative genius whose daemon exists only as it participates in "the great relationship," in "the true relatedness to the other," "the relation itself," which comprises "the quick and the central clue to life"—and which reveals the "Courage to accept the life-thrust from within oneself, and from the other person."[49] Art, Lawrence affirmed, cannot be a monologue.

IV

Modern literature shows that metaphysical issues and concerns cannot be easily dismissed, that all too often "the physical opens on the metaphysical." Indeed, it is one of the ironies of the modern age that it is imaginative artists who have nourished and sustained the relevance of metaphysics, in the face of, even in defiance of, the "style" of the times. Of course, as Professor Frederick J. Hoffman has admirably shown in his *The Mortal No,* the intruding presence of the secular in the midst of the religious—*e.g.,* the paradoxes of "secular grace," the merging of "assailant" and "victim," the spatialization of time, the transposition of "the metaphysical properties of the Trinity into areas of secular improvisation"—discloses that traditional and orthodox concepts of man and his universe are radically changing in the modern novel. "Man looks at the world," Robbe-Grillet wryly observes, "and the world does not return his glance." [50] Yet, when we read Hoffman's study carefully, we can hardly miss the implicit conclusion that modern writers are still very deeply and essentially obsessed with a view of the world; that whether their conceptions of the world are metaphysically organic or inorganic, man has once again been

forced to speculate upon the possibility of a means of transcendence, since he [cannot] long suffer the thought of mortality in and of itself; he [is] forced back upon the initial experiencing of the self in time, and [is] impelled to work in terms of a sensed immediacy of his participation in tempered flow; he [becomes] more and more interested in himself *as process,* and he [attempts] to rescue a value from the fact that he [exists] in the apparently endlessly repetitive process of becoming something else. . . .[51]

Whatever the differences in their artistic visions are, writers as different as F. M. Dostoevsky, Thomas Mann, Franz Kafka, Hermann Hesse, Nikos Kazantzakis, Ignazio Silone, and William Faulkner (to mention some representative figures) have powerful things to say in respect to such crucial questions as: What *kind* of universe do we inhabit? What constitutes the relationship of the immediate to the eternal? These writers are inevitably concerned with "the situation of our time" and with "the terrible things of life": alienation, incommunicability, loneliness, despair, anxiety, boredom. Consciously or unconsciously, they express in their art the metaphysical tensions that arise, on the one hand, from a view of the universe which concludes that "there's no way out" and, on the other hand, from a view which, with Charles Williams, François Mauriac, Graham Greene, J. F. Powers, and Flannery O'Connor, affirms "salvation with diligence." ("The poet is traditionally a blind man," Miss O'Connor remarks; "but the Christian poet is like the blind man cured in the Gospels, who looked then and saw men as if they were trees, but walking. This is the beginning of vision." [52])

Through a continuing preoccupation with metaphysical problems, modern literature attests what Pascal speaks of as *l'esprit de finesse* (the acute, or subtle spirit) as opposed to *l'esprit géométrique* (the geometric spirit). One of the supreme

ironies of this century, to iterate, is that creative writers have
seen fit to express metaphysical concerns: and to do so at a
time when strident forces both in theological and in philosophical circles have increasingly rejected metaphysics. We
need look only at "new radical theologians" like Thomas J. J.
Altizer, William Hamilton, and Paul M. van Buren, who
advocate a "secularized Christianity" and a theology in which
God "is not simply hidden from view . . . [but] is truly
dead," to comprehend a "style" which seeks for a reconstruc-
tion of metaphysics. Specifically, we are told that theology can
be an empirical science; that our "image" of God must go;
that speculative and abstract language must be cleansed, with
words like "God," "transcendence," "redemption," "creation"
seen in a new light, and terms like "up there" and "out
there" repudiated; that we now live in a "secular city" and
must give stress to "the secular meaning of the Gospel." *This*
is a "time for Christian candor," the late James A. Pike informs us.[53]

Among modern philosophers, *l'esprit géométrique* has been
particularly strong in the movement known as logical positivism
(*e.g.,* in the works of Ludwig Wittgenstein, Rudolf Carnap,
and A. J. Ayer). For the logical positivists, concerned as they
are with verbal analysis, with grammatical schemata, with
logical rules, with the nature of mathematics, with the meanings of "meaning," with the exactitudes of $2 + 2 = 4$, metaphysics lies outside the range of quantitative measurement and
is consequently "meaningless," inconsistent, and incommen-
surate with what G. E. Moore once spoke of as "the Common
Sense view of the world." Metaphysics as a term has, at the
hands of the positivists, taken on pejorative connotations.
It contains, to recall Hume's famous attack, "nothing but
sophistry and illusion." "The acme of *abstract* speculation,"
it signifies what is "neither true nor false but 'literally senseless,' " a "senseless obscurantism." It is the result of "mental
cramp." Such have been the charges brought against metaphysics in the modern period and embodies what has been
called the "style" of the times: a "style" which has been in
proliferating evidence since the breakdown of the traditional

value-structure and of the "single standard of faith," and which emerged with the Renaissance and triumphed in the post-Enlightenment world, when metaphysical meaning was negated through the substitution of the "dynamics of *becoming*" for "static *being*." [54]

That one should remain aloof from metaphysics, inasmuch as it is untenable and intangible, is an attitude that many modern theologians and philosophers have emphasized. "Trust the world"; say "yes to the world": this is the counsel of the radical theologians as well as of the logical positivists. (We are reminded here of Maritain's recent criticism of Teilhard de Chardin's "chronolatry," which he sees as part of the new trend in theology and ecclesiastic thinking—"a genuflection before the world.") It is counsel that underlines an outlook, a "style," that yearns for safeness and accuracy and comfort, secular qualities which preclude a quest for what lies beyond the sensible. "Matter," as Simone Weil astutely observes, "is [now] a machine for manufacturing good."

Imaginative art, however, is doomed to failure, to sterility, once it surrenders to such a "style." "To create today," Camus insists, "is to create dangerously." His words bear heed: For they focus on the mission of artists who are intensely preoccupied with the meaning of the world: "the world [which] is nothing and the world [which] is everything—this is the contradictory and tireless cry of every true artist—the cry that keeps him on his feet with eyes ever open." A metaphysics of art demands that a writer "speak up"—that he "speak up," or "speak forth" in a prophetic sense, truths of human existence. "One may long, as I do," Camus reflects, "for a gentler flame, a respite, a pause for musing. But perhaps there is no other peace for the artist than what he finds in the heat of combat." [55]

If modern theologians and philosophers have surrendered to the "style" of the times, to "literal-minded analysis" and "cautious 'empiricism' "—to the dictates of the geometric spirit—there are some creative writers who have chosen to express their views of the universe in dangerous terms. By "dangerous" one means the creative urge to respond to the

world without limiting vision to the secular dynamics of life:
a modern *alittérateur* like Samuel Beckett, for instance, illustrates in his drama and fiction just how dangerous the metaphysical quest for human meaning and truth can be. He is concerned with conveying a "sense of mystery, bewilderment, and
anxiety when confronted with the human condition, and . . .
despair at being unable to find a meaning in existence." Thus,
in metaphysical terms, Beckett sees "man as [a] lost soul,"
haunted by "an intolerable deprivation" and "an irreparable
absence." His is a desacralized world when, as Nietzsche would
have it, the shadow of God, lurking in caves, has been "conquered" at last.[56] Helplessness, worthlessness, meaninglessness, Beckett tells us, epitomize the condition of man. "But
what matter," we read in *Malone Dies,* "whether I was born
or not, have lived or not, am dead or merely dying, I shall go
on doing as I have always done, not knowing what it is I do,
nor who I am nor where I come from, nor if I am." [57]
Because he is unafraid to seek for metaphysical truth, for
what Gilson speaks of as "the problem without which there
would be no other problems," Beckett, we can agree with Professor Nathan A. Scott, Jr., when even "at his zero-point
there *is* no grace," is not unlike "a 'shepherd of being' unto
our time . . . enhanced by the very resoluteness with which
he plunges us into the Dark." [58] More than anything else,
Beckett is a writer whose metaphysical search leads to the
lowermost depths in his hope of finding, somehow, "the fundamental reality which would remain, once what is accessory
in man has been destroyed." "By dropping down into the
elementary void of existence, perhaps it is the soul that he
hopes to find in the end," Claude Mauriac says of Beckett.[59]
What we experience in Beckett's work is indeed the danger, the heightened and terrifying metaphysical danger, which
Camus emphasizes. The quest for metaphysical truth, we
must realize, refuses to bow to "aggressive reason" or be satisfied with "straight answers." This refusal constitutes the
strength and the glory of the artist; it is what compels us to
"face the full force of our existence." Surely, Beckett "has
materialized the impalpable . . . ; has almost enabled us to

touch the walls of our prisons." [60] Such is the power of an artist whose metaphysics must thrust him into "the heat of combat," into a world which is so close to us, yet so distant, so elusive: a world in which "the blind man's stick" is perhaps the only hope that one has, or needs, as he taps his way slowly and falteringly to the real truth beckoning from behind boundaries of darkness.

A metaphysics of art implies an artist's willingness to travel beyond the known world into the unknown, the unexpected, and to explore both worlds with an aim of realizing ultimate reality; to embark on that "expedition of truth," which Kafka envisioned; and to perceive the other world which some modern theologians and philosophers have been evading for fear of learning the real truth of the self and of the world. "For where I found truth," says St. Augustine, "there I found my God, Who is Truth itself." Increasingly, modern art has combined the highest function of poetry and prophecy and has attested to *l'esprit de finesse* by not failing to "write the vision, and make it plain upon tables, that he may run that readeth it." [61] "To-day, as always," Karl Jaspers declares, "art must . . . make Transcendence perceptible, doing so at all times in the form which arouses contemporary faith. It may well be that the moment draws near when art will again tell man what his God is and what he himself is." [62] Modern creative literature helps to bring us nearer to the moment of which Jaspers speaks and simultaneously reminds us of the timeless verity that "art is the grandchild of God." [63]

Notes

1. *A Gilson Reader,* ed. and with an Introduction by Anton C. Pegis (Garden City, N.Y.: Doubleday, 1957), p. 63.
2. *The Encyclopedia of Philosophy,* ed. Paul Edwards (New York: Macmillan, 1967), vol. V, p. 306.
3. *The Nature of Metaphysics,* ed. D. F. Pears (London: Macmillan, 1960), p. 131.
4. *Doctor Zhivago,* trans. Max Hayward and Manya Harari (New York: Pantheon, 1958), p. 90.

5. *Writers at Work: The Paris Review Interviews,* ed. and with an Introduction by Malcolm Cowley (New York: Viking, 1959), p. 55.

6. *Literary and Philosophical Essays,* trans. Annette Michelson (New York: Collier, 1962), pp. 84–85. D. H. Lawrence's concept of the relationship of art to metaphysics, as defined in his Foreword to *Fantasia of the Unconscious* (New York: Seltzer, 1922), is also pertinent here: "And finally, it seems to me that even art is utterly dependent on philosophy: or if you prefer it, on a metaphysic. The metaphysic or philosophy may not be anywhere very accurately stated and may be quite unconscious, in the artist, yet it is a metaphysic that governs men at the time, and is by all men more or less comprehended, and lived. Men live and see according to some gradually developing and gradually withering vision. This vision exists also as a dynamic idea or metaphysic—exists first as such. Then it is unfolded into life and art."

William Troy (1903–1961), counted among the best critics of this century, emphasized that an artist's works cannot be dissociated from "metaphysical problems," and that in the case of Gide, Proust, Mann, Joyce, and Lawrence, in particular, metaphysics is "the only relevant approach to these writers." "Of the various approaches to literature—the technical or esthetic, the historical, the socio-economic—the metaphysical alone," he insisted, "has the advantage of throwing light at one and the same time on both the form and the content of a work." See *William Troy: Selected Essays,* ed. and with an Introduction by Stanley Edgar Hyman (New Brunswick, N.J.: Rutgers University Press, 1967), pp. 123–124, 19, in the order of the quotations cited.

7. See "Un nouveau mystique," in *Situations I* (Paris: Gallimard, 1947); *Existentialism,* trans. Bernard Frechtman (New York: Philosophical Library, 1947), pp. 58, 60. See also Martin Buber, *Eclipse of God,* trans. Maurice S. Friedman (New York: Harper, 1957), Ch. V, "Religion and Modern Thinking," pp. 65–70.

8. "The Story," in *Aspects of the Novel* (New York: Barnes & Noble, 1963), pp. 28–29.

9. II Corinthians 5.17.

10. *Eclipse of God,* pp. 23, 24.

11. "Poetry, Man, and Things," in *Creative Intuition in Art and Poetry* (New York: Pantheon, 1953), p. 3.

12. See Eliseo Vivas, "Philosophy of Culture, Aesthetics, and Criticism: Some Problems," *The Texas Quarterly,* IX (Spring, 1966), 231–241; also his *D. H. Lawrence: The Failure and the Triumph of Art* (Evanston, Ill.: Northwestern University Press, 1960) and *Creation and Discovery* (New York: Noonday Press, 1955).

13. See his *Tolstoy or Dostoevsky: An Essay in the Old Criticism* (New York: Knopf, 1959), pp. 4–7.

14. *Against Interpretation* (New York: Farrar, Straus & Giroux, 1967), p. 14.

15. See his "Religion and the Mission of the Artist," in *The New Orpheus: Essays Toward a Christian Poetic,* ed. Nathan A. Scott, Jr. (New York: Sheed & Ward, 1964), pp. 59–73.

16. See his "Baptism in the Forest: Wisdom and Initiation in William Faulkner," Introductory Essay in *Mansions of the Spirit: Essays in Literature and Religion,* ed. George A. Panichas (New York: Hawthorn, 1967).

17. *Shakespeare and Spiritual Life* (The Romanes Lecture; New York: Oxford University Press, 1924), p. 24.

18. *Science and Poetry* (New York: Norton, 1926), p. 31.

19. Gabriel Marcel, Conclusion to *The Mystery of Being,* II: *Faith and Reality,* trans. René Hague (Chicago: Regnery, 1960), p. 208.

20. "A Memorable Fancy," in *The Marriage of Heaven and Hell* (*ca.* 1793).

21. Ernst Fischer, *The Necessity of Art: A Marxist Approach,* trans. Anna Bostock (Baltimore: Penguin, 1963), p. 200. See also Martin Jarrett-Kerr, C.R., "The Conditions of Tragedy," *Comparative Literature Studies,* II, 4 (1965), 363–366; Claude Mauriac, "A. Robbe-Grillet," in *The New Literature,* trans. Samuel I. Stone (New York: Braziller, 1959), pp. 225–234; Geoffrey Wagner, "Freedom to be a Thing: The 'New Novel' and Reality," and Thomas Molnar, "The 'New Novel' and the Future of Literature," *The Intercollegiate Review,* III, 1 (1966), 23–29 and 30–34, respectively.

22. These words are from the concluding lines of Wallace Stevens' "The Idea of Order at Key West" (1935):

> Oh! Blessed rage for order, pale Ramon,
> The maker's rage to order words of the sea,
> Words of the fragrant portals, dimly-starred,
> And of ourselves and of our origins,
> In ghostlier demarcations, keener sounds.

23. "The Way Back into the Ground of Metaphysics," in Walter Kaufmann, *Existentialism from Dostoevsky to Sartre* (Cleveland and New York: Meridian, 1956), p. 207.

24. "The Spirit of Place," in *Studies in Classic American Literature* (1923).

25. "The Responsibilities and Opportunities of the Artist," in *Moral Principles of Action: Man's Ethical Imperative,* planned and ed. by Ruth Nanda Anshen (New York: Harper, 1952), p. 475.

26. See *The Meaning of the Creative Act,* trans. Donald A. Lowrie (New York: Macmillan, 1962), especially Ch. X, "Creativity and Beauty: Art and Theurgy."

27. "John Dos Passos and *1919,*" in *Literary and Philosophical Essays,* pp. 95–96.

28. Paul J. Marcotte, *The God Within: Essays in Speculative Literary Criticism* (Ottawa: Runge, 1964), pp. 60–61.

29. Eliseo Vivas, *The Artistic Transaction and Essays on Theory of Literature* (Columbus: Ohio State University Press, 1963), p. vii.

30. D. H. Lawrence, *Women in Love* (1920), Ch. XIV, "Water-Party."

31. London: Hogarth Press, 1942, pp. 126–132.

32. See "'Ulysses': A Monologue," in *The Spirit in Man, Art, and Literature,* trans. R. F. C. Hull (New York: Bollingen, 1966), especially pp. 111, 112, 117, 119, 120, 124, 128.

33. "Fantasy," in *Aspects of the Novel,* p. 122.

34. *The Letters of D. H. Lawrence,* ed. and with an Introduction by Aldous Huxley (New York: Viking, 1932), p. 750. The letter containing these words is dated 15 August 1928 and is addressed to Maria and Aldous Huxley.

35. See *"Ulysses,* Order and Myth," in *James Joyce: Two Decades of Criticism* (New York: Vanguard, 1948), pp. 198–202.

36. Quoted in Richard Ellmann, *James Joyce* (New York: Oxford University Press, 1959), p. 410.

37. The quotations in this paragraph are from *A Portrait of the Artist as a Young Man* (1916), Ch. V.

38. Irene Hendry Chayes, "Joyce's Epiphanies," in *Joyce's "Portrait": Criticisms and Critiques,* ed. Thomas E. Connolly (New York: Appleton-Century-Crofts, 1962), p. 213.

39. "Morality and the Novel," *Phoenix: The Posthumous Papers of D. H. Lawrence,* ed. and with an Introduction by Edward D. McDonald (London: Heinemann, 1936), p. 532.

40. *Jerusalem* 4:6 (1804–1820).

41. *The Letters of D. H. Lawrence,* p. 631. Dated 17 November 1924.

42. See *The Idea of the Holy,* trans. John W. Harvey (New York: Oxford University Press, 1958).

43. "Sex *Versus* Loveliness," in *Assorted Articles* (London: Secker, 1930), p. 25.

44. The Foreword is included in *The Letters of D. H. Lawrence,* pp. 97–98.

45. *Apocalypse* (London: Secker, 1932), Ch. XXIII.

46. See George A. Panichas, *Adventure in Consciousness: The Meaning of D. H. Lawrence's Religious Quest* (The Hague: Mouton, 1964), especially pp. 31–61.

47. *D. H. Lawrence: Novelist* (New York: Knopf, 1956), p. vii.

48. *Eight Modern Writers* (London: Oxford University Press, 1963), p. 483.

49. *Phoenix,* p. 531.

50. Quoted in Frederick J. Hoffman, *The Mortal No* (Princeton: Princeton University Press, 1964), p. 366.

51. *The Mortal No,* pp. 346–347. For an incisive appreciation of this book see Melvin J. Friedman, "The Achievement of Frederick Hoffman," *The Massachusetts Review,* VI, 4 (1965), 862–867.

52. "The Role of the Catholic Novelist," *Greyfriar* [Siena College, Loudonville, N.Y.], VII (1964), 12. See also "A Collection of Statements" in *The Added Dimension: The Art and Mind of Flannery O'Connor,* edd. Melvin J. Friedman and Lewis A. Lawson (New York: Fordham University Press, 1966), especially pp. 226–237.

53. See Kenneth Hamilton's *Revolt Against Heaven* (Grand Rapids, Mich.: Eerdmans, 1965) and *God Is Dead: The Anatomy of a Slogan* (Grand Rapids, Mich.: Eerdmans, 1966) for a helpful discussion of the history of antisupernaturalism from pre-Reformation theology to neo-liberalism and for an analysis of the writings of the "Christian atheists."

54. W. H. Walsh, *Metaphysics* (London: Hutchinson, 1963), and *The Nature*

of *Metaphysics,* ed. D. F. Pears, contain excellent accounts of logical positivism in particular and of metaphysics in general.

55. See "Create Dangerously," in *Resistance, Rebellion, and Death,* trans. and
with an Introduction by Justin O'Brien (New York: Knopf, 1961), pp.
249–272.

56. *The Joyful Wisdom* (108):
   "New Struggles.—After Buddha was dead people showed his shadow for
   centuries afterwards in a cave,—an immense frightful shadow. God is dead:
   but as the human race is constituted, there will perhaps be caves for mil-
   lenniums yet, in which people will show his shadow.—And we—we have still
   to overcome his shadow!

57. New York: Grove, 1956, p. 52.

58. *Samuel Beckett* (London: Bowes & Bowes, 1965), p. 130. See also Josephine
Jacobsen and William R. Mueller, *The Testament of Samuel Beckett* (New
York: Hill & Wang, 1964).

59. *The New Literature,* p. 85.

60. *Ibid.,* p. 89.

61. Habakkuk 2.2.

62. *Man in the Modern Age,* trans. Eden and Cedar Paul (New York: Doubleday, 1957), p. 141. Similarly, St.- John Perse declares: "When the philosophers
abandon the metaphysical threshold, it falls to the poet to take upon himself
the role of the metaphysician: at such times it is poetry, not philosophy, that
is revealed as the true 'Daughter of Wonder.' . . ."—"On Poetry," trans.
W. H. Auden, in *Two Addresses* (New York: Pantheon, 1966), p. 11.

63. The phrase is taken from Dante, *The Divine Comedy,* in the *Inferno,* Canto
XI, line 105. There also comes to mind an analogous statement by Richard
Dehmel: "To be a poet means to embrace the world in love and lift it up
to God."

J. F. Powers' *Morte D'Urban*: Secularity and Grace

JOHN B. VICKERY · *University of California, Riverside*

> Theology is anthropology.
> LUDWIG FEUERBACH

THE FICTION OF J. F. POWERS poses, in particularly acute form, a crucial problem for the critic. Essentially a novel such as *Morte D'Urban* is a challenge to literary tact. In this it reminds us of the best work of F. Scott Fitzgerald, of, say, *The Great Gatsby*. Everything that ordinarily matters—character, theme, structure, all the rubrics dear to the professional critic—are absorbed into a stylistic surface of incomparable clarity and firmness. And the critic trembles at possibly being reduced to inarticulate murmurs of admiration and the helpless ostensiveness of endless quotation. Both Fitzgerald and Powers achieve such a full measure of realized concreteness and delicacy that interpretation threatens to limp far behind with the clubfooted gait of imaginative impertinence.

This is not to say, of course, that either Fitzgerald or Powers lies beyond the reaches of formalist analysis. Recently both John Hagopian and Martin Green have provided close and sustained commentaries on Powers' technical skills that

45

amply demonstrate the brilliance and solidity of his craftsmanship.[1] Given, however, the general cogency of their specific
comments as well as the character of the present volume, I
should like to adopt a critical strategy different from the
formalist one. In the past few years, we have witnessed a remarkable burgeoning of interest in the dialectical interplay
of literature and religion or theology. Father William Lynch's
Christ and Apollo, Murray Krieger's *The Tragic Vision,* the
late Frederick J. Hoffman's *The Mortal No* and *The Imagination's New Beginning,* Nathan Scott's *The Broken Center*
—all testify brilliantly to both the interest and its fertility of
insight for both disciplines. Nowhere perhaps is this mode
of criticism, which has been called "thematics," more relevant
than in the case of a Roman Catholic writer, such as Powers,
whose works are so redolent with the materials of his religion
and whose use of them has such critical implications for that
faith. What I should like to do is to bring to bear some of the
insights afforded by this most recent critical development on
Morte D'Urban as a work that peculiarly epitomizes issues
confronting the contemporary religious imagination.

It is no part of my concern to attribute conscious intention
of my argument to Powers either as a writer or as a practic-
ing Catholic. Indeed, the issues may be even more significant
if they form no part of his deliberate aim or even of his extra-
artistic thought. For in essence what I wish to question seriously is whether there is any meaningful sense, given the historical circumstances in which the modern world finds itself,
in which Powers can be regarded as a Roman Catholic writer.
In his chapter on Powers, Martin Green distinguishes three
senses in which one may be a "Catholic novelist." The first
consists in using Catholic material; the second in embracing
Catholicism as a religion and a philosophy; and the third is
connected with a literary tradition begun approximately a
hundred years ago. The first two may conceivably be either
extraneous or irrelevant or both to a specific writer. That is
to say, Powers uses Catholic material, but there is no logically
necessary connection with his adherence to the Catholic faith,
which in turn may not be substantially involved in his treat-

ment of his material. It is the third sense of "Catholic writer" that is of interest here. Mr. Green suggests that the tradition began with the nineteenth-century writer Barbey d'Aurevilly and developed three strains: the traditional or Balzacian, the mystical or prophetic as seen in Léon Bloy, and the psychology of sin developed most notably in François Mauriac. In the twentieth century, only the last two have played a significant role in shaping the work of such as Julien Green, Evelyn Waugh, Graham Greene, Flannery O'Connor, Muriel Spark, and Powers. Taken together, they represent, Mr. Green properly suggests, "an anti-humanist sensibility." More precisely, he says:

in these writers' novels, human achievements and modes of being are consistently and triumphantly shown to be inadequate, egotistic, evil, just in being themselves, in being human. Under stress all natural goodness breaks down; only grace-assisted goodness is valid, and grace-assisted badness is perhaps even better.[2]

In varying measures we can surely accept this appraisal of the writers in question. Precisely because of this, two questions are provoked and these lead on to the heart of the issue I wish to raise. The first questions whether the inadequacy of human achievements and natural goodness is sufficient to define a Catholic writer. Surely the massive if moribund evidence of American literary naturalism as detailed in Frank Norris, Theodore Dreiser, and Jack London would seem to dispute this. And what are we to do with James T. Farrell who mines both the naturalistic and Catholic veins? Is *Studs Lonigan* the product of a radically secular vision or of a transcendent religious imagination? And beyond this there is our second question. Assuming that the Catholic writer, having shown man's own shortcomings, wishes to underscore the primacy of grace—how is he to do so aesthetically? That is to say, is there a viable means of rendering the nature and experience of spiritual grace in an artistic economy so firmly grounded in secularity as the contemporary one is?

One of the things most striking about what is generally spoken of as Catholic writing is not only the absence of God

the Father as an actual presence or *persona* in the fiction but
also the substantive omission of suitable *figurae* for the descent of the Holy Spirit. It will not do, as Charles Glicksberg
does, to claim that God is always present in the background of
Graham Greene's fiction even though He never serves as
either protagonist or *deus ex machina.*[3] Nor do Muriel
Spark's hallucinatory telephone calls testify to a fictively satis-
fying spiritual presence, however much they dramatize the
underlying religio-cultural problem. Better in some ways is
Charles Williams' direct denial of natural law, as in *All Hal-
lows' Eve.* By straightforwardly including such phenomena
as magical transformations and creations and the spiritual
presence of the dead and their communication with the living,
he at least allows a clear-cut exercise of the reader's suspension of disbelief. Ultimately, of course, he pays the severe
penalty of moving his works from the ranks of fiction to those
of dramatized philosophical argument.

In short, we find that the modern Catholic writer—at least
of the order of seriousness mentioned above—has no positive
defining fictive characteristics that form both necessary and
sufficient conditions for his being so classified. To possess an
antihumanist sensibility precludes only those writers who possess a humanist sensibility, and clearly many antihumanists are
no more Catholic than they are humanist. As an exercise in definition, then, we find that there seems to be no satisfaction in
the label of "Catholic writer." This is not to say, of course,
that there are no Catholics writing; only that what they write
may not in any traditional sense be Catholic works. Such a
view obviously cannot stand in quite this unequivocal fashion.
Paul Claudel, for example, is clearly an instance of a writer
whose Catholicism is exactly coterminous with his imagination. And there are others. But for the most part modern
writers' sensibilities, especially in America, are shaped largely
by the secular world, which impinges on them virtually from
birth and in a thousand different forms. Consequently their
works become in some fundamental sense impure embodi-
ments of the Catholic imagination.

The logical question of definition, of whether any definition is possible, is obviously the root one. It underlies any and all concerns about the accuracy of any particular definition. That the Catholic writer or Catholic writing could be characterized in the past goes without saying. This fact suggests that the logical issue does not exist apart from history and the contemporary context. In other words, the religious climate, as well as its prospects for tomorrow, is of central importance to any understanding of J. F. Powers as a Catholic or Christian writer. Now, it is obvious that agreement on this issue is never going to be total, even among the religious and/or the devout. Nevertheless, one can fairly characterize mid-twentieth-century religious thought as uncertain of its rationale, uneasy about its future, radical toward the past and the need for change. Theologically, it is a time of crisis marked by a thoroughgoing questioning of basic religious assumptions and conventions. Even the most cursory glance shows us Tillich's existential monument, Bonhoeffer's "religionless Christianity," Bultmann's demythologizing activity, the death-of-God views of Vahanian, Altizer, Cox, and the others, and the new Catholicism of men like the late John Courtney Murray and Michael Novak. However divergent their opinions, they all share a profound concern with the interrelation of the religious and the secular, the temporal and the eternal. Unless they do interpenetrate in a significant and meaningful way, then Christianity is doomed. At the same time, these men are aware of the risks involved: the secular giant may crush or simply absorb the religious so that it either disappears totally or ceases to be relevant.

This last, some suggest, may already be more than a threatening possibility. Thus, the central contention in, for instance, Gabriel Vahanian's *The Death of God* is that the modern Western world is precisely a post-Christian era both theologically and culturally. It is so, he says, because Christianity has persistently confused its legitimate secularity with secularism. He distinguishes between these two as follows:

While the former is that realm in which religion can show its relevance, the latter is an inverted or concealed religious attitude. Secularism is a form of religiosity, for which the present and the immanent are invested with the attributes of the eternal and transcendent.[4]

Whether Vahanian's is an accurate historical analysis of the present age or not need not concern us here. It is a view that in a variety of forms a great many intelligent, sober, concerned persons hold and in support of which have advanced a series of significant arguments. Nor does the fact that this is fundamentally a Protestant interpretation of the contemporary scene materially affect the question. For, as one Catholic observer has remarked, "more and more, the significant theological questions are Christian questions, not 'Catholic' or 'Protestant' questions."[5] Its relevance remains constant regardless of its specific religious impetus. What does seem important is that if this view is tenable, then it is virtually impossible for a non-Christian age to yield Christian and hence Catholic imaginative works. And thus *Morte D'Urban* cannot be construed as an expression of the traditional Catholic vision. Certainly not in anything like the manner in which it customarily has been so regarded.

Such a position may at first glance look more like a *tour de force* than anything else. But there is rather more to it than that. It serves to project us out of two equally futile or limited critical stances toward Powers' novel. The first of these is amply documented by the reviews cited by Professor Hagopian in the course of his article. This view argues that in essence Powers identifies himself with Father Urban's sardonic appraisal of the clergy, his order, and the Church as an efficient administrative medium for religious action in the secular world. The second, ably represented by Professor Hagopian's article, endeavors to show how Father Urban's career in the novel follows a parabola from the secularistic to the spiritual, from what Vahanian calls the not-yet-holy to the holy. The first of these need not concern us to any extent, for patently Father Urban is not the lucid, undeluded intelligence he purports to be. Nevertheless, it does point up one important aspect that needs to be borne in mind. This is the fact that Urban's response to the smug, bumbling, ineffectual, petty stupidity of his fellow Catholics is an appropriate one. His proposed alternatives may be incomplete and superficial, but his perceptions of the Church's inadequacies in twentieth-century America are unerring and valid. To see him as a paranoiac compulsively distorting Fathers Wilfrid and Jack into dimwitted spiritual tyrants and plodding drones is to exaggerate Powers' techniques of perspective and point of view.

By the same token, the second critical view has a major weakness as well. It strives to suggest that Father Urban's developing sense of the complexity of the relationships obtaining between the sacred and secular orders and his change of heart from aggressive worldliness to diffident spirituality follows the traditional pattern of conversion or redemption. This, of course, is true in a sense, but what is really crucial is the way in which the novel diverges from or effects an important variation on that pattern. Powers' serio-comic sense is at its height when sanctifying grace is equated with the bishop's golfball striking Urban on the head. The same is true later when Urban, as new Provincial of the order, gains a reputation for increased piety by virtue of the effects of his severe headaches. There is no way in which such images and scenes can be regarded as other than farcical renderings of spiritual reality. To treat them straightforwardly as fictively viable representations of the entry of the divine into the human world is to strain credulity and to make primitive magic appear hard-headed by comparison. Consequently, such ironies call in question the precise nature of what one critic avers is Urban's "newly-won and unselfconscious state of grace." [6] Rather than view Powers' strategies for presenting grace as inept craftsmanship or deliberate religious self-delusion, it would seem intrinsically more probable to regard them as daring efforts to explore a borderline situation of the gravest order for the Catholic imagination.

Morte D'Urban is patently more than a remorselessly superficial critique of Catholic clerical and lay attitudes and manners, just as it is more than an ineffectual comic metaphor of the redemptive process. Powers is neither simply attacking the materialistic secularism of the Church nor evasively de-

fending (by making fiction serve as a mode of intellectual
fantasy) the realistic possibility of spiritual or religious life
in the modern world. What he is doing, it seems to me, is il-
luminating the post-Christian nature of that world through
his imaginative vision of American Catholic life. *Beowulf*, it
has been remarked, is a Christian vision of life before the
coming of Christ. And in a somewhat similar manner we
might say that *Morte D'Urban* is a post-Christian vision of
the disappearance of Christ. What it shows us is the idea of
the death of God working itself out in the Roman Catholic
imagination.

One Catholic student of the contemporary scene has asked,
"How long does it take before problems which agitate Protestant minds begin to agitate Catholic minds?" [7] An unequivocal answer is scarcely possible, but one can suggest, I think,
that in imaginative literature it has, as in *Morte D'Urban*,
Wise Blood, *The Violent Bear It Away*, and *A Burnt-Out
Case*, already occurred. To be sure, there is a wide range of
response in these authors to the issue of God's continuing
relevance to man's experiential universe. But they all reflect
through their ostensible themes and manifest techniques at
least an imaginative entertaining of the disappearance of God.
The agonizing of Greene's characters, the violence of image
and scene in O'Connor, and the remorselessly mundane perspectives in Powers—each points up the imagination's intima-
tions that it is being called on to make new beginnings. Quite
likely, spiritual agitation is a matter less of emulation than of
the inescapability of cultural context. Thus, Powers may be
totally oblivious to this issue and theme in his work and he
may be unaware of what is agitating Protestant minds. But
from the evidence of his fiction he certainly knows intuitively
some of the central issues agitating the imagination of his
time. And in registering them so sensitively his art serves a
unique role as the growing edge between the known and the
unknown.

The chief topic explored in *Morte D'Urban* is the problem
of secularity and the threat of secularism. It is this more than
anything else that accounts for the dual perspective on Father

Urban and his colleagues. As the novel opens, Urban is the priest in the world, aware that "in recent years . . . a little bit of community life went a long way with him." [8] At the same time he is presented as perceiving clearly that his order is doomed unless it can assume an active role in the secular society of the twentieth century:

Father Urban knew (none better) that the Order wasn't up to the job of being an effective influence for good on the near North Side, or any-where else in the fast-changing world of today, and it never would be, he knew, with men of Father Boniface's stamp calling the shots. There had to be a new approach. Ideally, it should be their own, recognizably theirs. Otherwise, it was only a matter of time before the Order died on its feet [pp. 19–20].

Thus, he desires a room in the headquarters of the order which would be "a rendezvous where passers-by would always be welcome to drop in and chat, to peruse the latest in worth-while books and periodicals" (p. 17). This is motivated by the desire to render more readily available access to and counsel with the spiritual world of the clergy and the Church. The austerity, ugliness and banality prized by Father Boni-face, the Provincial of the order, represent, ironically enough, a kind of puritanism of the spirit. Under its aegis the spiritual life is largely defined negatively, as the absence of secularity rather than as a positive presence.

In desiring to see his order renounce "the curse of medi-ocrity" (p. 18) under which it has always labored, Urban seeks the survival of the Church and the Christian faith in the modern age. His flaw is that he himself is more often than not unable to distinguish clearly and sharply between secu-larity and secularism. Thus, the converts he wishes for most are "the higher type" (p. 17), and his pockets fill up with mon-etary gifts because "he was true to his vow of poverty—to the spirit, though, rather than the letter" (p. 14). This blurred vision is best caught by his effort to improve the caliber of priests in the order. For, though several of his protégés are excellent prospects, it is nevertheless an ironic fact that "he had overshot the mark on occasion—two of his recruits had proved to be homosexual and one homicidal" (p. 19). Too often, particularly through the first half of the novel, Father Urban seems to invest practical intelligence, business sense, efficiency—all the ways of the present-day world—with eternal, transcendent qualities. They become almost ends in themselves with a value that is neither contingent nor limited.

But the burden of Powers' irony extends further than Father Urban himself. His limitations and shortcomings are limned in throughout the novel quietly and unostentatiously but unequivocally. Yet—and this is the devastating conclusion implicit in Powers' rendering—Father Urban is at the present time the best that twentieth-century American Catholicism has to offer. If he is incapable of perceiving accurately the difference between being in and being of the world, how much worse off are those less astute than he? Here the logic of Sir Thomas More's *Utopia* reappears in modern dress and with a negative emphasis. Where More argued from the merits of natural religion to the superiority of revealed religion, Powers dramatizes the inability of Christians adequately to define a viable relationship for themselves with the secular world. The best they can do, as Father Urban's example indicates, is "to make friends, as enjoined by the Scriptures, with the mammon of iniquity" (p. 20). And that is not good enough. For a religion of transcendent aspirations there must be something more, but that there is not is precisely what *Morte D'Urban* documents.

The novel's title is far from accidental, for it immediately and graphically charts the defining metaphor for twentieth-century man. As Frederick Hoffman observed,

Spiritual resources are an outgrowth of superstitions, of the sense of human limitation, and most significantly of man's fear of death. . . . Much of modern ideological history is taken up with the effort to secularize that fear and to realign the hope of immortality. The need for a City of Man to replace Augustine's City of God combines the history of man's disappointment in the Church as institution with his desire for absolutes.[9]

Though not of the same order of intensity as *Remembrance of Things Past* or *The Magic Mountain* or *The Sound and the Fury,* there is, nevertheless, a strain running through Powers' novel that makes it, too, a time-haunted book. Urban is almost perennially aware of the need for action within both the order and the community at large, because time is ceaselessly bearing them toward their own incipient termination.

In the beginning of the novel, Urban's career away from the novitiate is a busy and ceaseless round of spiritual activity in the secular world. He "stumped the country, preaching retreats and parish missions, and did the work of a dozen men" (p. 20). Later, at St. Monica's, he transforms it into "a busy, happy rectory" (p. 157), quickens both parish and town life, and then vitalizes The Hill through his preaching as well as through the installation of a golf course. And his plans and wishes are even more energetic, "but there just wasn't time for it" (p. 163). When he is most involved with the life of his parishioners, the ineluctable pressure of time reaches a peak of intensity:

At least he'd put in an appearance. "Look at that clock!" Off he'd go, and be late at the next stop. "And the worst of it is, I can't stay!" "OHHH!" So he'd relent and say a few words [p. 164].

The stupidity and pettiness he encounters are the accumulated dead weight of the human consciousness unaware of time's immanence. Thus, his confessor, Monsignor Renton, thinks that "any time not spent at the altar, or in administering the sacraments, was just time wasted for a priest" (p. 149), and so warns Urban against what he calls " 'overindulgence in spurious activity' " (p. 150).

Father Wilfrid and the rest avoid the spiritual pressures imposed by the reality of death through a sedulous concentration on bureaucratic piety conceived principally as a myopic concentration on the immediate moment. For them, there is only the spatial minutiae of sandpapering, painting and varnishing rooms, lettering cards, and planning gardens, each of which fills a lacuna created by their imaginative opacity to last things. Only Father Urban addresses himself to these, as when, at Father Phil Smith's funeral, "he spoke more of death itself than of the death of a priest" (p. 178). There he articulates in what the bishop ironically calls " 'a dazzling performance' " the orthodox Christian view of eschatology and immortality:

God Almighty wants *you!* That is the biggest, the best, fact of life! That is *the* fact of life! Death! Life and death and life—eternal life! *Who could ask for anything more?* [p. 179]

All the characters in their several ways effect strategies of evasion by which to circumvent the awareness of death. Even old Mrs. Thwaites's obsession with her own end and the nature of the afterlife is a way of bypassing the reality through a kind of casuistical cost-accounting applied to eschatology. She opts for what is in reality a parody of the traditional Christian and Catholic accommodation to death. Her God is not a living presence in a holy of holies but a manufactured screen bodying forth insubstantial images in a stiflingly hot room. The rest of the characters do not so much parody the religious sense of death as they attempt to secularize it. Sally Hopwood, Mrs. Thwaites's daughter, realigns the hope of immortality with intellectual and physical candor. For her a post-Cartesian clarity and a post-Freudian sexuality combine to create a hope of transcending mortality by making it a fact of consciousness which then is obliterated in physical ecstasy. The delusory character of this effort is indicated by her association with the golden calf, for her shoes, her only remaining item of clothing in the "Belleisle" chapter, not only carry the traditional allusion: they also testify to Powers' sense of the shriveled character of the symbol itself.

The fullest example, however, of this effort to secularize the religious response to death is, of course, Father Urban himself. Essentially, as Frederick Hoffman has suggested, it is the metaphor of grace that compensates for man's discovery of his mortality. But in the twentieth century "religious and secular images are confused with one another," [10] and as a result the myth of secular grace emerges, in which perfection and immortality are to be found in a future social state. Substantially this is what Urban seeks. His concern over and his multiform efforts to accelerate the perfecting of his order, the revitalizing of the parish, and the metamorphosing of society at large are ultimately efforts to achieve a state of secular grace. What Hoffman has said of this effort is peculiarly apt to Father Urban and his activities throughout the book:

It is one of the greatest risks ever assumed in human history: man somehow hopes to overcome the fear of death by thinking that immortality is available to him from an act of will, rationally disposed. Since he is not satisfied that it should exist beyond the grave but insists that it be available on this side, he must himself confront the fact of death in the expectation of a movement in time toward secular perfection.[11]

The profound ironies attendant on this risk account in large measure for the weary plangency that suffuses the final chapter, entitled, appropriately enough, "Dirge." Having devoted all his energies to improving and perfecting the secularity of the Church, Urban comes in the end to preside over an organization which all along has been the epitome of secularism. The dynamic changes expected from Urban are not forthcoming. Personnel changes are inexplicable, the order's lease on Billy Cosgrove's building is not renewed, the long-time weekly radio program lapses, the Avenue of Elms is cut down. Suddenly Urban seems to retreat from his old position and to assume that of the former provincial. In this, Powers captures one of his most brilliant insights. Urban turns back to the old order and ways of managing because in the twentieth century with its urban, industrialized, secularized universe secularity in the religious vision and institution is inevitably overwhelmed by secularism.

In short, Vahanian's distinction between secularity and secularism mentioned earlier can be made but not maintained. Actually they are historical developments of one another. When the Church or the religious spirit moves into the world of the twentieth century in all its temporal, immanent, mortal dimensions, it embarks on a course of secularity. But that world's intellectual, cultural, and imaginative pressures are so concentratedly secular that the delicate balance cannot be maintained, and secularism is the inevitable result. Thus, at the end of the book, Urban recognizes silently the precise congruence of his original aims with those of his order. Both are forms of secularism, the chief difference being that Urban's version aspired to greater efficiency by virtue of not recognizing its essential nature. All his efforts emerge finally as exercises in the vanity of human wishes. They represent the paradox of secular grace noted by Hoffman when he wrote:

Ironically, a strenuous effort to hasten the processes of history seem to have the effect of prolonging the conclusion toward which it is or should be proceeding. The ideal state (the vision of secular immortality) seems gradually to have assumed qualities of remoteness, inaccessibility, unreality, that have characterized the goal of spiritual grace from the beginning.[12]

By the time of "Dirge," Urban's vision of secular immortality as achieved through a religious society perfected in its secularity has become so remote that he cannot even remember it. What he is left with is a secular political analogue to his own religious position:

About these things [the various losses sustained by the order], and others, he had little to say, but reading the speeches of Winston Churchill, and coming to "I have not become the King's first minister in order to preside over the liquidation of the British Empire," he thought, "No, nor did Mr (as he was then) Attlee consider himself so called, but such was his fate" [p. 333].

Urban comes finally, given the cogency of his earlier analysis of the religious situation, to presiding over the dissolution of his order and, by implication, of the Christian faith and the Church as men now know it. The critical index that this is not simply the decline of an individual is the parabola of Urban's own development and its terminus. His movement

from secular efficiency and spiritual pride to chastened awareness and spiritual illumination of sorts does, as has been remarked earlier, seem to be cast in a pattern of redemption and
accession of grace. But it is important for Urban's case to
recall the relevant comment of Frederick Hoffman:

> The myth of grace . . . is a story of the movement of an imperfect
> spirit toward perfection, of the spirit's arduous labor to perfect itself
> and to make itself immortal—in other words, to defeat death, initially
> and always the most formidable of all threats to his security.[13]

The key phrase is that which links grace with the effort to
ensure immortality. This should be thought of together with
Hoffman's other point about the secular ideal's gradual assumption of the qualities of remoteness, inaccessibility, and
unreality. Then Urban's final state stands revealed in a quite
different, perhaps shocking, and certainly daring light. As
the "Dirge" chapter, together with several of the immediately
preceding ones, clearly demonstrates, Urban increasingly assumes these very qualities in the eyes of the rest of the characters and perhaps even of himself. And since he is also an
individual human being struggling for immortality, it would
appear that in effect he is engaged in a secular inversion of
the metaphor of the Incarnation. The golfing accident renders
the descent of grace or the Holy Spirit from a comic perspective that nevertheless seeks to authenticate its reality. Here,
however, Powers ironically reveals man endeavoring to ascend and become the father figure, God Himself.

In this very effort lies the ultimately total and complete
secularism of Father Urban, a secularism that is both poig-
nant, savage, and charged with futility for the religious mind.
For Father Urban acquires not only remoteness and unreality
as head of his order and secular surrogate for the father god;
he also attains ineffectuality. Like the provincial before him,
he modulates suggested changes and reforms into stasis and
an inscrutable impercipience about meaningful activity. He
presides, in effect, over a doomed holding-action in which his
own lack of wisdom and power point to the atrophying of

both the Church and the spiritual reality back of it. The really
devastating consequence to the imaginative logic developed
here by Powers is not the orthodox one of the overweening
spiritual presumption of the aspirant but precisely the reverse.
Father Urban is scarcely aware of the role in which he is cast
at the end of the novel. What is revealed through his secular
image is the weakened imaginative force of the idea of God
Himself in the twentieth century and in the very religious
world He is supposed to command. Urban's pallid, withdrawn, and halting regime is a quasi-secular or at least human
image of the supreme religious Father's command of the mid-
twentieth-century imagination. The Church, which Urban
epitomizes, both in its efforts and in its failures, at the end of
the novel, has itself become secularized and so ultimately a
non-Catholic institution. The traditional view of it is that
"for the Catholic the Church is a divine institution, but on
the pattern of the Incarnation itself." [14] That is, like Christ,
it is both human and divine, so that the imperfections and
blemishes of the one are transformed by the presence of the
other. But as the Church is represented in *Morte D'Urban,*
its divinity has dwindled in the wake of the disappearance of
God as a creative power in the imaginative economy of man.
It stands instead as a secular rampart and retreat for vested
interests who like the bishop are " 'always wanting something' " (p. 235).

It is no accident either that Urban's fatherhood should
be a travesty on religious and secular levels alike. He is the
individual embodiment of the city, the ambiguous symbol of
the human community and its potentiality. It is significant,
therefore, that he should, as the last sentence of the novel
tells us, abandon Chicago and its urban amenities and "think
of the Hill as home" (p. 336). Clearly, Powers uses the
pastoral motif to point up the desuetude of the city and to
suggest a spiritual vantage point from which to survey what
Eliot called "the immense panorama of futility and anarchy
which is contemporary history." [15] Yet it is equally clear that
Urban's settling on the Hill functions also as an elegiac au-
thentication of Urban's initial vision of St. Clement's. Moving

through a landscape of "rusty implements. Brown dirt. Grey
skies. Ice. No snow." (p. 39) and on out past a cemetery,
Urban thinks of "the silver flask in his attaché case" (p. 41)
and decides against it:

Many a good city man had gone down that drain. Yes, and even worse
fates, it was said, could overtake a city man in desolation—women,
insanity, decay [p. 41].

And when he finally arrives, "there was no sign of life" (p.
42).

Desolation, decay, and death are qualities that dominate
the Hill from the outset. Into these Urban finally settles not
simply as an individual but as the epitome of the City of God
in the twentieth century. And if he appears vastly shrunken
compared to Augustine's massively sustained symbol, that is
but the appropriate index of the cultural transformation
wrought by the intervening centuries. The clinching point in
his juxtaposition of scenic and dramatic irony lies in the idea
of "home." When Urban comes to think of the Hill as home,
he is returning to the townspeoples' original insistence on
calling the quarters of the order "The Home." This title
dated from the days when it had been "an old-people's home,
really a poorhouse" (p. 46). The closing implication of the
novel clearly is that Urban's final identification with the order
and the Hill is the assumption of spiritual residency in an
impoverished building for persons near the end of their lives.
That this building ultimately is the Church and the Christian
faith seems inescapable when one attends to the strategies of
secularization and grace developed by Professor Hoffman.

Such an ultimate significance needs, however, a more precise alignment with other thematic features in the novel than
has yet been offered here. And it is to this final aspect that I
wish to turn now. Earlier, I had discussed the two dominant
critical stances toward *Morte D'Urban*. In view of what was
said then, it might at this point be thought that the views
just enunciated are in accord with those that see Powers essentially as writing satire of a traditional order on stupidity,

vulgarity, and pettiness in a religious community. Throughout his career, Powers has shown a virtually unparalleled satiric sense of the foibles and failures of the American Catholic clergy. That this is not mere literary license but rather a penetrating awareness of the contemporary is shown by the similar discursive testimony of young Catholics writing in *The Generation of the Third Eye*. Summarizing the views there, Michael Novak has declared that

for nearly every contributor the ordinary parish life of the Church in America has been virtually bankrupt. The sermons are abominable, both in theology and in culture; the churches are run as "parish plants" rather than as praying and believing communities. The financial strain of building and maintaining parochial schools seems to have made practical materialists out of the Catholic community.[16]

Had Powers rested here with astringently chronicling the disparity between actual and ideal in American Catholicism, he would obviously be classifiable as a Catholic writer in one of the senses of Martin Green's alluded to earlier. The same is true of his efforts in *Morte D'Urban* to follow the movement of the protagonist's life and career from self-aggrandisement to a more genuine piety and contrition. Unquestionably, Powers intends Urban to represent the process of spiritual transformation that marks a man's movement from a secular to a religious perspective. But this, as has been indicated, is not all that he does.

Neither of the foregoing is the same thing as revealing the post-Christian vision of the irrelevance of God to self-knowledge. Beyond Catholic satire and the Christian myth of grace lies the motif of the death of God in the Catholic imagination. Looked at as functional coordinates, these three themes fall into place in a way that helps to explain *Morte D'Urban*'s role as an oblique seismograph attuned to the religio-cultural faults and quakes of mid-century. The satiric dimension begins by testifying to Powers' sense of the incompleteness and unsatisfactoriness of the American Catholic religious experience. Under its weight, he continues both to affirm the authenticity and to explore the implications of his perceptions, so that the post-Christian aspect of his novel is limned in obliquely but inexpungeably. But such implications as the disappearance of God pose too great a threat to his imaginative autonomy and integrity of his religious faith. As a result, the novel has Father Urban gradually grow and transform in the course of the book so that the traditional possibilities of salvation, redemption, and grace are enunciated in a symbolism that is not so much perfunctory as strained and devoid of verisimilitude.

It is a matter of extraordinary difficulty for Powers, as a Christian and especially as a Roman Catholic, to elucidate clearly the distinctive form of the post-Christian imagination. What pre-eminently conditions its shape can be gathered from Gabriel Vahanian's appraisal:

Today only the reality of the world, in all its immediacy and its immanence, provides man with a context for possible self-understanding. This self-understanding is amputated from any necessity of a fundamental knowledge of God. It is easier to understand oneself without God than with God. Modern man lives in a world of immanence. If he is the prey of anxiety, it is not because he feels guilty before a just God. Nor is it because he fails to explain the justice and love of God in the obvious presence of evil and injustice. God is no longer responsible for the world—since he is dead. But man is. He cannot avoid assuming full responsibility for a world of immanence, in terms of which he knows and understands himself or seeks to do so. The dilemma of Christianity is that it taught man how to be responsible for his actions in this world, and for this world itself. Now man has declared God not responsible and not relevant to human self-knowledge. The existence of God, no longer questioned, has become useless to man's predicament and its resolution.[17]

All Powers' works exhibit an acute ear for the rhythms and locutions of ordinary speech. They penetrate even the ostensibly august and formal propriety of the clergy and their finely realized sense of the minutiae and impedimenta of individual physical existence. By so doing, his works testify to Powers' sense of "the reality of the world, in all its immediacy and its immanence." Many of the stories, and in particular *Morte D'Urban,* also indicate his sharpened awareness of the uselessness to modern man of the concept of God. But this appears indirectly, through his inability to violate his imaginative integrity. No attempts are made to frame fictive means of incorporating any of the figures of the Trinity into his works in ways that mimetically render their essential religious functions. And when he does—as in the quasi-secular assimilation of the Father to Urban at the end of the novel—the result is unmistakably ironic. It testifies not to the Catholic reaches of Powers' imagination but to the post-Christian vision which he is powerless to deny. As a result, what he creates above all in the novel is a deeply disturbing prospect, that of an age of crisis and transition in which the Catholic imagination finds itself bereft of God not as a reality but as a relevance.

Vahanian has suggested that "our age is post-Christian; but it is still religious," [18] and this is an important qualification in Powers' case. Though he registers the insupportable possibility of a Catholicism demythologized or, better, detranscendentalized, he does not do so as an irreligious act. Instead, what he creates is a religious drama of the secular world's rendering God irrelevant, and holding this up to man as a possibility from which he can see no viable intellectual or imaginative escape. At the same time, the spirit in which this is done has nothing of the nineteenth-century exuberance and exultation of Nietzsche. The sad, cool, grey lucidity of *Morte D'Urban* bespeaks not of metaphysical emancipation and ethical release but of epistemological uncertainty and psychological reluctance. Recently Daniel Callahan called for a new logic of religion to match the "new freedom." This, however, is no part of Powers' achievement in *Morte D'Urban.* Instead—and perhaps more immediately appropriate to the prevailing climate—he provides only the courageous recognition that "there are fewer and fewer smug Christians to be found these days, especially those confident about the grasp their particular church has on the truth." [19] The "inner shambles" of Christianity and its cause are seen starkly and unrelievedly by Powers. This consists of the catalytic interaction of "the inner Christian world and the outer secular world." [20] It is in this vision of an order that is passing and that generates thereby a challenge to the religious mind equal to that of Nietzsche's in the nineteenth century or the Reformation earlier that the ultimate Grail significance of the novel's title resides. In tone, theme, attitude, and expectation, Powers' stance belongs more to Tennyson than to Malory, for in the former the realization is sharp that what is departing is less a moral code of unsurpassed nobility than the possibility of a transcendent religious order.

Notes

1. See John Hagopian, "Irony and Involution in J. F. Powers' 'Morte D'Urban,'" *Contemporary Literature,* IX, 2 (Spring, 1968), 151–171; Martin Green, "J. F. Powers and Catholic Writing," in *Yeats's Blessing on Von Hügel* (London: Longmans, Green, 1967), pp. 97–127.

2. Green, p. 74.

3. See Charles Glicksberg, *Modern Literature and the Death of God* (The Hague: Nijhoff, 1966), pp. 135–136.

4. Gabriel Vahanian, *The Death of God* (New York: Braziller, 1961), p. 67.

5. Daniel Callahan, *The New Church* (New York: Scribners, 1966), p. 214.

6. Hagopian, p. 160.

7. Callahan, p. 169.

8. J. F. Powers, *Morte D'Urban* (Garden City, N.Y.: Doubleday, 1962), p. 17. Subsequent references will be indicated in the text.

9. Frederick J. Hoffman, *The Mortal No* (Princeton: Princeton University Press, 1964), p. 98.

10. *Ibid.,* p. 6.

11. *Ibid.,* p. 109.

12. *Ibid.,* p. 108.

13. *Ibid.,* p. 106.

14. Michael Novak, *A Time to Build* (New York: Macmillan, 1967), p. 225.

15. T. S. Eliot, "'Ulysses,' Order, and Myth," in *Criticism,* edd. M. Schorer, J. Miles, and G. McKenzie (New York: Harcourt, Brace, 1948), p. 270.

16. Novak, p. 123.

17. Vahanian, p. 147.

18. *Ibid.,* p. 230.

19. Callahan, p. 214.

20. *Ibid.,* p. 215.

Flannery O'Connor's Sacred Objects*

MELVIN J. FRIEDMAN · *University of Wisconsin–Milwaukee*

THERE ARE FEW WRITERS as free from experimentation as Flannery O'Connor. She has diligently avoided the literary fashions of her time. She has maintained, in several interviews, that her work springs from an oral tradition; indeed, one notices in the two collections of her stories and in her two novels that the "spoken" seems always to triumph over the "written."

The only peculiarly twentieth-century technique she uses with any regularity is what critics have labeled indirect interior monologue: Miss O'Connor penetrates the minds of her characters but usually preserves the objectivity of the third person and the correctness of the syntax. There is nothing of Flannery O'Connor's consciousness in these monologues, only the consciousness of her characters; yet the sober controls exerted on the language are her own. A characteristic example is this third-person "quotation" from Tanner's mind in her last story to appear, "Judgement Day."

---

* An earlier form of this essay appeared in *The Added Dimension: The Art and Mind of Flannery O'Connor* (New York: Fordham University Press, 1966), pp. 196–206.

67

He laid his head on the back of the chair for a moment and the hat tilted down over his eyes. He had raised three boys and her. The three boys were gone, two in the war and one to the devil and there was nobody left who felt a duty toward him but her, married and childless, in New York City like Mrs. Big and ready when she came back and found him living the way he was to take him back with her. She had put her face in the door of the shack and had stared, expressionless, for a second. Then all at once she had screamed and jumped back.[1]

The digressiveness and absence of logical development in the third sentence is especially close to the milder forms of stream-of-consciousness used by many of Flannery O'Connor's contemporaries. We notice the objective narrative of the first sentence gradually giving way to an approximation of Tanner's idiom in the somewhat transitional second sentence—which could represent the point of view of either the omniscient author or the character.

The narrative procedures of this passage are evident in all of Miss O'Connor's fiction from her first published story, "The Geranium" (1946).[2] The devices are so natural to her that it would probably be wrong to connect them with any of the revolutions in fiction which we normally associate with the 'twenties and 'thirties. It may be the haunting and obtrusive presence of the Southern oral tradition which explains these near-monologues, often in local idiom, breaking into passages of description.

There is still another element in her fiction which seems to connect her stories and novels with the practices of certain of her contemporaries. This is her reliance on "a literature of Things."[3] Dorothy Van Ghent has admirably explained this phenomenon in an essay on Dickens' *Great Expectations*:

People were becoming things, and things (the things that money can buy or that are the means for making money or for exalting prestige in the abstract) were becoming more important than people. People were being de-animated, robbed of their souls, and things were usurping the prerogatives of animate creatures—governing the lives of their owners in the most literal sense.[4]

This is as precise a statement as we are likely to find anywhere to explain a set of literary circumstances which have characterized so much of modern fiction and poetry.

The exalting of "things," however, is not something new. Plutarch, in his life of Demosthenes, wrote: ". . . for it was not so much by the knowledge of words that I came to the understanding of things, as by my experience of things I was enabled to follow the meaning of words." In book IV, chapter 32 of *Tristram Shandy,* Tristram speaks of writing a "chapter of Things" and laments the fact "that things have crowded in so thick upon me, that I have not been able to get into that part of my work, towards which I have all the way looked forwards, with so much earnest desire. . . ."

This Shandyan lament is carried into the twentieth century in a series of prose poems, *Tropismes.* Nathalie Sarraute, in this early work, echoes Sterne:

Les choses! les choses! C'était sa force. La source de sa puissance. L'instrument dont elle se servait, à sa manière instinctive, infaillible et sûre, pour le triomphe, pour l'écrasement.

Quand on vivait près d'elle, on était prisonnier des choses, esclave rampant chargé d'elles, lourd et triste, continuellement guetté, traqué par elles.[5]

This passage may be said to have launched a new group of writers, who are occasionally referred to as *chosistes.* The inheritance of "things" has made its presence felt decisively in the novels of Samuel Beckett, Alain Robbe-Grillet, and Nathalie Sarraute herself. (We should not forget the title of an installment of Simone de Beauvoir's autobiography, *La Force des Choses.*) Almost all of Beckett's characters own hats, umbrellas, and bicycles which they treat with a certain reverence. No theatergoer can forget the vaudevillean moment in *En attendant Godot* when Vladimir and Estragon pass the hats ritualistically back and forth. The heroes of Beckett's novels are almost all feverishly attached to their bicycles—to the point that they seem to offer a new creatural dimension, which Hugh Kenner has classified as "Cartesian centaur." [6] Robbe-Grillet's novels depend heavily on physical objects, like the watches and the figure eight in *Le Voyeur*, or the eraser in *Les Gommes*. While Beckett's characters are fond of listing and cataloguing their "possessions," Robbe-Grillet's "narrators" describe objects in minute surface detail.

Flannery O'Connor's own reading probably did not include these "new novelists." Robert Fitzgerald mentions in his introduction to *Everything That Rises Must Converge*[7] that the only novels which she urged him to read during her stay in his Connecticut home were *Miss Lonelyhearts* and *As I Lay Dying*. Flannery O'Connor was evidently not drawn especially to French literature; as Fitzgerald reports: "Though she deprecated her French, now and again she would read some, and once carried off one of those appetizing volumes of Faguet from which I had learned about all I knew of old French literature" (*Everything*, p. xv). She would be unlikely to find out anything about *chosisme* (even in the broadest sense) from the pages of Emile Faguet. In the numerous interviews with Flannery O'Connor, the only contemporary French novelist whose name turns up is François Mauriac. And he is as far from the practices of the *nouveau roman* as it is possible to be.

We must, then, look in another direction to understand Flannery O'Connor's preoccupation with physical objects, with "things." Very much to the point, I think, are some remarks made by Mircea Eliade in his *The Sacred and the Profane*. After defining elementary hierophany as the "manifestation of the sacred in some ordinary object, a stone or a tree," he goes on to say:

It is impossible to overemphasize the paradox represented by every hierophany, even the most elementary. By manifesting the sacred, any object becomes *something else,* yet it continues to remain *itself,* for it continues to participate in its surrounding cosmic milieu. A *sacred* stone remains a *stone*; apparently (or, more precisely, from the profane point of view), nothing distinguishes it from all other stones. But for those to whom a stone reveals itself as sacred, its immediate reality is transmuted into a supernatural reality.[8] In other words, for those who have a religious experience all nature is capable of revealing itself as cosmic sacrality. The cosmos in its entirety can become a hierophany.[9]

The predominantly religious fiction of Flannery O'Connor, with its uneasy tension between the sacred and the profane, seems to be an exact literary application of this theory.

There are few characters in Miss O'Connor's work who are not irresistibly tied to some commonplace object. Hazel Motes, the self-appointed preacher of the new "Church Without Christ" in *Wise Blood,* has as his equipment a suit of "glaring blue," "a stiff black broad-brimmed hat," a black Bible, and "a pair of silver-rimmed spectacles." He holds on to the incongruously mated suit and hat almost as if they were religious objects, to the point at which (to use Dorothy Van Ghent's words again) they "were usurping the prerogatives of animate creatures—governing the lives of their owners in the most literal sense." The same can be said for the Bible and spectacles. They offer as ludicrous a combination as the suit and the hat. Hazel reads his Bible only when he is wearing the spectacles, despite the fact that "They tired his eyes so that after a short time he was always obliged to stop." [10] The "high rat-colored car" which he purchases later in the novel is treated with the same illogical reverence. Hazel Motes's "things" are perhaps the best illustration in Miss O'Connor's work of "immediate reality [being] transmuted into a supernatural reality" and of "nature [being] capable of revealing itself as cosmic sacrality."

Another character in *Wise Blood,* Enoch Emery, is characterized by Miss O'Connor as having "a certain reverence for the purpose of things." He presents Hazel with a shriveled-up mummy, stolen from a museum, to act as a new jesus for his Church Without Christ. A statement made by Paul Tillich in his *The Courage To Be* offers a gloss, perhaps, for Emery's action: "The man-created world of objects has drawn into itself Him who created it and who now loses His subjectivity in it."

Tarwater, the young hero of Flannery O'Connor's other novel, *The Violent Bear It Away,* shares Hazel Motes's regard for hats. When the novel reaches a kind of epiphany in the drowning-baptism of the mentally retarded Bishop, we note that both Tarwater and Bishop are wearing hats. Bishop, just before the drowning, is ominously described by Miss O'Connor: "The small black-hatted figure sat like a passenger being borne by the surly oarsman across the lake to some mysterious destination" (*Three,* p. 420). This Dantesque moment is underscored by the reference to the hat. Several pages later we understand the talismanic importance of the hat:

Bishop took off his hat and threw it over the side where it floated right-side-up, black on the black surface of the lake. The boy turned his head, following the hat with his eyes, and saw suddenly that the bank loomed behind him, not twenty yards away, silent, like the brow of some leviathan lifted just above the surface of the water. He felt bodiless as if he were nothing but a head full of air, about to tackle all the dead [*Three,* p. 431].

Despite the unpleasant symbolic reminders of Bishop's hat, Tarwater tenaciously holds on to his own through the final pages of *The Violent Bear It Away.*

Tarwater holds a corkscrew-bottleopener, which his uncle Rayber gives him, in the same awe: "He returned the corkscrew-bottleopener to his pocket and held it there in his hand as if henceforth it would be his talisman" (*Three,* p. 436). The hat and bottleopener are irresistibly linked to Tarwater and form part of a leitmotif which always identifies him.

Undoubtedly, Rayber's hearing-aid belongs in the same "hierophanic" category. The paradox is especially revealing here because of the two opposing views: Rayber treats the hearing-aid as the commonplace object it is for most people who are continually aware of its function; Tarwater has transformed it into a miracle box with special powers. " 'What you wired for?' he drawled. 'Does your head light up?' " (*Three,* p. 366). Later he asks, with quite the same naïve seriousness: " 'Do you think in the box . . . or do you think in your head?' " (*Three,* p. 367). Eliade has an explanation for this: "By manifesting the sacred, any object becomes *something else,* yet it continues to remain *itself.* . . ." For Tarwater, with his developed awareness of the sacred, it becomes something *ganz Anderes*. For Rayber, with his firm roots in the profane, it remains untransformed. If uncle and nephew can be viewed as conflicting parts of the same personality, as opposite sides of the same coin, their differing notions of the same object make for an interesting union between sacred and profane.

Flannery O'Connor's short stories offer the same reliance on "things" as her novels. The plaster figure of a Negro manages to exert a purging effect on the two main characters in "The Artificial Nigger"; it acts as an epiphanic agent on the story as it introduces a moment of illumination for both Nelson and Mr. Head:

They stood gazing at the artificial Negro as if they were faced with some great mystery, some monument to another's victory that brought them together in their common defeat. They could both feel it dissolving their differences like an action of mercy [*Three,* pp. 212–13].

Hulga's artificial leg is one of the central concerns in "Good Country People." The false Bible salesman makes off with it triumphantly at the end of the story; he adds it to his collection of unlikely objects which already includes a woman's glass eye. Flannery O'Connor mentions, as he departs, that he is wearing a "toast-colored hat"—a reminder of the hats which Tarwater and Hazel Motes rarely remove from their heads and the hat which Bishop throws in the water before he drowns. The Bibles which the salesman carries are hollow but are otherwise curiously similar to the Bible which Hazel reads with the spectacles which betray his eyesight: the Biblical text emerges with the same clarity in each instance. When Dorothy Van Ghent speaks of "things" as usurping the position of people and governing their lives, readers of Flannery O'Connor should immediately think of "Good Country People."

"The Partridge Festival" begins with a mention of a "small pod-shaped car." Its physical appearance is obviously quite different from Hazel's "high rat-colored car," but it serves much the same evangelical function. Hazel preaches his new creed, in good revivalist fashion, standing up in his car. Calhoun and Mary Elizabeth try to rescue their "Christ-figure" Singleton from the asylum with Calhoun's car. Hazel's Essex ends fatefully as a policeman pushes it off an embankment, thus ending the self-appointed preacher's itinerant career. The pod-shaped car is connected with the failed mission of Calhoun and Mary Elizabeth as it transports them from the asylum; the car is given special analogical importance: ". . . the boy [Calhoun] drove it away as if his heart were the motor and would never go fast enough." [11]

Mrs. Greenleaf's special cult of "prayer healing" (in "Greenleaf") is filled with Flannery O'Connor's special brand of prophetic vitality. Mrs. Greenleaf has a daily ritual of clipping "morbid stories" from the newspaper, burying them, and mumbling inaudible prayers over them. She evidently found "manifestations of the sacred," which had been abused, in these scraps of newsprint; the sounds pronounced over them transformed them into Eliade's category of *"something else,"* another experience of the "hierophany."

Perhaps the best example of the importance of "things" in the shorter fiction is in "The Lame Shall Enter First." This story is filled with the same physical objects, with their sacred possibilities, which we have seen in the two novels, especially in *The Violent Bear It Away*—but in larger supply.

Rufus Johnson (the Tarwater of the story) has a club foot which is insistently returned to, especially by his self-appointed mentor, Sheppard. Sheppard is anxious to have him fitted with a new pair of shoes which Rufus stoutly opposes. The shoe-fitting scene (a mockery of the foot-washing scene in Homer or John 13?) is especially instructive: "Johnson was as touchy about the foot as if it were a sacred object. His face had been glum while the clerk, a young man with a bright pink bald head, measured the foot with his profane hands" (*Everything,* p. 162). Surely the sacred *vs.* the profane is in evidence here.

Rayber's hearing-aid in *The Violent Bear It Away* has been turned into the telescope which Sheppard buys Rufus to dissuade him from his Bible-Belt superstitions. The telescope is used both symbolically and actually. It occasionally supplies a metaphorical function: "He appeared so far away that Sheppard might have been looking at him through the wrong end of the telescope" (*Everything*, p. 162). The telescope ends up as an object of betrayal, as do so many of the objects in Flannery O'Connor's work; it proves to be the undoing of Sheppard's neglected son, Norton. "The tripod had fallen and the telescope lay on the floor. A few feet over it, the child hung in the jungle of shadows, just below the beam from which he had launched his flight into space" (*Everything*, p. 190).

Sheppard also purchases a microscope for Rufus: "Since Johnson had lost interest in the telescope, he bought a microscope and a box of prepared slides. If he couldn't impress the boy with immensity, he would try the infinitesimal" (*Everything*, p. 171). The telescope and microscope, however, prove ineffectual in the face of the ever-present Bible which Rufus insists on referring to with righteous defiance. He counters all of Sheppard's scientific thrusts with gentle parries from Holy Scripture. Rufus' Bible seems more real than its hollow counterpart in "Good Country People" or its counterpart mated with silver-rimmed spectacles in *Wise Blood*. Instead of Mrs. Greenleaf's "prayer healing," which involves the burial of scraps of morbid newsprint, we find a reference to Rufus' grandfather involved in a Bible-burying expedition.

"The Lame Shall Enter First" is a splendid example of Flannery O'Connor's "literature of Things." It is a good stopping-point for our discussion. There are certainly other works in her canon which use objects in the way we have described, but multiplying illustrations would now seem rather unnecessary. The tattoos in "Parker's Back," for example, symbolically echo such religiously oriented objects as the Bibles, cars, and hats which abound in Miss O'Connor's fiction. Tanner's sitting "all day with that damn black hat on his head" ("Judgement Day") is still another reference to the special importance of hats (a preoccupation shared with Samuel Beckett).

Flannery O'Connor's work is thus a veritable community of objects.[12] She has made every effort (in Wylie Sypher's words, used in a different context) "to collaborate with things." It is tempting to connect her "objectal" bias with that of the *nouveau roman,* but literary history would not go along with us here. The more likely explanation is a religious one, in the direction of the hierophany with its clash between the sacred and the profane. This seems to me to be Flannery O'Connor's special contribution to Roman Catholic fiction of the twentieth century.

Notes

1. Found in Flannery O'Connor's posthumous collection of stories, *Everything That Rises Must Converge* (New York: Farrar, Straus and Giroux, 1965), p. 249. All subsequent references will be found in the text and will use the short title *Everything.*

2. Flannery O'Connor's career offers a pleasant symmetry if one examines her first story, "The Geranium," and her last story to appear, "Judgement Day." Both are concerned with displaced Southerners of advanced age, living with a strong sense of "exile" in New York City. These are the only two of her works, by the way, which are set in the North. Leon Driskell has recently argued that "Judgement Day" is actually a "rewritten version" of "The Geranium"; see his " 'Parker's Back' vs. 'The Partridge Festival': Flannery O'Connor's Critical Choice," *Georgia Review,* XXI (Winter, 1967), 479.

3. See J. Robert Loy, "*Things* in Recent French Literature," *PMLA,* LXXI (March, 1956), 27. See also the splendid pages on "things" in Harry Levin, *The Gates of Horn: A Study of Five French Realists* (New York: Oxford University Press, 1966), pp. 33–34.

4. Dorothy Van Ghent, *The English Novel: Form and Function* (New York: Harper Torchbooks, 1961), p. 128.

5. Nathalie Sarraute, *Tropismes* (Paris: Les Éditions de Minuit, 1957), p. 41. One might possibly think also of D. H. Lawrence's story "Things" in this connection, as well as Louis Simpson's poem "Things" (*The New Yorker,* May 15, 1965) and E. N. Sargent's poem "Things" (*The New Yorker,* March 12, 1966).

6. The connection between Beckett and Flannery O'Connor is not as far-fetched as it might at first seem. In his "Le petit monde de Flannery O'Connor" (*Mercure de France,* January, 1964), Michel Gresset suggests the possibility: "On pense à Bosch, à Poe, à Beckett même" (p. 142). See also my "Les romans de Samuel Beckett et la tradition du grotesque," in *Un Nouveau Roman?,* ed. J. H. Matthews (Paris: Lettres Modernes, 1964), especially pp. 42–44.

7. The title of this posthumous collection of stories is taken from Pierre Teilhard de Chardin. Claude Cuénot, in his *Teilhard de Chardin: A Biographical Study,* makes abundantly clear Teilhard's fascination with objects, especially with stones. Perhaps this renowned French clergyman has proven

to be something of an inspiration here. On the more secular side, we can look to another recent declaration of a fondness for things—this time on the part of the great Italian *littérateur,* Mario Praz: "Things remain impressed in my memory more than people. Things which have no soul, or rather, which have the soul with which we endow them, and which can also disappoint us when one day the scales fall from our eyes . . ." (*The House of Life* [New York: Oxford University Press, 1964], p. 333). Mario Praz, by the way, wrote an early piece on *A Good Man Is Hard to Find* in the 1956 *Studi Americani* ("Racconti del Sud").

8. Eliade gives special "sacred" properties to stones and mentions in a later passage of *The Sacred and the Profane* that "the stone reveals to man the nature of an *absolute existence,* beyond time, invulnerable to becoming." Three twentieth-century novels, all written in French, use stones in much the way Eliade suggests. The first of these is André Gide's *L'Immoraliste.* Near the end of this *récit* Michel, the hero, is seen manipulating rosary beads; on the final page we hear him exclaim: "look! I have here a number of white pebbles. I let them soak in the shade, then hold them in the hollow of my hand and wait until their soothing coolness is exhausted. Then I begin once more, changing the pebbles and putting back those that have lost their coolness to soak in the shade again. . . ." The reader is probably expected to connect the rosary beads with the "sacred" pebbles. Sartre, in *La Nausée,* refers several times to stones. The most revealing passage is the following: "Now I see: I recall better what I felt the other day at the seashore when I held the pebble. It was a sort of sweetish sickness. How unpleasant it was! It came from the stone, I'm sure of it, it passed from the stone to my hand. Yes, that's it, that's just it—a sort of nausea in the hands." Sartre connects the stone with his theory of nausea—which happens to be at the creative base of his existentialism. Finally, there is a ten-page section in Beckett's *Molloy,* probably indebted to both Gide and Sartre, which describes the manipulation of sixteen "sucking stones." For a detailed discussion of this section, see my "Molloy's 'Sacred' Stones," *Romance Notes,* IX (Fall, 1967), 8–11.

9. Mircea Eliade, *The Sacred and the Profane: The Nature of Religion,* trans. Willard R. Trask (New York: Harper Torchbooks, 1961), p. 12.

10. Flannery O'Connor, *Three* (New York: Signet, 1964), p. 17. All subsequent references will be found in the text and will use the title *Three.*

11. "The Partridge Festival," in *Critic,* XIX (February–March, 1961), 85. For an interesting discussion of Hazel Motes's automobile, see Jonathan Baumbach, "The Acid of God's Grace: *Wise Blood* by Flannery O'Connor" in *The Landscape of Nightmare* (New York: New York University Press, 1965), pp. 95–96.

12. For a discussion of imagery patterns and their significance in Flannery O'Connor's work see Irving Malin's excellent *New American Gothic* (Carbondale: Southern Illinois University Press, 1962); also his "Flannery O'Connor and the Grotesque," in *The Added Dimension: The Art and Mind of Flannery O'Connor,* edd. Melvin J. Friedman and Lewis A. Lawson (New York: Fordham University Press, 1966), pp. 108–122.

The Ordeal of Evelyn Waugh

BARRY ULANOV · *Barnard College*

IT IS ALL BUT A FIXED CONVENTION in the critical presentation of the work of Evelyn Waugh to date his decline, in mid-career, with the appearance of *Brideshead Revisited* in 1945. The novels written before it are comic masterpieces. Those that come after, with the possible exception of *The Loved One* (1948), are blighted by the disease of Brideshead, an egregious inclination to take religion seriously, accompanied by a marked distaste for the world that does not share that inclination—the modern world.

Waugh was immediately taken to task, on the appearance of *Brideshead Revisited,* for his shocking display of religious sentiment and his apparent loss of the satiric spirit. He answered his American critics as publicly as he could in the pages of a journal not generally thought of as literary—*Life* magazine. Modern novelists, Waugh explained,

try to represent the whole human mind and soul and yet omit its determining character—that of being God's creature with a defined purpose. So in my future books there will be two things to make them unpopular: a preoccupation with style and the attempt to represent man more fully, which to me means only one thing, man in his relation to God.[1]

79

The work that followed *Brideshead Revisited,* two years later, was a corrosive political satire, a novella called *Scott-King's Modern Europe*. It is the tale of the misadventures of the Classical Master of a second-rate English public school in Neutralia. He has been invited to this "typical modern state, governed by a single party, acclaiming a dominant Marshal, supporting a vast ill-paid bureaucracy whose work is tempered and humanised by corruption," because of his celebration in an essay in a learned journal of the qualities of Neutralia's Latin poet Bellorius. Bellorius is about to suffer—along with Scott-King and the reader—the tercentenary of his death. With the heaviest possible irony, Waugh describes his narrative as "the story of a summer holiday; a light tale." It is not a light tale; it is a ponderous satire which brings Scott-King back to his public school by way of "No. 64, Jewish Illicit Immigrants' Camp, Palestine." The headmaster suggests that Scott-King think about teaching another subject alongside Classics— "History, for example, preferably economic history." After all, parents no longer send their boys to school to become " 'the complete man.' . . . They want to qualify their boys for jobs in the modern world. You can hardly blame them, can you?" Scott-King's answer is direct: "Oh yes," he says. "I can and do." The last bits of dialogue permit Scott-King to put the modern world in its place.

> "But, you know, there may be something of a crisis ahead."
> "Yes, headmaster."
> "Then what do you intend to do?"
> "If you approve, headmaster, I will stay as I am here as long as any boy wants to read the classics. I think it would be very wicked indeed to do anything to fit a boy for the modern world."
> "It's a short-sighted view, Scott-King."
> "There, headmaster, with all respect, I differ from you profoundly. I think it the most long-sighted view it is possible to take." [2]

Waugh did not need the cumbersome apparatus of *Scott-King's Modern Europe* to make clear his disenchantment with the modern world. Nor did he need the pages of *Life* magazine to make public pronouncements about his "preoccupation" with style and the relation of man to God. He had been making such pronouncements for almost two decades before *Brideshead Revisited,* but obliquely, in variously light and heavy explorations of the allegory of irony. Waugh was not finished with allegorical devices, nor did he relinquish the ironic pose after *Brideshead*; but the indirections of satire were no longer all. It was as though his presentation of "The Sacred and Profane Memories of Captain Charles Ryder" had evoked in him the spirit of the confessional. Like the most unconscious character in Chekhov, he seemed determined now to reveal his working purposes. In some curious way, his two creeds, as writer and as Christian, would be made to coincide. In *The Loved One,* he mocked the happy hunting-grounds of the American ways of death, human and animal, which sought certainties where none were to be found. In *Helena* (1950), he praised the simple faith of the woman who was canonized by tradition for her perseverance in seeking the wood of the True Cross, a woman of a time "Once, very long ago, before ever the flowers were named," the mother of the Roman Emperor Constantine, and, in Waugh's version of sacred history, a Briton and the daughter of Old King Coel.

In-between the clammy humors of California Gothic and the dry atmosphere of Celtic-Roman hagiology, Waugh followed the confessional urge where it led—to the opening pages of a collection of stories of conversion to Catholicism by well-known figures of the late 1940s. Waugh's piece was called "Come Inside." In five short pages he moved across the bare facts of his religious life, from beginnings in the Church of England and a "family tree" which "burgeons on every twig with Anglican clergymen," and an early intention of becoming a clergyman himself:

The enthusiasm which my little school-fellows devoted to birds' eggs and model trains I turned to church affairs and spoke glibly of chasubles and Erastianism. I was accordingly sent to the school which was reputed to have the strongest ecclesiastical bent. At the age of sixteen I formally notified the school chaplain that there was no God. At the age of twenty-six I was received into the Catholic Church to which all subsequent experience has served to confirm my loyalty.[3]

Waugh's little piece is savage in its rejection of his own attempts to deal with the brambles of the higher criticism, as uncovered by a skeptical Oxford theologian ("now a bishop"), and the thickets of metaphysics, as presented in Pope's *Essay on Man* and in Leibniz, to whom he was sent by the notes in his edition of Pope.

I advanced far enough to be thoroughly muddled about the nature of cognition. It seemed simplest to abandon the quest and assume that man was incapable of knowing anything. I have no doubt I was a prig and a bore but I think that if I had been a Catholic boy at a Catholic school I should have found among its teaching orders someone patient enough to examine with me my callow presumption. Also, if I had been fortified by the sacraments, I should have valued my faith too highly to abandon it so capriciously.[4]

What Waugh found in the Church was tradition, the Catholic structure omnipresent in European life, customs, ceremonies, and disciplines of learning. Americans may lack this; their world certainly does. Europe in general and England in particular may not look upon the Church as simply one of a series of splendid sects. The Church underlies everything in Waugh's world. It is his inheritance. After being admitted into the Church, he tells us in carefully weighed words, his "life has been an endless delighted tour of discovery in the huge territory of which I was made free." [5] What he does not tell us in this 1949 piece, but does confess in the novels, the stories, the occasional pieces, the columns of liturgical controversy—in nearly everything that followed upon it—is that more and more he became a furious partisan, fighting for the survival of ancient values, ancient worlds, ancient rituals. He moved with sour obstinacy against the new liturgy produced by the Second Vatican Council. He was made sick with something like shame by the translation of the words of the Mass into the

English vernacular. In this vulgate tongue, they clearly lacked unction. They were not in the ancient style. They were not in any style that he could respect. They lacked that universality and coherence that made the terrors of modernity, if not tolerable, at least endurable as a preface to a world of endless grace. He had extended his invitation to the non-Catholic to follow him inside the Church:

You cannot know what the Church is like from outside. However learned you are in theology, nothing you know amounts to anything in comparison with the knowledge of the simplest actual member of the Communion of Saints.[6]

Could one still believe this, still feel this, after the depredations of Vatican II?

Waugh mocks the "shallowness" of his "early piety," clearly demonstrated "by the ease with which I abandoned it." To his interest in "chasubles and Erastianism" he attributes a depth comparable to the devotion to birds' eggs and model trains of his contemporaries at school. But there is something quite different in kind about his penchant, at the age of eleven, for Anglican churchmanship, the intense curiosity he describes in his autobiography: "about church decorations and the degrees of anglicanism—'Prot, Mod, High, Spiky'—which they represented." [7] The pursuit of grace at eleven may have been confined to a shrine he constructed for the night-nursery, complete with plaster saints, an *art nouveau* edition of Newman's *Dream of Gerontius,* and his own attempt at the subject of Newman's long poem, Purgatory—an effort "in the metre of Hiawatha" which he calls "long and tedious" in one place, "deplorable" in another. But it was grace he pursued, tediously perhaps, certainly at length. The comings and goings of his faith, now Anglican, now atheist, finally Roman, were surely never as inconsequential to him or for him as his ironic autobiographical narratives suggest. He was always a ceremonialist, always caught up in some ritual or other, as feckless student and schoolmaster, or as despairing socialite. It is ritual that fascinates him in his several worlds, even when it is altogether fatuous. It is ritual he gathers so entertainingly into his early satires. When the satire wears thin and the end in view ceases to be entertainment, the ritual remains. Only now it is no longer quite so fatuous. There is faith in it. The pursuit of grace has become, like the explorations of the allegory of irony, far less oblique.

If one sees the pursuit of grace in the work of Evelyn Waugh, sees it in the inverted and perverted rituals of *Decline and Fall* (1928), *Vile Bodies* (1930), *Black Mischief* (1932), *Scoop* (1938), and *Put Out More Flags* (1942) as much as in the open courtings of the supernatural in *Brideshead Revisited, Helena,* and *Sword of Honour,* one is not so easily put off or surprised by the sentimentality of the later work. One sees Waugh constantly soliciting a deeper coherence than the ceremonies of the social life or the customs of international politics are likely to reveal. One sees Waugh's meticulous notation of custom and ceremony as being in the service of grace, and not at all lacking in meaning because it deals with people who have little or no meaning and are determined to do everything to escape meaning. One sees Waugh's narratives, from the beginning, as severely moralized—though not (in the beginning at least) very clear in their moral purpose. One sees an allegorist sharpening his instruments, perfecting his ironic moral tone, so that when the pursuit of grace can be made more open, when grace can emerge from the chilling shadows of a world that holds it in contempt, there will be a machinery skillful enough to deal with it and to make it recognizable.

Nowhere is this honing of the tools so evident as in *A Handful of Dust* (1934). There all that Waugh had learned in his early tales of the rituals of the fatuous is displayed with an ironic detachment that can easily be interpreted as withdrawal from the moral lists—or worse, as accidie. The world of the aristocracy has collapsed. Tony Last—a name at least as roundly allegorical in intent as any in the novels of Henry Fielding—brings that world to its inexorable end, condemned to spend his final days—and they are clearly to be many—reading Dickens aloud to a madman in a South American jungle. While this allegory of attrition is worked out, Tony Last's wife, Brenda, works out her salvation in the service of a personification of nullity, John Beaver, whose name spells nothing but an industrious boredom. The book takes its title from *The Waste Land,* and perhaps some of its hauteur as well. But where Eliot communicates his distaste for the modern world in fragments, Waugh polishes his periods in an elegantly sustained continuity, with every detail fitted firmly into place. Disaster leads to disaster in an orderly succession of horrors which everybody can accept, for the disasters and horrors follow so faithfully the ordinations of high society and never lose the approved tones. Thus the ironic echoes of Proust in two chapter titles: "Du Côté de Chez Beaver" and "Du Côté de Chez Todd"—memorializing in these cases no elegant or gifted men, but a middle-class bore and an illiterate son of a missionary with a savage devotion to the works of Charles Dickens.

The part played by Dickens in the allegorical structure of *A Handful of Dust* is particularly engaging to the reader of Waugh who has gone so far as to search out his occasional reviews. In 1953, examining Edgar Johnson's two-volume biography of Dickens for *The Spectator,* he confesses that

We all have our moods when Dickens sickens us. In a lighter, looser and perhaps higher mood we fall victim to his "magnetism." . . . It is this constantly changing mood of appreciation that makes everyone's fingers itch for the pen at the mention of his name.

Waugh gratified the itch in this review in such a way that one understands perfectly the particular irony of Todd's fixation upon Dickens:

—the pity of it—the more we know of Dickens, the less we like him.

His conduct to his wife and particularly his announcement of the separation were deplorable. His treatment in middle age of Maria Beadnell was even worse. His benefactions to his family were grudging and ungracious. Faults which would be excusable in other men become odious in the light of Dickens's writing. He frequented the demi-monde with Wilkie Collins. He probably seduced and certainly kept the young

actress Ellen Ternan, to whom he left £1,000 in his will, thereby putting her name in disrepute while at the same time leaving her miserably
provided. All this is very ugly in the creator of Little Emily and
Martha. He claimed a spurious pedigree and used an illicit crest—a
simple weakness in anyone except himself who vehemently denounced
the importance attached to gentle birth. In success he was intolerably
boastful, in the smallest reverse abject with self-pity. He was domineer-
ing and dishonourable in his treatment of his publishers. He was, in
fact, a thumping cad.[8]

Clearly a model for Waugh's grotesque tale, this reading of
Dickens is allegorical of all the large hypocrisy and emotional
emptiness that masquerades in *A Handful of Dust* under the
small pieties of upper-class social life. What better writer
could Waugh have found with whom to torment Tony Last—
and the gullible reader who has been incautious enough to look
for some deliverance for Tony or anyone else in this allegory
of a world without grace and thus without any chance of fulfillment?

The landscape of *A Handful of Dust* is perfectly pieced
together, as an allegorical landscape must be. The surfaces of
buildings, as of people, are described with a splendid and an
unmistakable precision. The rooms within, like the interior
dispositions of the people, are carefully decorated. Waugh
is following the example of his tutors in the allegory of irony
—Henry Fielding and Laurence Sterne. He has left behind at
this point the epicene shallows of Ronald Firbank, an earlier
guide in the tones and textures of irony. The depths in which
he finds and leaves his allegorical figures are those of Hierony-
mus Bosch and the elder Pieter Brueghel, not perhaps because
he has sought those depths but because they have sought him.
This world of a pettiness so acute that it has become an almost
diabolical kind of hallucination was the world which sat for
its portrait in Waugh's studio. This world of evasions, of
shadows in retreat and of shadows in pursuit, this world that
Eliot prepared for burial in *The Waste Land*—"I will show
you fear in a handful of dust"—Waugh drew from its winding
sheets and stood end to end in its native flats and country
houses. This world of the living dead Waugh painted as Bosch

and Cranach and Brueghel did—in allegorical precision. This was the world without grace, its rituals superbly ordered inversions of Christianity, its instruments so perfectly tuned that one could hardly hear the difference. One had to look very closely indeed to see that the laughter bared too much gum and popped the eyes too much to be the laughter of entertainment.

For some readers, the entertainment dropped out of Waugh's novels after *A Handful of Dust,* never to return. He simply did not get the facts of Mussolini's invasion of Ethiopia straight in *Scoop,* and to the hollow humors of his novel of the cold war, *Put Out More Flags,* he added an embarrassing tinge of patriotism. Real heroism, even if inadvertent, seemed to be popping up beneath the mock heroics. The sounds of the indecorous war that had brought *Vile Bodies* to its conclusion had given way to noisier exchanges in a war that shattered more than mere decorum. The comic-opera struggles for power in the African kingdoms of *Black Mischief* and *Scoop* did not amuse any longer; they had been replaced by a deadly warfare in the desert in which men Waugh loved and admired were losing their lives. The terms of the allegory were irremediably changed. The deadly sins were still there—lust, gluttony, greed, and especially sloth, of which Waugh had appointed himself the patron devil. But now there were, of all things, virtues to be dealt with. Grace hovered overhead, even appeared now and then in the lives of the Halberdiers of Waugh's trilogy about the war: *Men at Arms* (1952), *Officers and Gentlemen* (1955), and *Unconditional Surrender* (1961; *The End of the Battle* in its American edition). In fact, some of Waugh's fictional regiment seemed to be positively maddened by grace, not the least of them that improbable hero of the trilogy, Guy Crouchback, who seems dedicated to moral ambiguity—that is to say, dedicated to the contradictory textures of the human condition, the only textures in which grace can comfortably appear.

The leading figures of Waugh's suddenly uprighted world are not very different from those of the inverted one. They have gone to the public school of *Decline and Fall,* to the parties of *Vile Bodies,* to the hunts of *A Handful of Dust*; they have served their own mad little corners of the cold-war bureaucracy of *Put Out More Flags,* and scratched their way to the top—or the bottom—of African kingdoms. Even in their weaker moments, they have more often achieved the look of lechery and the manners of sin than the matter. Their moral failures have been most frequently failures to be immoral, which in the *old* days could be shrugged off in the giggling manner of *Vile Bodies*—

"What I always wonder, Kitty dear, is what they actually *do* at these parties of theirs. I mean, *do* they . . . ?"

"My dear, from all I hear, I think they do."

"Oh, to be young again, Kitty. When I think, my dear, of all the trouble and exertion which we had to go through to be even moderately bad . . . those passages in the early morning and mama sleeping next door."

"And yet, my dear, I doubt very much whether they really *appreciate* it all as we should . . . young people take things so much for granted."

"*Si la jeunesse savait,* Kitty . . ."

"*Si la vieillesse pouvait.*" [9]

In the *new* days, the days of Brideshead and the Halberdiers, some sense is made of all this patchwork of immorality wished-for and morality achieved in spite of one's dearest hopes. The coherent patterns of a moral theology supervene. The revels, achieved or postponed, are permanently interrupted. The great romance of Brideshead, for example, into which the reader, following Waugh's sentimental lead, has poured so much expectant feeling, is dashed on the rocks of canon law. Julia Mottram must accept the terms of her marriage, as set forth in the positive legislation of the Church. She and Charles Ryder must separate. She must say goodbye. Ryder asks what she will do. She will not, she explains, lead a life of lies, on one side or the other:

"Just go on—alone. How can I tell what I shall do? You know the whole of me. You know I'm not one for a life of mourning. I've always been bad. Probably I shall be bad again, punished again. But the worse I am, the more I need God. I can't shut myself out from His mercy. That is what it would mean; starting a life with you, without Him. One can only hope to see one step ahead. But I saw today there was one thing unforgivable—like things in the schoolroom, so bad they are unpunishable, that only Mummy could deal with— the bad thing I was on the point of doing, that I'm not quite bad enough to do; to set up a rival good to God's. Why should I be allowed to understand that, and not you, Charles? It may be because of Mummy, Nanny, Cordelia, Sebastian—perhaps Bridey and Mrs. Muspratt—keeping my name in their prayers; or it may be a private bargain between me and God, that if I give up this one thing I want so much, however bad I am, He won't quite despair of me in the end.

"Now we shall both be alone, and I shall have no way of making you understand." [10]

Non-Catholic readers can surely be forgiven their revulsion at the seeming smugness of this dismissal of love. The set speech comes so easily from the rhetoric of the rectory. God has made the laws, down to their last canon, and we who have been initiated into His great legal fraternity, we understand. Pity we cannot make others understand.

Was Waugh trying to make others understand when he constructed his canonist's copybook adultery? Had he given up irony for apologetics? The same question can be asked about the sterile marriage which haunts Guy Crouchback, made twice as barren by the unyielding law of the Church which prevents any satisfaction to Guy in the relationship. His attempt to seduce his former wife is ruined when he informs her that the seduction is entirely licit since their marriage had never been dissolved by the Church; she runs, appalled, from his arms. He can only remarry her, to make legitimate her child by a brother officer, a malingerer and moral neutral with the precisely allegorical name of Trimmer, who has become a hero *malgré lui,* in a series of events typical of the activity of grace in the *Sword of Honour* trilogy. Grace pursues its victims in the Crouchback novels in the ancient manner, makes heroes of trimmers and withholds the trappings of honor from those who have performed with virtue. Grace achieves the textures of irony in these books. When it lands on a hero's head, it dents his skull; it marks him a fool. If Waugh has turned to apologetics, he has not relinquished the allegory of irony to do so. He has discovered, like the Flemish painters before him, where that allegory leads.

Irony, now that it is to be employed in the precincts of grace, must make chivalry seem gauche, a hopeless anachronism; charity, the always underlying virtue in these quarters, must appear the refuge of fools. Guy Crouchback forms himself, as best he can, in the image and after the likeness of a medieval knight, Roger of Waybrooke, and grace confounds him, after having long confused him, by supporting his insane sentimentalization of the past. He finds his appropriate roles, is splendidly victimized in war and peace, and ends up, *mirabile dictu,* with a marriage that works, after his first wife has died. The original, British-edition title of the last of the Crouchback novels, *Unconditional Surrender,* is the final irony in the saga: everyone, everything concedes; grace settles on Guy's head with all the sweet finality of happy events at the end of a novel by Charles Dickens. Guy, it is clear, is a thumping saint. To the consternation of the conventional hagiologist, he is a saint rewarded on earth, although not exactly with public honors and a grand justification of his follies. His rewards come in retirement from the battles, to the family estate which is as much his inheritance as are the motions of chivalry. His life in retirement opens before him in the manner of the last years of the medieval knight. The moves are classical. Guy is, as his name makes abundantly clear, a throwback, a minor aristocrat in the annals of the blood, a major aristocrat in the annals of the spirit. One has to look twice to find him, in either set of records, crouched, like a self-conscious gargoyle, hiding beneath the benches, not of royalty or the first families of the realm, but of the quieter and less heralded families at the periphery. But one finds him—or rather grace does. And we respond—or rather grace permits us to, if we accept the terms of Waugh's allegory—in spite of all our inherited distaste for religious sentiment and the coincidences and inadvertencies which it keeps stirring up.

It is silly to reproach Waugh with the coincidences and in-

advertencies of his books, whether they are the contrivances of
a late religious romanticism or those of an early dyspeptic
expressionism; almost as silly as the accusation that his figures
are without objective reality. An allegorist's figures, like his
landscapes, are deliberately contrived. Events in an allegorist's
world are chained together by coincidence and inadvertences
which are quite without spontaneity. Causal connections are
made by the logic of the imagination and tied firmly together
by the webs of dogma—whether of art or of religion or of
both. Waugh's allegories take root in the real world, but they
flower in no world that ever was, no matter how close their
world may seem at times to the world we know. Their reality
is a spiritual one, which is not to say a rational one or one that
seeks the balance it does not have. The reality of the spirit
may be a deranged reality or a supremely sane one. Who is
to say whether the world of Brideshead and the Crouchbacks
and the Halberdiers is more or less deranged than that of
Tony and Brenda Last or the public-school and party-going
folk of the early satires—such as Captain Grimes, Agatha
Runcible, Ambrose Silk, Basil Seal, Margot Metroland, and
Mrs. Ape? From beginning to end, it is the reality of the spirit
that concerns Waugh. He is relentless in his efforts to get at
it and ruthless with the devices of fictional realism. His novel
is the novel of the eighteenth century. His techniques of
characterization and narration are those of the originators
of the English novel. And so in his novels, right to the end,
we live with personifications and placards—Lord Outrage
and Lady Circumference and Lord Tangent, Miss Tin and
Miles Plastic, Mr. Joyboy and Aimée Thanatogenos, Trimmer and Major Hound. Like the titles of his books, the names
of his characters signify much in the construction of his allegories. He is never shy about extending meanings beyond
the uncertainties of chance and the imprecisions of the laws
of probability.

In reading Waugh, one does well to meditate, for a few
moments at least, on his contrivances. They are not schoolboy
jokes, as they may at first appear, nor are they allegorical
commonplaces. They are lines into a world of moral specu-

lation in which every image is a potential icon and every proper
noun a likely emblem. They begin as counters in a game of
great comic gusto. They end as the blazons of a devout and
complex heraldry.

It would be a great mistake to overestimate the depth of
Waugh's allegories, to see either in the comic counters or in the
heraldic clutterings a profound insight into the human condition. It would be a distortion of these materials to find anything entirely fresh or novel in them, and from Waugh's point
of view an impertinence. His allegories are of an ancient kind
and their content as far outside the philosophy, psychology,
and sociology of this century as his devices could make it and
as a vocabulary intelligible to modern readers would permit.
To find more than a passing joke or a lingering sentimentality
in Waugh, one must surrender to his world of the spirit and the
style in which it is encased. One must, in a sense, accept and
undergo the ordeal of Evelyn Waugh as a kind of spiritual
exercise. For that, surely, is what Waugh's performance
amounts to, looked at as an entity. It does represent a complete
oeuvre, I believe, a unity not always sought but somehow
usually found. Working with the materials of a dying society,
a society in which such values as could be discovered were inevitably blurred and sometimes impossibly opaque, Waugh
found coherences and even more—an underlying structure:
the "Catholic structure [that] still lies lightly buried beneath
every phase of English life; history, topography, law, archae-
ology everywhere reveal Catholic origins." [11] That revelation
of coherence and structure, and of underlying design and
purpose, led to another revelation for Waugh: it was possible
to give the history and topography of his novels an unmistakable coherence, structure, design, and purpose, and not simply
to allow those qualities to appear as the functions of a rigor-
ously measured prose style. An irony that accidentally produced
an allegory of sorts gave way to an allegory of irony dedicated to the exploration and even, sometimes, to the explication of Christian values. A covert regard for the ridiculous
people with whom he lived out his public-school and college
and party-going youth became an open sentiment of support

for the soldiers who survived the opening ceremonies of World War II long enough to fight with style—in whatever task, fatuous or glorious, they were assigned—for Christian values, whether or not they understood or even professed those values.

Waugh had discovered some years before he died that, as he explained in the introductory note to *The Ordeal of Gilbert Pinfold* (1957), "Hallucination is far removed from loss of reason." He was explaining that he himself had undergone "a brief bout of hallucination" very much like that described in the novel. "The reason works with enhanced power," he went on, "while the materials for it to work on, presented by the senses, are delusions. A story-teller naturally tries to find a plot into which his observations can be fitted." [12] That, it seems to me, is the point of Waugh's work, a point made with more and more clarity and precision as his life wore on, and with more and more warmth that sometimes settled into sentimentality. Hallucinations and all the other demonstrations of human fallibility, Waugh's fables tell us, and tell us with particular strength of conviction at the end, are also opportunities for a show of reason. That is his faith. It makes, finally, even the modern world endurable for him.

Notes

1. Evelyn Waugh, "Fan-Fare," *Life,* XX, 14 (April 8, 1946), 56.
2. Evelyn Waugh, *Scott-King's Modern Europe* (Boston: Little, Brown, 1949), pp. 88, 89.
3. Evelyn Waugh, "Come Inside," in *The Road to Damascus,* ed. John A. O'Brien (London: Allen, 1949), pp. 12–13.
4. *Ibid.,* p. 14.
5. *Ibid.,* pp. 15–16.
6. *Ibid.,* p. 16.
7. Evelyn Waugh, *A Little Learning* (Boston: Little, Brown, 1964), p. 93.
8. Evelyn Waugh, "Apotheosis of an Unhappy Hypocrite," *The Spectator,* 191 (October 2, 1953), pp. 363–364.
9. Evelyn Waugh, *Vile Bodies* (New York: Jonathan Cape and Harrison Smith, 1930), pp. 180–181.
10. Evelyn Waugh, *Brideshead Revisited* (Boston: Little, Brown, 1945), p. 340.
11. O'Brien, p. 15.
12. Evelyn Waugh, *The Ordeal of Gilbert Pinfold* (Boston: Little, Brown, 1957), p. v.

The Deceptions
of Muriel Spark

IRVING MALIN · *City College of New York*

—*For* ROBERT CHAPPETTA

THE NOVELS OF MURIEL SPARK deal with religious themes in
a deceptive manner. It is easy to misread them, as does
Frederick R. Karl in *The Contemporary English Novel*: "they
are so involved with the eccentric event and the odd personality
that they have virtually no content. . . . She can write about
murder, betrayal, deception, and adultery as though these
were the norms of a crazy-quilt society." Mr. Karl apparently
believes that novels should have clearly defined ideas and
"normal" characters. He does not see that the "eccentric
event" and the "odd personality" are deliberately chosen for
religious, artistic ends.

Mrs. Spark is concerned with "miracles." She attempts to
capture in novelistic form those events which are so extraordinary that they demonstrate the beautiful complexity of
cosmic design. She uses the "odd personality" because he (or
she) is often involved with conversion and salvation, making
him extremely aware of "other voices, other rooms." She is
not content, in other words, to accept human relationships as
clear or rational.

95

Perhaps two passages will clarify the matter before I an-
alyze her novels in detail. In *Memento Mori* Charmian and
her former lover, Guy, have this exchange:

"The characters," said Charmian, "seemed to take control of my
pen after a while. But at first I always got into a tangle. I used to say
to myself,

> 'Oh what a tangled web we weave
> When first we practise to deceive!'

Because," she said, "the art of fiction is very like the practise of deception."
    "And in life," he said, "is the practise of deception in life an art too?"
    "In life," she said, "everything is different. Everything is in the Provi-
dence of God. . . ."[1]

Their conversation implies the paradoxical nature of art and
life. Both worlds cannot be scientifically measured; both use
deception—or are deceptive—to signify the design of a Higher
Power. By presenting the vague, playful, or uncanny occurrence, Mrs. Spark refuses to preach doctrine. Her religious
message is consciously elusive—at times it is so beyond us that
we can partially agree with Mr. Karl.
    In *The Mandelbaum Gate* there is another passage which
suggests the nature of the novels. Barbara Vaughan, the
Catholic convert, muses as she lies in bed:

And, she thought, we must all think in these vague terms: with God, all
things are possible; because the only possibilities we ever seem able to
envisage in a precise manner are disastrous events; and we fear both
vaguely and specifically, and I have myself too long laid plans against
eventualities. Against good ones? No, bad ones.[2]

She believes that our "precise" plans cannot account for the
"eccentric event" which simultaneously shows human limitation and divine complexity. We cannot fathom cosmic meaning,
but this spiritual fact is the very center of the Plan. Mrs.
Spark, however, can represent such painful, vague paradoxes

by presenting the "impossible" and the "unnatural" *as possible and natural*. She can teach us by deception.

The Comforters, written only three years after her con-version to Roman Catholicism, is Mrs. Spark's first novel. Caroline Rose, the heroine, is a critic of the modern novel. She is writing *Form in the Modern Novel,* but she is "having difficulty with the chapter on realism," especially after she begins to believe that she is herself a character in the novel we are reading. She hears voices which repeat her thoughts: "But the typewriter and the voices—it is as if a writer on another plane of existence was writing a story about us." When Caro-line tries to indicate her odd belief to those around her, she is merely "comforted." She remains alone with the voices and learns to accept them.

Although we have read about unnatural voices speaking from other worlds to saints, we have not encountered a novel in which the novelist uses for her descriptions the very lan-guage of the voices. Occasionally we are made to feel that Caroline Rose is more than "Caroline Rose" in *The Com-forters—that she has a spiritual identity of her own beyond the one given to her.* Unfortunately, we can never go beyond this box-within-box quality of the novel because, once she gives us the voices, Mrs. Spark does not know how to go on. (Would any writer?) Her "miracle" is not thoroughly worked out, and we are left with Caroline's easy acceptance.

The Comforters opens with a meeting of smugglers. We learn later that Mervyn and Andrew Hogarth transport their stolen goods from the Continent in religious figures and rosary beads. Are we to take these goods as symbols of some religious truth? Can they—and their carriers—be related to Caroline's predicament? Mrs. Spark is content to play with the *secret* quality of both smuggling and voices, but she does not evalu-ate it. Therefore we are baffled. We want to "connect," but she does not permit us to do so. Perhaps this is the underlying message of the title—although we would like to *comfort* ourselves with solutions to these relationships (and the strange death of Mrs. Hogg), their meaning escapes us. Mrs. Spark may, indeed, be playing with lies—as her characters lie to each other and to themselves—to show us that ultimate meaning lies beyond our detections. We remember an early passage in which Mervyn (a liar at times!) says to Louisa: "You have the instinct for unity, for co-ordinating the inconsistent elements of experience; you have the passion for picking up the idle phenomena of life and piecing them together." Mrs. Spark attacks our "instinct for unity" as she gives us many false clues and arbitrary associations. But then we and she are at a standstill. *The Comforters* raises unsuccessfully the problem which is to recur in the later novels: How can artistic deception be employed to symbolize cosmic design? But it offers no answer except to imply that life is an inconclusive puzzle.

Robinson is set on an exotic island which is likened to a "landscape of the mind." The island is an appropriate landscape because as January Marlow, the heroine, maintains, "all things are possible" here. Immediately we expect the unexpected.

January and Robinson, the owners of the island, are Catholics; they quarrel about the "irrationality" of the Church. Robinson believes that devotion to Mary is unnecessary— it interferes with our need for rational understanding. He has come to the island to create his own design and, in effect, to be his own Master. January, on the other hand, accepts Marian devotion as necessary and important. It does not offend her sense of logic. She is, indeed, *remarkably open to wonder* and her receptivity to the miraculous and the paradoxical (like that of Caroline Rose) is her "redeeming" quality.

Robinson disappears in the middle of the novel. This event resembles Caroline's voices; it too is "miraculous"—or so it seems. January prepares to find the reasons for the disappearance. She seeks clues, hints, and ambiguities. She refuses the "systematic," one-sided explanations of Tom Wells, the astrologer-blackmailer. She realizes that meanings are hidden but ironically purposeful. Thus her detection is like that of Caroline—she searches alone for mysterious truth and she attempts to describe it in her journal.

But *Robinson* falters here. When Mrs. Spark explains the reasons for Robinson's disappearance and reappearance—he left because he could not stand their company!—we feel cheated. We have been so involved with the "supernatural" that the psychological cause seems needlessly simple. There is again the possibility that Mrs. Spark wants us to feel disturbed, so that she can demonstrate that even our desire for secret meaning can be self-deceptive. *To expect always the unexpected is as dangerous as never expecting it.* She suggests, in other words, that January reaffirms her faith in the cosmic design by accepting the miraculous *and* the usual, the high *and* the low. In any event we are let down; we remember the quest, not the answer(s), in *Robinson*.

Memento Mori is more successful than the previous novels. The voice(s) on the phone that says *"Remember you must die"* occupies a central position; all the aged characters hear the message but interpret it in different ways. Therefore the novel is tight and intense (as well as comic); each incident helps to underline the obscure meaning of the phone calls.

Again we have a "detective story." Who is responsible for the calls? What does he (or she) want? Can the calls be stopped? The various old people assume that simple materialism is the answer; but as the calls persist in spite of police efforts, we realize that a "miracle" is taking place. We eagerly listen to the spiritual advice of Inspector Mortimer and Jean Taylor.

Mortimer's meeting with Lettie Colston, Charmian Piper, Godfrey Colston, Mrs. Pettigrew, Alec Warner, and Janet Sidebottome is placed in the middle of the novel, so that the answers given can serve as a motivating force for the rest of their lives. The Inspector suggests that after considering all the evidence, he believes the offender is Death himself. Death is calling to remind the aged to re-examine their actions and to reform their ways: "If I had my life over again I should form the habit of nightly composing myself to thoughts of death. I would practice, as it were, the remembrance of death. There is no other practice which so intensifies life." For the most part, this explanation—it is a symbolic sermon—goes unheeded. Alec Warner continues to study the symptoms of old age; Godfrey continues to brood about his wife's knowledge of his past infidelities; Lettie continues to believe that a criminal is the caller. Eventually they die without any great change of heart. They are not "saved."

Jean Taylor, the former maid of the Colstons and a Catholic convert, comes to the same conclusion as Mortimer. She lies in the home for the aged—symbolically isolated from the others—and thinks constantly of first and last things: "she mused upon her condition and upon old age in general." Her meditations are juxtaposed to the frantic activities of the other characters; they are at a still point. Even before she hears of the phone calls, she has remembered "the four last things": Death, Judgment, Hell, and Heaven. She is ready to die. She does not fear it. The novel ends with a list of the diseases which finally claim the aged. We are not given their feelings or thoughts—their lives have been empty!—except in the case of Jean Taylor who, we read, "lingered for a time, employing her pain to magnify the Lord, and meditating sometimes confidingly upon Death, the first of the four last things to be remembered."

If we examine the spiritual wisdom of Jean Taylor, we are led to believe that she is "saved." She has been able to understand the mysterious truth of the phone calls and to accept it. Is her insight Catholic? Does it depend upon dogma? Can non-Catholics follow it? Mrs. Spark does not really answer these questions; she implies that Catholicism has been a source of spiritual strength, enabling one old woman to cope with the "eccentric event" of death. But Miss Taylor's personality was, at least, partially formed before she converted; *she brought something to the Church which made her embrace its doctrines.* This ambiguity is the final strength of *Memento Mori*: we are not ultimately sure about Catholicism as the *only means of salvation,* but we recognize that it offers one meaningful answer to the phone calls.

In *The Bachelors* Mrs. Spark introduces us to a special world which resembles the island of *Robinson* or the aged of *Memento Mori*; here we see only bachelors as they go about their daily business. By employing an isolated, quirky group, she can present unusual tensions and doubts.

Perhaps the key to the many bachelors lies in the nature of their deceptions. Ronald Bridges hides the fear that his memory may be going. He constantly tests himself, remembering friends' birthdays and historical events. His deception is relatively minor. It is appropriate that he is an expert in graphology because he traces forgeries; he can see underlying truths. He "bridges" worlds of deception and honesty, of secularism and religion. When his faith in himself and others falters, he chooses to recite a passage from the Epistle to the Philippians which begins: "All that rings true. . . ."

Patrick Seton is a spiritualist medium who deceives others by means of his trances. He forges letters; he blackmails women; he even contemplates murder. He is able to get far—at least before his conviction—because he apparently offers insight into universals and explicates the cosmic design without faltering. He is, we can say, the metaphysical confidence-man. Because he is so dramatically opposed to Bridges—his trances are symbolically linked to the other's epileptic seizures—there is great excitement when they comfort each other (really for the first time) in the courtroom, and this scene is probably the most memorable one in all of Mrs. Spark's novels.

The Bachelors ranges from the "public" excitement of the courtroom to the private soul of Bridges. It opens and ends with an account of his "condition." We see that his illness is the cross which lifts him out of the ordinary and gives him special lucidity. It is his "vocation." (It is ironic that epilepsy has prevented his becoming a priest because it has helped him to understand his spiritual motives and to *confirm* the religious quality of his life.) Although he is "diseased," he is healthy enough to see that "being Catholic is part of his human existence." He attends Mass; he fights Seton's spiritualism; he is aware of original sin; he regards humanity without disgust—if not with complete love. Thus his meditations lead him to final wonder or amusement, and relate him to Caroline Rose, January Marlow, and, less so, to Jean Taylor.

We are getting close to the special quality of Catholicism for Mrs. Spark. It emerges as a "rock," a position from which the believer can survey the human condition. It helps him (or her) to note the twists of motivation—including his own—and to be amazed at such devious complexity. It fights simple surrender to various human deceptions. It offers, finally, an exalted view of pervasive meaning. For these reasons the four Catholics I have discussed are "saved." Their lives are differentiated from those of their friends and relatives because of their quirky insights. This is not to say that Mrs. Spark lacks irony. She demonstrates that some Catholics like Mrs. Hogg in *The Comforters* and Robinson—to mention only the most obvious ones—lack special "wonder and amusement," and, as a result, are defective in their vision. They don't *see through deceptions*; they remain trapped in grotesque, self-centered patterns.

The Prime of Miss Jean Brodie is even more ironic than the previous novels because it suggests that conversion itself may not "save" us.

It begins with one short paragraph:

The boys, as they talked to the girls from Marcia Blaine School, stood on the far side of their bicycles holding the handlebars, which established a protective fence of bicycle between the sexes, and the impression that at any moment the boys were likely to be away.[3]

The "protective fence" implies that there is a barrier between boys and girls, but we also find that it eventually symbolizes the separation of teacher from student, experience from innocence, the world from the convent.

Miss Jean Brodie has somewhat Fascistic opinions about politics, women, art, and religion. She expresses these to her girls, hoping that, in effect, they will "convert" to her views. Why does she take such special care? There is no doubt that superficially she wants them to live full lives—to enjoy their "prime" ("the moment one was born for"). But at the same time she tries to fight their eventual fulfillment. She inhibits their actions; she commands them to obey her laws. She suggests, for example, that Rose should become Teddy Lloyd's mistress. It is appropriate that she is likened by Sandy Stranger to "Providence"; unconsciously, she does want to create "the beginning and the end."

When we first meet Sandy, we note that she does not listen to the lecture. Her attention is "wandering"—to use Miss Brodie's word. The "fence" between her and her teacher (and the other girls) is established subtly here. We never completely learn why she is a "stranger," but as the novel progresses, the "stranger" quality assumes control. Sandy rebels against the "psychological Calvinism" of Miss Brodie; she refuses to be confined to playing a role for her. Although she is instructed to "spy" on Rose and Teddy Lloyd, she really spies, instead, on her teacher, and informs the school authorities that she is an evil influence. She reaches her "prime," as it were, in rebellious betrayal. The ironies are compounded. By asserting her "freedom" in this way, she becomes as falsely "divine" as Miss Brodie—perhaps even more so. She cannot forgive herself; she discovers that she has been "transfigured by the commonplace"—to use the title of the book she eventually writes. She becomes a nun to build a protective fence against the "others."

Sandy apparently finds "no wonder and amusement" in her new-found position. She continues to feel trapped behind the fence: "She clutched the bars of the grille as if she wanted to escape from the dim parlour beyond, for she was not composed like the other nuns who sat when they received their rare visitors, well back in the darkness with folded hands." She wants to flee—but where? She cannot live peacefully in any world. The "clutching" differentiates her from the four converts to Catholicism: January Marlow, Caroline Rose, Jean Taylor, and Ronald Bridges. She is more desperate, more solitary, and more disgusted with humanity than they are. Why? Can we attribute the cause only to her act of betrayal? Is her conversion just punishment? Mrs. Spark does not answer these questions. She leaves the case open; she wants us to feel that there are elements in human nature which remain beyond our simplistic psychological understanding. She frustrates us with great skill.

Although the title of *The Girls of Slender Means* suggests that the girls are the central concern, they are less important than Nicholas Farringdon. We first hear about him when Jane Wright, the gossip columnist, calls her friends to inform them that he has been martyred in Haiti. This introductory contrast between gossip and martyrdom, frivolity and seriousness, runs throughout the novel.

The May of Teck Club is a haven for young ladies "who are obliged to reside apart from their families in order to follow an Occupation in London." In 1945 it is inhabited by Joanna, an "elocution" teacher; Jane, a publisher's assistant; Selina, a flirtatious beauty; and several other girls described in detail. We get to know their outstanding qualities as Mrs. Spark employs symbolic repetitions. Selina, for example, is interested in "poise" so that she can be attractive to men; she reminds herself that *"Poise is perfect balance, an equanimity of body and mind, complete composure whatever the social scene."* Joanna expresses her religious fervor (she is the daughter of a clergyman) by reciting *The Wreck of the Deutschland.* Their voices are counterpointed to reinforce the contrast between the "social scene" and spiritual devotion.

Nicholas Farringdon visits the May of Teck Club because he is in love with Selina. He uses the excuse of having dinner with Jane Wright (who can help get his book published). *He is full of contraries.* He writes *The Sabbath Notebooks* and he sleeps with Selina. He dislikes war and joins the Army. He is an idealist and he forges a letter for his self-advancement. He is "a bit of a misfit," as his brothers claim. Because Nicholas is so completely ambivalent, he strongly embodies the thematic contrast between the "social scene" and the religious world I have already mentioned.

Mrs. Spark employs one "miraculous" event to transform him. Early in the novel we are told by Greggie, one of the three spinsters, that an unexploded bomb lies in the garden. It is referred to a few times so that it begins to assume symbolic importance as the dark force underneath our feet. Finally it explodes when we and the girls least expect it; in the resulting fire Joanna is trapped and dies, "mechanically re-

citing the evening psalter of Day 27, responses and answers,"
while Selina steals a Schiaparelli dress and escapes unharmed.
Nicholas is there and crosses himself; he realizes that "nowhere's safe."

In later years the girls speculate about his conversion to
Catholicism. What moved him? Was he really in love with
Joanna's purity? Did he go mad? The following conversation
suggests one answer (Jane is speaking to Nancy):

> "It's Jane. Look, I've just got another question to ask you, quickly,
> about Nicholas Farringdon. Do you think his conversion had anything
> to do with the fire? I've got to finish this big article about him."
>
> "Well, I always like to think it was Joanna's example. Joanna was
> very High Church."
>
> "But he wasn't in love with Joanna, he was in love with Selina.
> After the fire he looked for her all over the place."
>
> "Well, he couldn't have been converted by Selina. Not converted."
>
> "He's got a note in his manuscript that a vision of evil may be as
> effective to conversion as a vision of good." [4]

Nicholas did not convert merely as a result of viewing Joanna's death; he was even more disturbed that Selina (and
the "social scene" she represented) used the opportunity for
her greed. He chose (or was chosen) to give up the "slender
means" of materialism. But our psychological understanding
is as empty as Jane's "news" because it does not completely
explain his transformation. Thus he remains beyond our grasp
—like ambiguous Sandy Stranger and Ronald Bridges. It is
fitting that his death occurs far away and yet tantalizingly
close to the girls and us.

The Mandelbaum Gate seems to represent a departure. It
does not give us a tight society; it does not dwell upon one
miraculous event which transforms the individual; it does
not deal primarily with English manners. But the more we
think about this comic, suspenseful, and exotic novel, we realize that it shows another way Mrs. Spark has used her abiding themes.

Every event and conversation in the novel deals with deception. Joanna, the English woman, says about the Arab men-

tality: "They think in symbols. Everything stands for something else. And when they speak in symbols it sounds like lies." One spying ring makes believe that it is an insurance company. Barbara Vaughan dresses as a nun. Suzi hides her in the house. Ricky, the cold schoolteacher who apparently cares little for men, is found in bed with Joe Ramdez: "What had been overlooked was perfectly obvious. . . ." Violence is expected in the Holy Land—but is it Holy?—but it occurs off-stage in England. The Eichmann trial is said to be "highly religious." It is no wonder that Freddy, who acts so bravely for the first time in his life, cannot remember exactly what happened to him during his cloak-and-dagger adventures with Barbara: his amnesia perfectly captures the vague, suspended condition which plagues humanity.

Barbara Vaughan is a half-Jewish Catholic convert. She is on a pilgrimage in the Holy Land not only to see the religious shrines but to be close to her lover. She wonders whether the Church will permit her marriage. Her "obscure" position reinforces the crazy goings-on. Barbara resembles Mrs. Spark's other heroines—Caroline, January, and Jean Taylor—because she is open to "wonder and amusement"; even when she is at the point of danger or illness, she can smile at her condition. She believes that "either religious faith penetrates everything in life or it doesn't. There are some experiences that seem to make nonsense of all separations of sacred from profane— they seem childish. Either the whole of life is unified under God or everything falls apart" (p. 344).

The Mandelbaum Gate tries to unify life by moving swiftly from half-truths to complete faith. It ranges from spy-story thrills to religious humor. It is even more deceptive than the previous novels because it substitutes many "comic coincidences" for one miraculous event. It ends fittingly enough with this sentence:

[Freddy] walked round the city until at last, fumbling in his pocket for his diplomatic pass, he came to the Mandelbaum Gate, hardly a gate at all, but a piece of street between Jerusalem and Jerusalem, flanked by two huts, and called by that name because a house at the other end once belonged to a Mr. Mandelbaum [p. 369].

The first impression we get from the sentence—and the novel —is that things are divided and isolated ("between Jerusalem and Jerusalem"), but we also see that someone can go "round" the city and thus bridge its divisions. The house once belonged to one man, Mr. Mandelbaum, before the barrier was built; things were unified, and if we look closely enough, they still are.

Mrs. Spark returns again and again to thematic deceptions and conversions as she tries to deceive and convert us. Although she cannot make us accept her Catholicism as the true faith, she supports our belief in the ultimate design of our apparently divisive, "funny" lives. She gives us, in the end, "wonder and amusement."

Notes

1. *Memento Mori* in *A Muriel Spark Trio* (Philadelphia: Lippincott, 1962), pp. 575–576.
2. *The Mandelbaum Gate* (New York: Knopf, 1965), p. 319. Subsequent page-references appear in the text.
3. *The Prime of Miss Jean Brodie* (Philadelphia: Lippincott, 1962), p. 9.
4. *The Girls of Slender Means* (New York: Knopf, 1963), pp. 173–174.

Children's Faces:
Graham Greene

ALBERT SONNENFELD · *Princeton University*

ONE OF MY PRINCETON UNDERCLASSMEN cavalierly dismissed *Brighton Rock* as the least valuable selection on the syllabus because "it's like reading a *Hardy Boys* book." It was a perceptive criticism, I believe. The stock situations and facile black-and-white characterizations of juvenile fiction, from *Tom Brown's Schooldays* through Dixon's glorification of "hardy" boys, are indeed a basic ingredient in Greene's formula for serious adult novels: "[Mr. Colleoni] was a small Jew with a neat round belly . . . and his eyes gleamed like raisins." [1] Clearly a villain! And when that suspiciously foreign name is compared to such sterling first names as Rose and Pinkie, Greene does indeed seem to have stacked the allegorical odds. And yet even in his first "Catholic novel," *Brighton Rock* of 1938, the novelist moves away from primary colors and into half-tints and blends: *Rose, Pinkie Brown*, Molly *Pink*. For Greene, the adolescent, the schoolboy, the apprentice criminal is in a transitional world between the purity of babyhood and the malevolence of the adult. When Pinkie returns to his birthplace at Paradise Piece, he meets a crippled child:

. . . it was like the dreadful appeal of innocence, but *there* was not innocence: you had to go back a long way further before you got innocence; innocence was a slobbering mouth, a toothless gum pulling at the teats, perhaps not even that; innocence was the ugly cry of birth [pp. 204–205].

Those of us who have interpreted Greene's work in the light of our admiration for the Christological children in Dostoevsky and Bernanos have unwittingly attenuated his very literal belief in original sin; we have forgotten the children in Brighton's amusement tunnel with their paper sailor caps marked "I'M NO ANGEL." The adolescent, acting out the ancient schoolboy pattern of initiation into the class, of making the team, is suspended between innocence and guilt, between heaven and hell:

The gulls which had stood like candles down the beach rose and cried under the promenade. The old man found a boot and stowed it in his sack, and a gull dropped from the parade and swept through the iron nave of the Palace Pier, white and purposeful in the obscurity: *half vulture and half dove.* In the end one always had to learn [italics mine; p. 190].

And in the lounge-bar of *Lureland*:

Siphons stood about on blue-topped tables, and on the stained-glass windows medieval ships tossed on cold curling waves. Somebody had broken the hands off one of the statuettes—or perhaps it was made like that, something classical in white drapery, *a symbol of victory or despair.* The Boy rang a bell and a boy of his own age came out of the public bar to take his order; they were oddly alike and allusively different— narrow shoulders, thin face, they bristled like dogs at the sight of each other [italics mine; p. 333].

Those who are only in the anteroom of damnation, for whom all hope has not yet been abandoned, are invariably seen as adolescent schoolboys. The decrepit yellow-toothed lawyer, Mr. Drewitt, knows that Brighton is hell; he uses the same words of Marlowe's Mephistopheles that Greene himself will apply to the "Metroland loneliness" surrounding his school in the "Prologue" to *The Lawless Roads* (1939): " 'Why, this is Hell, nor are we out of it.' " Drewitt's shameful urge to expose himself ("No money can heal a mind diseased. This is Hell. . . . How much could you spare?") would seem to damn him irrevocably, were it not for the vestiges of adolescence which the author carefully leaves him. Drewitt is "an old Lancaster boy" with a photo of the school group on the wall and memories of field days with Harrow. Like a schoolboy, Drewitt has "grubby and bitten nails" on the shaky hands "which were the instruments of pleasure." His addiction to masturbation strangely becomes that of puberty rather than the vice of a married adult who watches the typists going by and dreams of embracing "their little portable machines" (pp. 307, 308). In this most Freudian of Graham Greene novels (he once called his own psychiatric treatment "perhaps the happiest months of my life"), the proselyte author forgives his characters more than they, Jansenists to the core, are willing to forgive themselves.

"J'écris pour l'enfant que je fus," Bernanos was fond of saying. Graham Greene, for whom Christ's *revelasti ea parvulis* prefigures Freudian theory, writes for the lonely and tormented schoolboy he had been. "I was, I suppose, thirteen years old," he writes in beginning his 1939 Mexican journal, *The Lawless Roads* (in the American edition, *Another Mexico*):

> And so faith came to one—shapelessly, without dogma, a presence above a croquet lawn, something associated with violence, cruelty, evil across the way. One began to believe in heaven because one believed in hell, but for a long while it was only hell one could picture with a certain intimacy—the pitchpine partitions of dormitories where everybody was never quiet at the same time; lavatories without locks . . . ; walks in pairs up the suburban roads; no solitude anywhere, at any time.[2]

The initiation into belief, into acceptance of the reality of Hell, comes through the apprenticeship in the world of adults that we call adolescence but which for Greene seems to go back to the traumas of childhood. The boy Philip, in the revealing story *The Basement Room* (1936), loves to keep secrets and to listen to Baines telling stories, but discovers that the sharer becomes an accomplice in a sordid adult plot and that the childhood adventure stories turn into novels of adultery:

> A kind of embittered happiness and self-pity made him cry; he was lost; there wouldn't be any more secrets to keep; he surrendered responsibility once and for all. Let grown-up people keep to their world and he would keep to his, safe in the small garden between the plane-trees. "In the lost childhood of Judas Christ was betrayed"; you could almost see the small unformed face hardening into the deep dilettante selfishness of age.[3]

"The lost childhood of Judas." That line from AE's *Germinal,* which became the title of one of Greene's most moving essays, seems to combine psychoanalysis with theology: can one explain, and perchance excuse, the archetypal betrayal by the determinism of a trauma repressed or buried in a long-lost childhood? Or does the very loss of childhood constitute the formation of a Judas? Both are doubtless true, yet we should never forget that even childhood is theologically far removed from the "ugly cry of birth" that is innocence. As Ida Arnold says to Rose who had naïvely maintained that "People change" (Greene has cleverly reversed the roles here, making the non-believing Ida the spokesman for the Catholic truth of original sin):

> "Oh, no, they don't. Look at me. I've never changed. It's like those sticks of rock: bite it all the way down, you'll still read Brighton. That's human nature." She breathed mournfully over Rose's face—a sweet and winy breath.
> "Confession . . . repentance," Rose whispered.
> "That's just religion," the woman said. "Believe me. It's the world we got to deal with" [*Brighton Rock,* p. 291].

And so the Philip of *The Basement Room* will not be able to keep to his safe world in the small garden; even with the dilettante selfishness of age he will keep his small unformed face, but his essential sinfulness (to be born is to take the first step toward adulthood and toward death) is as present in every fiber in the fabric of his being as the name of Brighton in that Churchless "rock."

II

> The possibility of damnation is so immense a relief in a world of electoral reform, plebiscites, sex reform and dress reform, that damnation itself is an immediate form of salvation—of salvation from the ennui of modern life, because it at least gives some significance to living.
>
> It is better to do evil than to do nothing: at least we exist.

T. S. Eliot's oft-quoted remarks define the two forms of purgatory in Greene's imperfect, and for that reason all the more revealing, first Catholic novel. There is the purgatory of the adolescent who by definition *is* "possibility of damnation" and therefore possibility of salvation; there is the purgatory of the lukewarm, of the non-believer or unbaptized, who will be spewn forth, as the Apocalypse foretells, or cast into the circle of a Hell which leads nowhere. And these two forms are *physically* rendered: there are the fully grown adults and there are the still growing children or adolescents: "Un mystique à l'état sauvage," Claudel once called that prototypical adolescent, Rimbaud. Mr. Colleoni is not only the evil Jew of Victorian edifying literature for juveniles; he is also the successful adult (*Colleoni,* the Venetian warrior, does sound rather like *coglione,* too). He owns the world Pinkie seeks to penetrate: "the whole visible world, that is: cash registers and policemen and prostitutes, Parliament and the laws which say 'this is Right and this is Wrong.' " Every trait both in his setting and in his person confirms an impression of fullness and maturity. The Cosmopolitan Hotel (where else would a Jewish ganglord be found?) has an acre of deep carpet, deep velvet couches, overweight clients in furs and jewels; Colleoni himself has a round belly, plump thighs, a gold lighter and long cigar. Small wonder that Greene con-

stantly refers to Pinkie allegorically as "the Boy" ("You are
not Mr. P. Brown?" Colleoni had asked. "I expected someone
a good deal older" [pp. 85ff].) ; for the relationship between
the two "criminals" quickly becomes that of father to rebellious son, of schoolmaster to insolent pupil. "You're wasting
your time, my child," Mr. Colleoni says after the Boy had
threatened violence. The same parental attitude, superficially
affectionate but profoundly corrupting, marks Ida's encounters with Rose as she tries to get the evidence to convict
Pinkie of murdering Hale: "Pardon, dear. You see we can
get along all right when we are together. I've never had a
child of my own and somehow I've taken to you. You're a
sweet little thing" (pp. 174–175). Late in the novel, Ida
practices an even crueler deception, literally passing herself
off as Rose's mother to gain admittance to her rooms:

> "I know." Rose ran upstairs; it was the biggest triumph you could
> ever expect: to greet your mother for the first time in your own house,
> ask her to sit down on your own chair, to look at each other with an
> equal experience. There was nothing now, Rose felt, her mother knew
> about men she didn't know: that was the reward for the painful ritual
> upon the bed. She flung the door gladly open and there was the woman
> [p. 287].

Ida even moves across the floor as if she intended to take
Rose in her arms, explaining "Why, you poor little thing, I
pity you." Pity is that adult substitute for Christlike compassion which will distort Scobie's self-imposed Calvary in *The
Heart of the Matter,* as we shall see. In contrast, Pinkie looks
at the greying hair of Spicer, his next victim, with "no pity
at all; he wasn't old enough for pity" (p. 134).

If we examine Greene's careful presentation of Ida's total
physicality, the same impression of maternal fullness and
maturity is reinforced. (What Ida Arnold represents in the
theological structure of the novel has, of course, been adequately defined by numerous critics and will not concern me
further here.) Ida smells of soap and wine, comfort and
peace and a slow sleepy physical enjoyment; with her "big
tipsy mouth," "her large cool pastry-making hands," "her

big breasts, which had never suckled a child of her own," Ida, as her name indicates, is the embodiment of the plenitude of life. She accepts the comfort of the deep couch and the gaudy furnishings of her place of assignation with Mr. Corkery "like an aphrodisiac in her tea." Above all, Ida Arnold joyfully accepts sex: "It doesn't do anyone any harm that I know of. It's human nature." As she undresses in surroundings so similar to Colleoni's ("big padded pleasure dome of a bedroom, deep soft rug, red velvet hangings"), she thinks of popular phrases "A Night of Love," "You Only Live Once" and works "her plump toes" in the rug. At the very moment that Pinkie is *buying* Rose from her moody parents (they ask for guineas not pounds in one of the true revelations of grown-up venality) and dreading the inevitability of consummation, "the horrifying act of a desire he didn't feel," Ida is consuming the Host of her religion of uninhibited eroticism:

[She] bit an éclair and the cream spurted between the large front teeth. She laughed a little thickly in the Pompadour Boudoir and said: "I haven't had as much money to spend since I left Tom." She took another bite and a wedge of cream settled on the plump tongue [p. 209].

In contrast to Ida's "Bacchic and bawdy" cult and ample physical endowment, Pinkie and Rose are slight, almost monastic (he had wanted to be a priest: "They know what's what. They keep away" [p. 240]), and physically and psychically incomplete. Pinkie has little experience of the adult world despite his career in the protection rackets:

He knew everything in theory, nothing in practice; he was only old with the knowledge of other people's lusts, those of strangers who wrote their desires on the walls in public lavatories. He knew the moves, he'd never played the game [p. 166].

Brighton Rock narrates Pinkie's conversion from theory to practice. "I don't drink" (p. 7), he admitted in the first pages; he will begin drinking and shortly before his death downs

two double brandies. "I don't bet" (p. 146), he tells Spicer,
but he will gamble on his salvation. He acquires the habit of
lying (Greene explains that he wasn't used to lying). He is
taunted by Spicer's girl, Sylvie: "I bet you don't go with girls
either" (p. 192), yet much of the novel is devoted to his
initiation into sex; from a kiss ("his mouth missed hers and
recoiled. He'd never yet kissed a girl" [p. 130]) to the mar-
riage-bed (" 'It's Saturday night,' he said with a bitter taste
on his tongue, 'it's time for bed.' " [p. 263]). Each movement
toward adulthood is accompanied by the imagery of juvenile
fiction. When Pinkie reviews his brief but effective career in
murder, Greene tells us "He had graduated in pain. . . .
He had a sense now that the murders of Hale and Spicer were
trivial acts, a boy's game, and he had put away childish
things" (p. 243). A wedding night in mortal sin fills him
"with a kind of gloomy hilarity and pride. He saw himself
now as a full-grown man for whom the angels wept." His
last gesture of satanic defiance, the recording of his message
of hatred and damnation to Rose, forces him to absent himself
from his gangland mission, giving him "the sense of playing
truant from his proper work—he should be at school, but he
hadn't learned his lesson" (p. 258). And in a simile that reveals the author's essentially adult pity toward the Boy,
Pinkie is described after his wedding as being "like a child
with haemophilia: every contact drew blood" (p. 218).

   If one tries to reconstitute a portrait of Pinkie from the
details scattered throughout the novel by Greene, the obsession with adolescence betrayed by the opening of *The Lawless Roads* becomes all the more striking. The nervousness of
puberty shows in his close-bitten nails (Pinkie's first victim,
Hale, who had been both son and lover to Ida, had bitten
nails and inky fingers), in his reflexive gesture of "licking
an indelible pencil, his mouth was stained purple at the corners" (p. 82), in his slight tic "through the soft chicken down,
where you might have expected a dimple" (p. 29). His face
is "like a child's, badgered, confused, betrayed" (p. 352),
and the years of hard experience are called "fake years." In
those rare moments of self-revelation when Pinkie sings, it is

"in his spoilt boy's voice" (p. 71) or in "his high adolescent voice" (p. 151). His repressed sexuality finds an outlet in cruelty, as he systematically tears an insect's wings off (" 'She loves me,' he said, 'she loves me not' " [p. 134]) or crushes a wounded moth underfoot; or else in uncontrolled fits of rage as he shouts "I want service," smashing a salt sprinkler down on the table with "a little spurt of vicious anger" (p. 33). Only one form of experience seems to take him beyond the immediate physical impulse, and that is music. For Ida Arnold, music (" 'One night in an alley,' Lily [Ida] sings, 'Lord Rothschild said to me' " [p. 6]) had been an incitement to the physical; for Pinkie music is a dangerous enemy, stirring in his brain "like poetry," speaking to him "of things he didn't understand" (p. 71). Small wonder that he is unwillingly prompted to sing softly the words of the Mass (of the *Agnus Dei, qui tollis peccata mundi, dona nobis pacem* particularly) by even the most vulgar popular songs. "Music was the nearest he knew to sorrow." Pinkie weeps in a movie when he hears a leading man moaning "I know in my heart you're divine," the trite lyrics suddenly assuming a literal meaning like "a vision of release to an imprisoned man" (p. 261). Christ was in the music as much as in the Host; here was an area of adult experience that was not pity but compassion, was far removed from the physicality of Colleoni and of Ida:

Only the music made him uneasy, the cat-gut vibrating in the heart; it was like nerves losing their freshness, it was *like age coming on,* other people's experience battering on the brain [italics mine; p. 62].

What irony then that the record he cuts should not be the song of "something loving" requested by Rose, but the message of hatred, "the worst horror of all."

The record will be Rose's future; that betrayal was prepared in Pinkie's lost childhood. Two literally formative traumatic experiences constitute Pinkie's psychic inheritance and provide the matrices for the novel's imagery. When Pinkie drives with Rose along the road to Peacehaven, stopping at Lureland to prepare the bogus suicide pact which will eliminate her as potential witness against him, he encounters Piker, his double, a former schoolmate from Catholic school days; and his tortured past as victim and as would-be priest comes back to him when he sips the double brandy in a bizarre communion parody:

> The Boy rang a bell and a boy of his own age came out of the public bar to take his order; they were oddly alike and allusively different— narrow shoulders, thin face, they bristled like dogs at the sight of each other [p. 333].

. . . .

> He looked with loathing into the past—a cracked bell ringing, a child weeping under the cane. . . [p. 346].

. . . .

> . . . fake years slipped away—he was whisked back towards the unhappy playground [p. 352].

One has the feeling that Pinkie's career in murder is a re-enactment of the playground scene where he stabbed a "bullied brat" with the dividers as well as a revenge for beatings received from parental figures in the school—characteristically, he acts upon ineffectual, childlike figures: Hale, Spicer, Rose. "He had graduated in pain: first the school dividers had been left behind, next the razor. . . . Murder had only led to this—this corruption" (p. 243). The corruption is sex, "the frightening weekly exercise of his parents," "bouncing and ploughing": "If you were ignorant of that one dirty scramble you knew nothing" (p. 216).

Pinkie will come to knowledge, if not to pleasure, but the pervasive sense of a prolonged puberty is conveyed by a carefully contrived series of phallic substitutes, actually masturbatory in quality, which distort Pinkie's erotic energies. His assaults by stabbing and slashing, his pricking of Rose's arm with his one unbitten nail, his constant fingering and "tickling" of the vitriol bottle which he keeps in his pocket, are distinctly sexual gestures. When Pinkie fails so miserably in his first sexual "scramble" with Sylvie in the back seat of a car ("he was aware of nausea and retched. Marry, he thought, hell,

no; I'd rather hang" [p. 196]), Greene draws attention to
the Boy's pointed shoes slipping on the wet tiles near a swimming pool where two lovers were swimming together. These
shoes, mentioned repeatedly, cannot help but remind us of
Greene's more than passing acquaintance with psychoanalysis,
as do, in a comically vulgar way, the gang's wedding presents
to Pinkie and Rose:

a tiny doll's commode in the shape of a radio set labelled: "The smallest
A.I two-valve receiving set in the world," and a mustard pot shaped
like a lavatory seat with the legend, "For me and my girl" [p. 215].

These images of sublimation lead inevitably to the real thing,
to direct experience. "You're growing up, Pinkie—like your
father," Dallow says after the wedding:

Like my father . . . The Boy was shaken again with his nocturnal
Saturday disgust. He couldn't blame his father now . . . it was what
you came to . . . you got mixed up, and then, he supposed, the habit
grew . . . you gave yourself away weekly [p. 320].

Pinkie's entire career in violent crime had been an attempt
to ward off, to defer, sexual experience. Kite, the gangleader,
had picked him up, adopted him; Kite had died, but Pinkie
had prolonged Kite's existence, "not touching liquor, biting
his nails in the Kite way, until *she* came and altered everything." For Pinkie, Kite was a father unblemished by the
horror of Saturday-night procreation. (Psychoanalysts have
written often of that shattering discovery that "father and
mother" are "lovers" to each other.) The death of the father-
substitute left him with the legacy of "his duty never to leave
for strange acres" and a mission of revenge. Ironically, it will
be the "maternal" Ida (" 'What, she? She's old enough to
be my mother' " [p. 201].) who will drive the Boy to self-
destruction at the very moment Rose may already be carrying
his child.

Symbolically, the movement of the novel from adolescence
to the malevolence of adulthood is reversed by Pinkie's death.
As he mutilates his own face with vitriol and leaps over the

cliff, "he looked half his size, doubled up in appalling agony; it was as if the flames had literally got him and he shrank— *shrank into a schoolboy* flying in panic and pain, scrambling over a fence, running on" (p. 352). Rose, whose innocence had been detailed repeatedly ("She didn't even know the name of a drink" [p. 67]), becomes a mystical reincarnation of the childlike Virgin thanks to her husband's self-immolation. She too had lived an apprenticeship ("She was like a child in a new school . . ." [p. 284]), but her grossly enlarged and distorted image reflected in a bottle of Extra-Stout ("It seemed to carry an enormous weight of responsibility" [p. 247].) is transformed into that of one of the dolls ("like Virgins in a church repository") that Pinkie had won in the shooting gallery. In the confessional an old priest begs her: "Pray for me, my child" (p. 358).

III

The excessively contrived network of children's faces in *Brighton Rock* reflects the adult author's pity for his creation. One does get the feeling that Greene is trying too hard, that along with blatant allegory (Paradise Piece, Liberty Hall, Lureland, etc.) he is still too close to his own experience of faith coming through belief in hell, too eager to communicate that strategy of salvation to a reader who probably shares the modern worldly ethic of an Ida Arnold. His virtual Manicheanism is reflected in the reversal of the ethics of the school-boy novel: here the self-designated "good" are evil and cast into hell, whereas those who commit murder and suicide achieve at least an initial groping toward salvation. That Greene continues to hold to this belief can be seen in the epigraph to one of his most perfected mature works, *The Heart of the Matter* (1948):

Le pécheur est au coeur même de chrétienté. . . . Nul n'est aussi compétent que le pécheur en matière de chrétienté. Nul, si ce n'est le saint.

One should note, however, that in his mature fiction Greene has retreated somewhat: the saint is linked to the sinner, not to the criminal. In *The Heart of the Matter,* the novelist has shifted the burden of bearing adult pity for the childlike onto his protagonist, Scobie. It will be *his* failing to see "children's faces" everywhere, just as it had been the failing of Greene's narration in *Brighton Rock* to be too consistent in its imagery. One scene seems to me to be crucial. Scobie actually becomes the narrator of a *mysterium iniquitatis* worthy of the school-boy-novel liturgy of *Brighton Rock.* A Protestant missionary asks Scobie to read a story to a little boy rescued from a torpedoed boat, assuring him that the novels in her library are not "novels," but safe. The titles include *Twenty Years in the Mission Field, Lost and Found, The Narrow Way*—happy-ending books. Scobie selects *A Bishop among the Bantus,* and in telling it makes it into a boyhood tale of Arthur Bishop, a secret agent of the British Government, who lets himself be captured by the Bantus in order to discover their secret pass-words, hiding places, and plans of raids. He falls in love with the daughter of the captain of the Bantus and turns "soppy." But there are lots of fights and murders before the end, Scobie insists. This is, of course, a foreshadowing of Scobie's own betrayal by Wilson; it seems, in addition, to parallel Ida Arnold's pursuit of Pinkie Brown, though here Wilson, "the old boy," who subscribes to the *Old Downhamian,* is track-ing down the "adult" Scobie.

The novel opens with Wilson's arrival, as he sits "stroking his very young moustache" and looking down on the world of vultures and pye-dogs, of brothels and corruption that Scobie has long been familiar with in his job as deputy police com-missioner. Wilson, seen by Scobie the adult, is very much like Pinkie viewed by Greene:

> There was something defenceless, it seemed to Scobie, in his whole attitude: he stood there waiting for people to be friendly or unfriendly— he didn't seem to expect one reaction more than another. He was like a dog. Nobody had yet drawn on his face the lines that make a human being.[4]

But then Scobie finds the childlike and pitiable in everyone, as we shall see. The author himself is rather harder on Wilson, while remaining faithful to his basic pattern of imagery. The police spy has "bald pink knees," a smooth-skinned face "pink and healthy, plump and hopeless" (p. 3), and wears his mustache "like a club tie." His friendship with his fellow Downhamian, the middle-aged Harris, is a desperate attempt to organize chaotic experience by schoolboy rules. A cockroach hunt with a slipper and a scorecard ("The Cockroach Championship") becomes an obstacle to their relationship when Wilson refuses to abide by the rules of "the inventor of the game":

> "My rules are the Queensberry rules in this town."
> "They won't be for long," Wilson threatened [p. 75].

Still, Harris and Wilson decide to "room together" with thoughts of an Old Downhamian Dinner rejected by the irritable and defensive Wilson:

> He was one of those, it seemed to Harris, who always knew what was on: who gave advance information on extra halves: who knew why old So-and-so had not turned up to school, and what the row brewing at the Masters' special meeting was about. A few weeks ago he had been a new boy whom Harris had been delighted to befriend, to show around. . . . But Harris from his first year at school had been fated to see how quickly new boys grew up . . . [p. 178].

In fact, Wilson is more like the transfer student who had been sent down elsewhere. While Harris (who had meanwhile composed a newsy letter for the alumni magazine) sips barley water with lime, Wilson drinks whisky. He goes to the brothel "impelled by a passion of curiosity more than of lust," and after a momentary revulsion like Pinkie's he surrenders: "he felt as though his dead veins would bleed again" (p. 190). The so-called "new boy" had clearly served his apprenticeship in adult evil elsewhere. Unlike Pinkie who learns deviousness in the course of the novel, Wilson's "profession was to lie." He lies particularly about his love of poetry ("he absorbed it

secretly—like a drug"), which becomes the basis for his love
for Louise, Scobie's wife: "Have I really found a friend?"
The schoolboy falls in love with the headmaster's wife, one
might say: the signs of adolescent awkwardness mark Wilson's
publication of his poem "Tristram" in the *Old Downhamian,*
his stubborn nosebleed after a slap from Louise (staining the
poem on the torn-off page), his undisguised tears in a rare
moment of sincerity ("He looked at the man who had seen
his tears with hatred."), his fond memories of the movie
"Bengal Lancer," his constant recourse to threats ("One
day I'll ruin you, Scobie."). Despite these vestiges, the betrayal
of Scobie originates in the lost childhood of Wilson. He had
mastered what Pinkie was only learning: lying, bribery, blackmail, deceit. And the cruelest betrayal of all is his only too-
well-founded insinuation to the Pharisee Louise that Scobie
had committed suicide. Only Father Rank's belief in the
mystery of God's ways ("don't imagine you—or I—know a
thing about God's mercy" [p. 306]) can undo that betrayal
and lead Louise to acknowledge albeit reluctantly that Scobie
had loved no one else except God.

The implicit analogy with Judas' betrayal of Christ is really
the heart of the matter. Scobie is a would-be Christ; his career
of sacrifice would seem to be a true *imitatio,* were it not that
he too is psychologically rather than mystically driven. He
feels an adultlike pity toward children, rather than a Christlike compassion. He will take pity and accept his own moral
corruption because he sees even in adults a projection of his
dead daughter, his only child, "who had died at school in
England three years ago—a little pious nine-year-old girl's
face in the white muslin of first communion." And so when he
finds an illegal letter to a daughter in Germany in the toilet
of the Esperança, he not only sees the Captain as a father like
himself but metamorphoses him into a child:

The man had lowered his bulk onto the edge of the bath as though it
were a heavy sack his shoulders could no longer bear. He kept on wiping
his eyes with the back of his hand like a child—an unattractive child,
the fat boy of the school. Against the beautiful and the clever and the

successful one can wage a pitiless war, but not against the unattractive: then the millstone weighs on the breast [p. 49].

Scobie will not turn in the letter. The next stage in his downfall, a foreshadowing also of future suicide, is his trip across a Styx-like river to view the body of a dead district commissioner who had been deeply in debt:

> When Scobie turned the sheet down to the shoulder he had the impression that he was looking at a child in a night-shirt quietly asleep: the pimples were the pimples of puberty and the dead face seemed to bear the trace of no experience beyond the class-room or the football field. "Poor child," he said aloud [p. 88].

Scobie, too, will contract debts to Yusef in order to send his wife to haven in South Africa. Pemberton's suicide note to "Dad" ("It was like a letter from school excusing a bad report.") will lead to Scobie's own deception in his diary. Even his adulterous love affair with Helen Rolt confuses passion with pity. She, too, is a reincarnation of his dead daughter, as he first sees her clutching a stamp album "from her loving father on her fourteenth birthday." Scobie brings her presents of stamps (his spilling gin on a stamp anticipates Wilson's nosebleed on the poem), and shortly before he kisses Helen for the first time, he sees her as ugly, "with the temporary ugliness of a child." Her love letter to Scobie, reminiscent of Pemberton's suicide note, only confirms Scobie's mistaken impression:

> *My dear my dear leave me if you want to or have me as your hore if you want to.* He thought: She's only heard the word, never seen it spelt: they cut it out of the school Shakespeares [p. 217].

It is Scobie's inability to treat Helen as anything but the schoolgirl who excels "at net-ball" (she is for him daughter and mistress much the way Hale had been son and lover for Ida) that will lead him to disaster. After she has denounced him for only taking pity, never loving, Scobie feels impelled to write a letter to Helen the adult:

How much older she is than she was a month ago. She hadn't been capable of a scene then, but she had been educated by love and secrecy: he was beginning *to form her. . . . In my school,* he thought wearily, *they learn* bitterness and frustration and *how to grow old* [italics mine; p. 194].

His written declaration of love will be stolen and then used to blackmail him. But its most important consequence is to lead him to suspect his houseboy Ali of having betrayed him to Yusef and Wilson.

Scobie's complicity in the retributive death of Ali marks the penultimate station in his Calvary of theological corruption. Here, too, children's faces provide psychological evidence. Along with Helen Rolt and the little boy to whom Scobie told his tale of a Judas-like betrayal, one other rescued passenger from the torpedoed boat attracts his attention. A little six-year-old girl for whose distraction Scobie makes shadow-pictures on the wall becomes in his mind's eye the image of his own dead daughter ("he saw a white communion veil over her head: it was a trick of the light on the pillow and a trick of his own mind"). He utters a self-sacrificing and Christlike prayer: "Give her peace. Take away my peace for ever, but give her peace." This prayer will be answered, since in consequence Scobie's spiritual itinerary toward suicide and damnation soon becomes manifest. But in many ways more important in hastening his suicide is the death of Ali. At the very moment that he is about to cross the Styx into the world of Pemberton's suicidal death, Scobie dreams a dream which defines Ali's symbolic role in the novel as a pagan child of *before* the Fall:

He was walking through a wide cool meadow with Ali at his heels: there was nobody else anywhere in his dream, and Ali never spoke. Birds went by far overhead, and once when he sat down the grass was parted by a small green snake which passed onto his hand and up his arm without fear and before it slid down into the grass again touched his cheek with a cold friendly remote tongue [p. 82].

Looking into the rearview mirror, Scobie sees Ali "nodding and beaming," as though he represented that reflection of innocence in Scobie's soul which allowed him to think "that this was all he needed of love or friendship." But Ali will die, a victim of Scobie's pity for Helen's disdain of his pity. When one can suspect innocence of betrayal, one has truly been corrupted. Scobie finds his way "quickly and unhesitatingly to the body as though he had himself chosen the scene of the crime." And Ali becomes, for a moment, Christ Himself. His body lay coiled like the image of God coiled at the end of Scobie's broken rosary (he had given the rosary to Ali as a token of identification to his murderers) : "O God . . . I've killed you" (p. 277), Scobie says in a deliberately ambiguous prayer. The death of Ali will fuse with that of his daughter in Scobie's diary: "*Ali found murdered.* The statement was as plain and simple as that other time when he had written: *C. died.*" And the mendacious entries that will follow transform that former vehicle of self-knowledge into a log-book of the journey toward suicide and damnation:

"O God, I offer up my damnation to you. Take it. Use it for them" [p. 250].

This prayer, too, will be answered.

It is ironic that a character who sees virtually everyone as a pitiable child should be himself deprived of childlike traits by an author who lavishes a not inconsiderable amount of affection on him. Perhaps this very absence constitutes Scobie's fall from grace. Certainly, one of the most successful effects created by *The Heart of the Matter* is that of Scobie's age and weariness, like the rusty handcuffs and the broken rosary. But Greene's art is too consistent to deny Scobie completely. The most convincing emblem of Scobie's corruption in death is taken from juvenile fiction:

That night he dreamed that he was in a boat drifting down just such an underground river as his boyhood hero Allan Quatermain had taken towards the lost city of Milosis. But Quatermain had companions, while he was alone, for you couldn't count the dead body on the stretcher as a companion. He felt a sense of urgency, for he told himself that bodies in this climate kept for a very short time, and the smell of decay was already in his nostrils. Then, sitting there guiding the boat down the midstream, he realized that it was not the dead body that smelt but his own living one. He felt as though his blood had ceased to run: when he tried to lift his arm it dangled uselessly from his shoulder. He woke, and it was Louise who had lifted his arm. She said, "Darling, it's time to be off."

"Off?" he asked.

"We're going to Mass together" [p. 246].

In the lost childhood of Judas Christ was betrayed. It is most appropriate that AE's poem was entitled *Germinal,* for the loss of childhood or its perversion is an organic process. Spiritually, this growth can in no way be considered as qualitatively progressive. On the contrary, as Scobie fully realized:

Is it because here human nature hasn't had time to disguise itself? Nobody here could ever talk about a heaven on earth. Heaven remained rigidly in its proper place on the other side of death, and on this side flourished the injustices, the cruelties, the meannesses, that elsewhere people so cleverly hushed up. Here you could love human beings nearly as God loved them, knowing the worst [p. 32].

Graham Greene's first penetration of the disguise and his first gropings toward faith came to him at "The School," as he told us in *The Lawless Roads.* It may have been a childhood lost and betrayed, the imagery of his fiction shows; but it was a past that remained forever present as a well-spring of his imagination, a past to be recaptured by the act of creating a fictional world that revealed Man as God loved him, knowing the worst.

Notes

1. Graham Greene, *Brighton Rock* (New York: Viking Press, 1938 [repr. Viking Compass Books, 1956]), p. 84. Subsequent page-citations to this work appear in the text.
2. Graham Greene, *The Lawless Roads* (London: Heinemann, 1960), p. 5; *Another Mexico* (New York: Viking Compass Books, 1964), p. 3.

3. Graham Greene, *Twenty-One Stories* (New York: Viking Compass Books, 1962), p. 26.

4. Graham Greene, *The Heart of the Matter* (New York: Viking Press, 1948 [repr. Viking Compass Books, 1960]), p. 25. Subsequent page-citations to this work appear in the text.

Spirits in Fiction:
The Example of Bernanos

ROBERT CHAMPIGNY · *Indiana University*

BY *fiction* (OR *novel*) I SHALL MEAN a narrative piece of writing designed to be enjoyed aesthetically. The logic of a narration is temporal: nothing which is not an event (or an aggregate of events), linked to other events by temporal relations, can take place in the world of what is narrated.

However, this physicalistic bias does not preclude other aspects. On the contrary, it requires them. For no entity, even in physics, can be reduced to its spatio-temporal location. A blue spot is blue and blue is not an event. A dramatic performance is an event, but not the play which is performed. An action can be narrated as a sequence of events, but the relation between means and end, which defines it as an action, is not temporal. I may be thinking now of what happened yesterday, but the relation between thinking and what is thought of is not temporal.

This is enough to ensure that the introduction of supernatural entities (gods, demons) need in no way endanger the integrity of a novel *as narration*. I see two possibilities.

The spirits may be embodied in their own right, be it only as voices. Thus, they acquire physical location—in other words, their citizenship in the spatio-temporal world. The embodiment of a god or demon may be multiple. In this respect, spirits

are like plays, poems, or symphonies, which may be performed
in several places at the same time, but unlike human beings,
according to our current concept of the human.

A narration may also introduce them outside of any specific
embodiment, in the way a theologian, a demonologist, or a
philosopher might speak about them. The condition, of course,
is that a character, himself embodied in the spatio-temporal
world, act as theologian, demonologist, or philosopher: at a
certain time, in a certain place, a certain character will speak
about a demiurge, or about Aphrodite. His thoughts, or
speeches, are presented as events temporally related to other
events. This kind of introduction denies them the status of
full-blown entities which they might enjoy in an essay. Consider also this example: if I pray to Saint Anthony (or rather
Saint Antoine, since I am not capable of praying in English),
Saint Anthony is, for me, a separate entity; but, insofar as I
consider that I am praying to Saint Anthony, he is not, for my
reflecting self, an independent entity.

These two ways of introducing spirits may be mixed: thus,
descriptions of cases of possession, in which a spirit takes up
lodgings, assumes a location, in a body already claimed by a
human soul. There need not be a one-to-one relation between
body and spirit: one spirit may have many incarnations; one
body may serve several spirits. Think also of the Homeric
world in which a god may send a dream, like a messenger, not
only to, but into, a mortal.

II

An ontologist might well see the seeds of analytic trouble in
the preceding remarks.[1] But I do not think that they raise any
theoretical difficulties for narrative literature. The threat
which the insertion of gods and demons may pose to the coherence and integrity of a fictional world appears to me much
less likely to center on the relationship between physical and
metaphysical than on the distinction between history and
fiction.

Like the novel, history uses the narrative approach—that is to say, temporal relations—as basic. But, if a piece of writing is viewed as historical, not fictional, it is viewed cognitively, not aesthetically. Historical events take place in the same spatio-temporal field as the events in the life of the reader, which are also historical. Fictional events, on the other hand, take place in their own closed world. We, authors and readers, are not related to them spatially and temporally: this allows for a basic aesthetic "distance," characteristic of the novel as a genre. Care must be taken to distinguish, at this point, between *fictional* in the sense of false (in this sense, an historical piece of writing may be rejected as "fictional"), and *fictional* in the sense of neither true nor false: I use the term in this second sense only.[2]

Spirits can be introduced into the historical field in the two ways which have been distinguished. Whether or not they are introduced in the first way depends on the metaphysics and epistemology which the historian, or biographer, or auto-biographer, is pleased to adopt: spirits or no spirits, names of spirits, functions, rules of manifestation, rules of evidence. Thus: Isis or Mary? Can the Virgin Mary appear naked? Is she allowed to say: "I am not the Virgin Mary"? Can the Devil disguise himself as the Virgin Mary? If so, what telltale evidence is he required to give? Note that the decision to use spirits or not can be viewed as stylistic: how far should the device of personification extend? Is there any reason why it should be confined to human beings? Or, for that matter, should human beings be personified?

The second way of introducing spirits into the historical field raises no such questions: the historian does not use spirits; he mentions them. He quotes reports of manifestations, records stated religious beliefs. This is enough to bestow on certain spirits a socio-historical type of existence, comparable to the existence of Paris as the political capital of France, or to France as a nation (but not as a country). It is the fictional conversion of such consecrated spirits which creates a problem.

I reject the conception of art as imitation of reality, and of fiction as imitation of history. I see no reason to consider that the novel exemplifies Ideas less directly than history. This applies to logical syntax: the Form of time is not specifically designed for cognitive use. And, generally speaking, this also applies to vocabulary.[3]

However, there are special cases to consider. There is nothing in the Idea of spirit which would seem to confine its illustration to historical discourse. On the other hand, the case of human beings would be less easily disposed of: the notion that we are historical and the notion that we are human appear to be tightly linked. Yet we see nothing wrong in saying: "Suppose that a man. . . ." Shall we agree to let the class of human beings cover the fictional as well as the hypothetical range? We may fashion our concept of the human so that it includes the property of being a spatio-temporal individual, though not necessarily a historical individual. But what about proper names?

Suppose that, in a novel, a town is named *Paris*. The capital of France is not the only geographical city named *Paris*; besides, I know *Paris* as a family name and as the name of a ship. By itself, its use as the name of a fictional city appears as innocuous as the use of *Jason* or *Mary* to name a fictional character. But suppose that extensive details are given (names of streets and buildings, topography, allusions to public events), which coincide with what I know about the capital of France. I then waver between two interpretations. On the one hand, the presence of fictional details (fictional inhabitants, connections with fictional places) makes it still possible for me to see in this Paris and in the capital of France two distinct individuations of the Idea of Paris. On the other hand, I am tempted to separate the two kinds of information (fictional and not fictional) and apply to these two cities the principle of the identity of indiscernibles. Literary critics generally adopt the latter interpretation. Thus: "The action takes place in Paris during the reign of Louis-Philippe." That is to say: "The fictional action takes place in the capital of France during the historical reign of Louis-Philippe." Ontologically, this is nonsense.

The names of socio-historical spirits, such as *Apollo* or *Lucifer,* are another case in point. To pursue my enquiry in this direction, I shall draw my examples from some of the writings of Georges Bernanos which are commonly labeled *novels.* Namely: *Sous le soleil de Satan, L'Imposture, La Joie, Journal d'un curé de campagne.*[4]

III

In these texts, spirits are generally introduced in the second way: their names appear in the speeches and verbalized thoughts of situated characters. There is, however, one passage which deals with spirits in the first way: in *Sous le soleil de Satan,* which is told in the third person, a "natural" character, Donissan, meets another character who appears to be the ephemeral embodiment of a supernatural spirit (pp. 167–184). Another case of manifestation is suggested in the pages which follow, but the clues are less definite.

The names of spirits which appear in these texts offer no departure from the repertory of a socio-historical religion— Christianity; more precisely its Roman Catholic branch. Thus: *Dieu* (God), *Notre Seigneur* (Our Lord), *Jésus-Christ, Satan, Lucifer, diable* (Devil), *Esprit Saint* (Holy Spirit), *Sainte Vierge* (Holy Virgin), and other names of well-known saints (Paul, Theresa, Ignatius).

Other coincidences with historical entities are provided by names of towns and regions (*Valenciennes, Calais, Avranches, Paris, Allemagne, Coutances, Bayeux, Flandres, Boulonnais*), names of writers (*Péguy, Goncourt, Renan, Lemaître, Freud, Anatole France*), and by names of political and social institutions, in particular religious institutions which appear to be identical with those of the Roman Catholic church.

Add to this comments, judgments, apostrophes, and rhetorical questions, which, except in *Journal d'un curé de campagne,* cannot be interpreted as either conceived or spoken by a character situated in the fictional field (see, for instance, pp. 153,

381, 560). These elements remain impervious to fictional assimilation. And it must be further noted that names of spirits appear in such passages.

The number and interconnections of the ingredients mentioned in the preceding paragraphs are such that one may wonder whether it would not be advisable to try to view these texts as something other than straight fiction. I see two possibilities.

IV

In *Sous le soleil de Satan, L'Imposture* and *La Joie,* the outside comments and judgments are like refractory lumps which refuse to dissolve into the fictional sauce. But why not, instead, consider them as basic? Why not consider these texts as essays with a strong rhetorical flavor: as sermons? If we adopt this perspective, we do not have to be concerned with the socio-historical aspect of the names of spirits. As for fictional characters like Donissan, Mouchette, Cénabre, Chevance, Chantal —they could be interpreted as hypothetical examples. Their names would be used like *John, Bill,* and *Mary* in philosophical essays. And the mixture of fictional and historical characters, such as the comparison of Donissan with the vicar of Ars (p. 232), would not be troublesome either. Whether the examples are fictional, or historical, or both, makes no difference to the basic integrity and coherence of an essay, or sermon, as such. For, in this perspective, fiction and history are converted into hypothesis.

Unfortunately, in the three texts under consideration, the dramatic and narrative load is too heavy to allow a conversion of story into example and of fiction into hypothesis. Let us try another kind of interpretation.

In subject and style, the texts are more reminiscent of hagiographies than of sermons. No doubt, the strong fictional aspect prevents them from being interpreted as straight hagiographies. But this fictional aspect, more precisely the mixture of fictional and socio-historical aspects, would fit very well a satirical pastiche of hagiography in general. Quite a few things could be said in defense of this interpretation.

The commentator is allowed to lapse into unctuous gestures, pompous poses, and flights of pseudo-lyricism with exclamations galore. With the addition of religious spicing, this style strikes me as a caricature of the way we were taught to write literary essays in high school.

Among the stylistic details which tend to make the commentator ridiculous in the eyes of the reader, there is also his abuse of such phrases as: "The eminent master" (p. 296), "the author of *The Life of Gerson*" (p. 351), "the author of *The Life of Tauler*" (p. 634). When labels of this sort are applied to characters he appears to dislike, it can be assumed that the commentator intends to be ironical. But the irony turns against him, as a would-be hagiographer, when he writes: "I did not ask for that, exclaimed the future saint of Lumbres, with sudden vehemence" (p. 228).

The fictional status of "the future saint of Lumbres" contributes to the ironical effect. And the same could be said about the following sentence, which refers to the same character: "The second part of this book, based on authentic documents and testimonies, reports the last episode of his extraordinary life" (p. 232). At the end of this episode, after a passage printed in italics and replete with exclamation marks, we find this comment: "Such was, probably, on this earth, the supreme lament of the vicar of Lumbres . . ." (p. 308).

The theatricality of the commentator's attitudes extends to the speeches and verbalized thoughts of the characters he invents. Some he dislikes, some he likes and tries to extol.[5] But the result of his clumsy presentation is that they all appear basically as comedians. Donissan, the "saint of Lumbres," is set against Saint-Marin, "the harmonious chatterbox who talked only about himself . . ." (p. 297). Unfortunately, that is also how the favored characters are, for the most part, presented to the reader (and this could also be said about the diarist of *Journal d'un curé de campagne*).

In *La Joie*, the commentator heralds the words of Chantal de Clergerie with an aura of verbal incense: "A supernatural, disinterested sadness, similar to the reproach of angels. And so simple too, so limpid, with such a thrill of innocence and suavity . . ." (p. 658). Burdened with such exacting stage-directions, the quoted speech, whatever it may be, can only fall flat on its face. On the whole, the speeches of the heroine leave me with the impression of an upperclass ado- lescent who tries her hardest to sound exquisitely cute. Though a commoner, the Isabelle of Giraudoux would beat her at this kind of game.

The basic error of the would-be hagiographer is of course to let his favored characters speak and to verbalize their thoughts. The way in which he goes about it compounds the mistake. The main trouble with his analyses of inner life is a confusion between the mystical and the moral which subverts them both. The subversion of the moral is the more obvious and it is a common feature, not only in hagiography, but in the tradition of the *moralistes*: we are dealing with an aestheticism. Instead of being tied to action, good and evil are used as labels which are supposed to help map out a *carte du Tendre,* in con- junction with names of feelings, inner attitudes, and super- natural spirits.[6] The result is that we are left with a good and an evil which bear hardly more relation to morals than the St. Louis Cardinals and the Los Angeles Rams bear to zoology.

In the preceding paragraphs, I have attempted to show how *Sous le soleil de Satan, L'Imposture,* and *La Joie* could be interpreted as parody. This is a tempting perspective; but one must be careful not to abuse a strategy common in con- temporary criticism which consists of endeavoring to justify any text by stamping it as ironical. In order to adopt this perspective in the case of the three texts under consideration, we should have to be able to posit the commentator as a first- degree character writing about second-degree characters, which is what I have done implicitly in the preceding paragraphs. In this way, what is ludicrous about him would not compromise the work as a whole. Unfortunately, the texts provide little support for this operation: they give us comments, rather than a commentator. They do not allow the reader to distinguish clearly between the total work as parody and a commentator as comic character.

V

The two possibilities which I have investigated (sermon and parody) do not offer satisfactory avenues of escape. Let us, then, be content to accept these three texts as straight fiction with refractory elements. And the fourth text, *Journal d'un curé de campagne,* can be added again to the list. What is to be done with the names of spirits?

Several commentators of the texts have apparently thought it made sense to wonder whether this or that character could be considered as "saved." [7] A preliminary question would be: saved by a socio-historical god, or by a fictional god?

The factors of identification are so strong that a socio-historical god, more precisely the Roman Catholic God, is the obvious choice. But the notion that this god should be concerned with the salvation of fictional characters is, to say the least, heretical. This God incarnated Himself as a historical being, not as a fictional character. Consider also the case of the "saint of Lumbres." Donissan is not a Roman Catholic saint; and I do not think that the Roman Catholic Church has ever canonized a being whom it held to be fictional. It follows from these considerations that the god of the texts cannot be the Roman Catholic God.

Since I know of no other socio-historical god who would fit, I am now led to try a fictional god. This fictional god and all the elements of the fictional metaphysics which go with him might prove to be analogous to the Roman Catholic God and religion. But note that, in this perspective, coincidences in the repertory of proper names no longer count as sources of information. I cannot infer fictional traits and relationships from the sole fact that certain characters in a novel happen to bear the same names as my father, my mother, my uncle, and I.

In other words, we have to act as if the names of spirits in the texts were foreign to us and see what the context tells us about the entities which they name. I must confess that I have not pushed this experiment very far. But it is obvious that the texts rely heavily on socio-historical identification. And it is safe to assume that, by themselves, they furnish very few semantic pieces of the spiritual puzzle. How, for instance, are we going to connect "the Father" and "God" (p. 355), if we discount what we know about the tricky dialectics of the Trinity?

This paucity of information would not necessarily be an aesthetic flaw. The type of reading which I have suggested might endow the texts with a charm akin to that of *Waiting for Godot*. Or a poetic kind of mystery might radiate from the proper names. But an attempt to justify the use of the names of spirits along these lines would fail to show why they were not invented.

VI

The various remarks I have made are not directed against the use of metaphysical elements in fiction. I have shown that they are inevitable; and the art of the novelist could be said to consist basically in arranging tensions between the physical and metaphysical elements, and between the metaphysical elements themselves. Furthermore, I see nothing wrong with the use of individual spirits as metaphysical elements. I should not say, for instance, that this is an anachronistic device: as long as we, humans, consider ourselves somehow as individual spirits, the concept of individual spirit will remain in force and its extension will remain open.

What I did intend to make clear is that the coherence and integrity of a fictional world depend on the fictional authenticity of its significant elements. If supernatural spirits are to play an important part in the structure of a fictional creation, then it is important that they be created.

Notes

1. The difficulty would consist in deciding which kinds of entities to include in the ontological scheme. The kinds I have mentioned (colors, works of art, actions, thinking, spirits) are a disparate bunch. Selecting kinds of beings (not singular beings) for ontological existence is a basic aesthetic decision for the analyst.

2. No doubt, a *quotation* from a novel can be true or false; but it is so because it can be verified in our historical world. Note also that, within the world of the novel, the distinction between true and false may reappear: for instance, testimonies in a detective novel.

3. The aesthetic attitude is often characterized as a "suspension of disbelief." This formula is pointless if it is not taken to mean a suspension of disbelief *and* belief. Belief and disbelief should be conceived as the two poles of one kind of attitude. Concerning language, there is no reason to decide that this kind of attitude is basic.

4. References are to the Pléiade edition (Paris: Gallimard, 1961).

5. Though he pays due respect to Charity, the commentator is rather petty at times. This would provide another ironical point.

6. The commentators of Bernanos' fiction have devoted much attention to the topography of this *carte du Tendre*.

7. Bernanos encourages this kind of speculation in a prefatory note to his *Nouvelle Histoire de Mouchette*. Referring to two of his characters, he exclaims: "May God have mercy on both!"

The Novels of
François Mauriac

GERMAINE BRÉE · *University of Wisconsin–Madison*

I FIND IT DIFFICULT TODAY when rereading the novels of François Mauriac not to entertain some misgivings about their ultimate viability. It may be that a critic like me who approaches them without sharing Mauriac's Catholic beliefs is at a disadvantage. It may be too that it is difficult today to respond wholeheartedly to some of Mauriac's themes and stylistic idiosyncrasies. Mauriac's fictional world developed in the 'twenties—the 'thirties did not greatly add to its basic characteristics—at a time when, under the impact of Freud, some French writers were revising traditional conceptions concerning the processes of individual experience and the nature of human motivations; while, under the impact of World War I and the Russian Revolution, others were re-examining the foundations on which their culture rested. By temperament and perhaps because of his provincial upbringing, Mauriac seems to have remained insulated from the more extreme ideological currents, attitudes, and literary experiments of those years. But instinctively, almost surreptitiously, at the very outset of his career as novelist, he broke away from the then decried novel of analysis with its smooth cause-and-effect mechanisms and its preoccupation with the surface of everyday reality. The particular realm he exploited—the essentially

141

elusive modalities of sexual attraction and obscure individual revolts—the vivid but not logically explicable narrative line of his stories and their intensively personal atmosphere all appealed to readers avid for new literary experiences. His techniques as novelist were freer. Steeped in an atmosphere of sustained emotion, his short narratives relied for their dynamism on a visionary kind of lyricism reminiscent of Chateaubriand and the Romantics. Barrès was his literary patron. What endeared Mauriac to some critics was this "beautiful harmonious language," the "spiritual music" of his style,[1] the familiar cadences of the Romantics. Today these cadences have lost their seduction, an obstacle rather than an advantage.

It is not easy for most of us to share Mauriac's intense but vague anguish concerning the omnipresent but seldom concretely evoked "sins of the flesh." Half a century of research into the workings of human emotions have accustomed us to more searching inquiry into our own. Sensuality is no longer solitary or hidden, a hideous form of disease; and we can no longer indiscriminately attribute the human perturbations it causes to the fascinating voice of Satan avid for the possession of our souls. Nor is it easy, in our strife-torn society, to accept unquestioningly as a criterion of moral lucidity Mauriac's contemptuous rejection, at least for fictional purposes, of the simple joys of private affections and everyday living. It is not, however, these peculiar components of Mauriac's fictional universe that limit his efficacity as novelist but rather a certain conflict and confusion apparent in the patterning of his style and which deeply affect the basic coherence of his fictions.

Mauriac is the author of many kinds of books: twenty novels or so, a few plays, essays on the novel and narrative techniques, memoirs, a *Journal,* and poems. Whole sentences and paragraphs could be shifted from one category to the other without causing the slightest disturbance in atmosphere.[2] Their relevance then, when they appear in the novels, is not to the specific concrete situations and individual experiences narrated. They refer us to the private world of the author, a realm of discourse common to characters and novelist alike whereby the ones are absorbed into the inner life of the other. Picked at random, the following examples are characteristic; one could align other examples of this kind almost endlessly:

How numerous the creatures for whom his approach proved fatal! Nor does he know how many existences he oriented or disoriented. He does not know that because of him a woman killed a germ in her bosom,[3] a girl died, a friend entered the seminary . . . [*Le Désert de l'amour*].

The childhood of Thérèse? Snow at the source of the filthiest river [*Thérèse Desqueyroux*].

The life of most men is a dead path that leads nowhere. But others know, from childhood, that they are moving toward an unknown sea. Already the bitterness of the wind astounds them, already the taste of salt is on their lips—while beyond the last dune an infinite passion lashes them with salt and spray. All that remains is to sink into the abyss or turn back [*Les Chemins de la mer*].

In all these instances theme, cadence, and images echo the traditional hortatory eloquence of the pulpit.

In the first example, to amplify the impact of the moral point he is making—a young seducer's egotistical disregard of his responsibility to others—Mauriac makes a cumulative use of the characteristic devices of the preacher: the use of the exclamatory form to heighten the emotional tension; emphasis by reiteration: "nor does he know . . . he does not know . . ."; accumulation by enumeration and suspension. The portentously charged vocabulary underscores the effect: fatal, killed, died; and the indeterminate "numerous," "many" add an aura of the unimaginable to the young man's devastating power. The paragraph is rhetorical in structure and hortatory in purpose. But it fulfills another function—it authenticates Mauriac's rather tedious story, a father–son rivalry for the favors of another man's unresponsive mistress. The rhetoric obliquely guarantees the weighty moral seriousness of the case. Let us make no mistake: we are not in the world of vaudeville.

In the second instance, who but the reader is presumed to have put the question rhetorically echoed by the novelist, "Thérèse's childhood?" Mauriac is unashamedly prompting his reader, creating a pause, a moment of suspense, but in the rhetorical structure of his text, not in the narrative development of the story. The perfectly gratuitous suspense and pause prepare for the theatrically introduced metaphor "snow" and the tension suggested by the absolutely contrasting "filthiest river": clearly the function of the metaphor is to release a certain response in the reader, a wave of intense emotion and commiseration at the horrible sullying of a life. The brusque syntax may mask the banality and even the inappropriateness of Mauriac's metaphor,[4] but it cannot hide the banal poverty of the thought: even a Thérèse once knew the-pure-innocence-of-childhood. I have hyphenated the words because the-pure-innocence-of-childhood is one of those psychological commonplaces from which Mauriac draws a number of appropriate tremolos. In the case under scrutiny the author and the prompted reader can share the same head-shaking emotional involvement, not so much with the suffering of Thérèse as with the general inevitable perversion of innocence, which is the human lot. As in the first example the rhetoric is defensive: Mauriac is obliquely engaged in defending his story as a source and example of moral truth.

The long, elaborate metaphor in the third example develops according to the familiar cadences of oratorical style, the voice rising through increasingly ample sentences to the central statement "already the taste of salt is on their lips" then coming to rest in a shorter, slightly asymmetrical movement on the "turn back." Mauriac here develops a moral parable in two panels. It suggests at first the Biblical example of the straight and narrow path of salvation contrasted with the broad and easy road to perdition. But a closer examination of the metaphor reveals a rather puzzling lack of relevancy to any coherent meaning. What the "dead path that leads nowhere" is we may vaguely infer. But what does the path of the "chosen few" toward the "unknown sea," "beyond the last dune," represent, with its "infinite passion" projected in the static but intensive lashings of wind, salt, and spray, and the melodramatic choice presented at the end? The spatialized image here quite evidently has only very little rapport with reality. The landscape, vague as it is, may be slightly reminiscent of the Bordelais coast, but the entire perspective is psychological, an emotional enactment of the inner state of mind that purportedly separates Mauriac's "lambs" from the herd. The fervid intensity with which the metaphor is developed, amplified, and built up to its climax is the rhetorical substitute for the suggested but absent revelation of some kind of high truth. What it does reveal is the premium put by an intensely Romantic writer on inner intensities and torments. The somewhat tedious flow of pious neo-"Christian" commonplaces and imagery[5] disguised by such tricks of rhetoric is Mauriac's attempt to bridge the gap between the private world of his imagination and the antagonistic moral emotion it creates in him. He further reinforces this attempt by interlacing the narrative with aphorisms, interchangeably pronounced by novelist and characters alike, and addressed in the classical traditions of the moralists to "us," all mankind: "We have all been molded and remolded by those who love us, and if they are at all tenacious we are what they have made of us." "But desire transforms the being who approaches us into a monster who has no resemblance whatsoever with that being. . . ."

Mauriac's own uneasy relation with his stories was brilliantly attacked by Sartre, though on rather specious grounds. And indeed, as the above brief analysis shows, Mauriac's fictional world is not self-contained.[6] This characteristic seems to point to a deep fissure in Mauriac's own personality. Yet undoubtedly his world has a certain power of imaginative persuasion and undeniable intensity and coherence. This is perhaps because Mauriac's direct intervention in his narrative, as manifest in his stylistic mannerisms, engages his emotions, not his intelligence, or, in fact, any system of belief. As he has very often made quite explicit, what he pursued as novelist was the concrete dramatization of inner fantasies based on the intense emotions that welled up inside him. Mauriac has never been reticent about his work and has made it quite clear over the years that as writer he took only slight interest in the commonplace reality about him. Until the Spanish Civil War—that is, until he was in his fifties—he lived, he said, withdrawn in a private universe of dream.[7] Houses, land, people observed all served to give shape to the dramas and "monsters" of his imagining. It is because the narrative and the commentary originate in the same violent emotivity that, in the best of Mauriac's stories, they can coexist in an uneasy equilibrium, contributing thereby to the dramatic impact of the work. Where the equilibrium is not maintained, fiction turns into a particularly insidious form of self-dramatization. Mauriac is not really, as he would have it, engaged in a "drama of salvation" as much as in a specious kind of equivocation, unwilling to take the responsiblity for his own imaginings.

From this point of view he was well served by one of the current literary ideas of the day concerning the relation between the novelist and the characters he creates. The character, so it was argued, once he or she emerged, took on in Pirandellesque fashion an autonomous life which the novelist could record but was powerless to mold. So Mauriac, in relatively good faith, could claim a kind of innocence with regard to Thérèse Desqueyroux in the famous apostrophe placed by Mauriac as foreword to the novel,

> Thérèse, there are many who will say that you do not exist. But I know you exist, I who for many years have watched you, waylaid you, stopped you as you went by, unmasked you.

Metaphor and reality neatly overlap. But the confusion can hardly excuse Mauriac's incredibly pharisaic "envoi,"

> I should have liked your suffering, Thérèse, to have delivered you up to God. . . . But many of those who nonetheless believe in the fall and redemption of tormented souls would have denounced the sacrilege. . . . At least on the pavement where I abandon you, I hope you are not alone.

This is doubly equivocal coming from the man who claimed at one time that it was his self-appointed task "to make perceptible, tangible, and odorous the Catholic universe of evil." And the equivocation is only compounded when we consider that Mauriac also stated his intent in slightly different terms "to make perceptible, tangible, and odorous a world full of criminal delights." The equivalence established is curious.

In point of fact, Mauriac's universe draws its visionary power from what seems to be an imagination mired in a latent semiunconscious sexuality rather than from the "Catholic universe of evil." The dramas enacted in the stories, the characters that emerge in them, live in a kind of interzone between two realities connected through the particular rhetoric of Mauriac's language: intense sexual desires felt by characters enclosed in the "prison" of flesh, verbal frustration, and impotence; and a vague sense of impending spiritual doom suggested from without by the writer. "The river of fire," "the fetid swamps," "the prison bars" link the two worlds of lust and damnation, not logically but by the force of insistent evocation. To these two realms Mauriac relates the conduct of his characters, and not to any objective system of reference, Catholic or otherwise. What we see enacted are not moral conflicts, nor even, as Mauriac sometimes suggests, the ravages of destructive passions, but a submerged ritual of possession, destruction, and punishment. In *Le Baiser au lépreux,* Jean Péloueyre expiates his single night of possession of his wife's alluring body; Thérèse all her life must pay for that moment of intense delectation when she held power over Bernard's life; in *Genitrix,* Félicité Cazenave, the strongest, most unforgettable of Mauriac's characters, and her son are in turn "possessed" and destroyed by each other.

At the source of Mauriac's creations there is a turbulent power, a fear and a revolt manifest in the nature of his stories. Their simple narrative line, as Mauriac progressed, acquired somewhat more complexity through the use of the flashback or the fictional journal. But it remained uncluttered, involving only a very few characters. Timeless, anachronistic stories, in spite of a few vague attempts at establishing temporal perspectives, they are played out against the static hierarchical background of a society clearly outlined and projected in the typical Mauriac "décor," the isolated estate surrounded by its vineyards or pine forests. The vivid pictorial scenes depicted can be, on occasion, unforgettable in intensity: a gigantic Félicité dancing with fury on one of the platforms she had had erected in every room so that she could watch her son, refusing to accept his marriage; Thérèse, sequestered in her room, imprisoned behind the endless rows upon rows of pine trees, endlessly stubbing out her cigarettes. A few outside characters trapped and passively going to their doom—unchanged, unchanging, inexplicable; a world of "dead paths," of moral irresponsibility in which every character, submissive or not, unique or mediocre, is eventually preyed upon or preys. These are the well-known characteristics of his best novels. Schopenhauer, not Christ, is at the heart of Mauriac's world with an added dash of Nietzschean contempt for the "sick animal," man, and his addiction to mediocre happiness. A book, Mauriac once said, is a violent act, a kind of rape. The force of his own work comes perhaps from the intensity of an inner struggle, Schopenhaueresque in kind.

Guilt-ridden, Mauriac seems to have sensed that his attempt to extinguish in himself the turbulent "lust," which he denounced as "the will to evil," was to extinguish his own power to create. He seems to have associated that power with the Satan of his childhood anguish, a Satan feared because of the invisible fascination of his appeal and whom he felt he must resist, and yet could not resist, trapped thereby in his own closed hell.

The weakness of his work seems to me to stem from an inner cleavage, from an unwillingness to accept his fictional world, in all its ambivalence, as coming from himself, and from his paradoxical fear of being contaminated by the proliferation of his own myths. Hence, his refuge in the fiction that the "evil" embodied in his stories, like the evil in the world, did not come from himself as creator, but from the world itself. Hence, too, Mauriac's tendency to draw the reader away from the narrative toward the commentary and to replace the unresolved tensions in his writing by a rhetorically imposed unity. He is undoubtedly sincere when he claims, as he has claimed ever more emphatically with the years, that he aims at direct or indirect edification and that his fictional universe has a metaphysical dimension. The claim is not convincing. It is apparent that, Sartre notwithstanding,[8] Mauriac was primarily an artist, albeit a reluctant and hesitant one, who did not fully accept the artist's responsibility for and involvement in his creation.

Notes

1. See in particular André Rousseaux, *Littérature du vingtième siècle,* Vol. I (Paris: Albin Michel, 1938), p. 150.
2. See for instance the quotations in page after page of Jacques Robichon's *François Mauriac* (Paris: Éditions Universitaires, 1953).
3. Mauriac uses the word "sein" in order to avoid the too precise "womb"; to evoke abortion without naming it, he introduces a noble periphrasis in the neoclassical style of the early French Romantics. In the same way, to create the solemn aura he needs he prefers the word "existences" to "lives," the more appropriate term in this context, and "creatures" to "people."
4. Mechanical rhetorical momentum sometimes leads Mauriac into a curiously inept expanse of Biblical images—such as, in relation to Thérèse Desqueyroux, the well-known image of the diseased limb that must be severed from the body. "Opprobrium could only be avoided" by the Desqueyroux family, "by severing the gangrened limb, rejecting it, repudiating it in the sight of men." A "repudiated" Thérèse is one thing; a repudiated gangrened limb is another. And the end of the sentence, Biblical though it be, is quite inappropriate to the limited circle of people known to the Desqueyroux. As in the case of the "snow" image, the effect is ludicrous rather than intense. And what are we to make of an "eye that never ceased measuring the abyss of dead time"?
5. It is, I think, unnecessary to recall a vocabulary so often analyzed, usually rather indiscriminately. Mauriac uses, it seems, two registers of imagery, one purely abstract and censoriously moralistic, the other sensuous and alive. It is difficult to take seriously his "sewers" of iniquity, "fetid swamps," "iniquitous flesh," "bodies of mud," and the mechanical, reiterated "désert," used adjectivally or as a noun, to the point of meaninglessness: the Seine is "déserte"; eyes are "déserts"; the year is "déserte"; days are "déserts," endlessly. Nor can one be particularly moved by the labels—stinking, putrid, abject, depraved, ignominious—which he liberally tacks on to his characters; or be affected by the monotonous "gémissements" that recur throughout his work.
6. This in itself puts Mauriac in a different category as artist from Racine with whom, at his own suggestion, he is often compared. There is in fact nothing in common between the two. Each one of Racine's plays draws us into a coherent world in which vision and representation are completely correlated. Not so Mauriac, in whose works subjective and objective unity are seldom completely achieved.
7. Madeleine Chapsal, *Les Ecrivains en personne* (Paris: Julliard, 1960), pp. 121–142. This interview gives a vivid sense of the seventy-year-old Mauriac's

personality. It was because of the pressing issue of the Spanish Civil War, he states, that he gave up writing fiction.

8. Sartre's article, "M. François Mauriac et la liberté," which was first published in the *Nouvelle Revue Française* in Feburary, 1939, and included in *Situations, I* (Paris: Gallimard, 1947), pp. 36–57, ends with the rather facile thrust: "God is not an artist; neither is M. Mauriac."

Julien Green: Structure of the Catholic Imagination

JEAN ALTER · *University of Pennsylvania*

IS JULIEN GREEN A CATHOLIC WRITER or merely a writer who was a Catholic, lost his faith, then recovered it? In other words, is it possible, and meaningful, to place his novels within the stream of religious fiction, or should they be set apart? There is little doubt concerning works published after Green's "conversion" in 1939; from *Moïra* on, critics had no trouble pointing to their religious message. For the earlier writings, whether torn by violence and sin, like *Léviathan* or *Adrienne Mesurat,* or opening into imaginary escapes to quasi-surrealistic dreamlands, like *Le Visionnaire* or *Minuit,* it is fashionable to use the demonstration *per absurdum*: the nightmarish aspect of life is said to prove the novelist's conscious or unconscious despair in a world forsaken by God. Green himself encouraged this approach by proposing a fundamentally religious outlook as a constant source of his inspiration. Thus he was writing in his 1949 *Journal*:

I do not try to make Catholic novels out of my books. . . . But I believe that all my books, however removed they may seem from the usual and generally accepted notion of religiosity, are nonetheless religious by nature. The anxiety and loneliness of my characters can be always reduced to what I remember calling the dread of finding oneself in this world.

151

Coming after his conversion and, so to speak, with hindsight, this claim may appear suspect, especially since the "dread of finding oneself in this world" does not have to be necessarily religious. On the other hand, in the absence of specific counter-indications, there is no cause to dismiss this confession without an honest attempt at a more objective verification. It is such a check that we intend to carry out here, using a method that for want of a better word may be called a structural approach, inasmuch as it addresses itself to the basic structures of a novel.

II

Furthermore, in order the better to test the validity of Green's assertion, we shall examine one of the least known of his novels: *Epaves,* written in 1932, and quite appropriately described by Henri Peyre as "the most desolate of all." [1] It is indeed significant that Peyre himself offers no further comments, and that most critics deal very rapidly with that work; many studies do not even mention it, and it rarely finds its way into selective bibliographies of the novelist's fiction. Yet it was one of Green's favorites, and no one denies its value as a novel. But apparently it does not fit well in the pattern devised for his other writings during the "non-religious" period. It contains neither dramatic crimes nor magic visions—no revolt, as it were, but a resigned acceptance of despair, all the more pessimistic because no explosion or escape suggests the intuition of something other than this world, even if only an absent God. In fact, very little of any significance happens in *Epaves.* A man in his thirties realizes his mediocrity and loses some illusions of his youth; a neglected younger wife continues an already stale affair; a child is brought home from a boarding school, and sent back to study; and a frustrated sister-in-law who runs the household finally gets the man. None of them is much happier or more miserable after all is said and done; they simply sink a little faster into their dim but comfortable middle-class half-world, unaware of any other choice. The main outline of the plot points to the dull world view of a realistic novel rather than to the tragic inspiration of a religious conscience.

This does not mean that *Epaves* is totally devoid of obvious religiosity. While God and religion are rarely mentioned, even in abstract terms, a certain number of themes, symbolic representations, and author's comments, could be brought up to justify the hasty classification of the novel among Green's early fiction, still marked by Catholic reflexes. There is no need to go beyond the traditional approach to notice that hell provides the dominant image. Paris, the sole setting of *Epaves*, is shown enclosed on all sides by dark walls, with a dark low sky in the daytime; at night, under "the dark vault of the heavens," where "not a single star is shining," the hellish atmosphere comes into its own, exhaling "a vegetal death" and horribly flickering in "the vast incendiary glimmering that rises each evening from Paris and surrounds it with a red halo" (p. 15). In addition, there is at least one symbolic representation of hell: the meeting of the board of trustees, introduced and closed by gratuitous allusions to purgatory; and a closer reading reveals several other partial representations: the motion-picture theater, the cellar, etc. The frequent references to "calls" and "impulses of love" also betray a religious bent, especially when they are associated with "charity," as in the episode of the beggar, where the play on the two meanings of the word (charity and alms) discloses its symbolic value (p. 33). Both Philippe and his sister-in-law Eliane are prey to Green's usual embodiment of evil: the flesh, in the very spirit of Catholic tradition; and Eliane at least, though only in the first part of the novel, tries to be "good" before giving up all pretense. Finally, when he manages to forget his narcissistic preoccupation with his own body, Philippe now and then experiences the intuition of a transcendent truth known in "former ages when instinct still moved the hearts of men" (p. 30), wonders whether he "might have been born free" (p. 31), entertains the fleeting notion that this world's existence may be "more vague and futile than a dream" (p. 35), and suspects that "in this

world which makes no sense to us, everyone is blindly fulfilling
a secret fate which he may never understand" (p. 39). There
are about a dozen of these relatively clear manifestations of
a religious orientation in the novel.

These indications should not be discounted. Considered
together with arguments drawn from other novels, situated
within the general evolution of the writer, reinforced by his
own comments and by the helpful hints of critics, they may
be barely sufficient to force *Epaves* into the scheme of a religious Green. After all, in 1934, i.e., not long after the com-
pletion of the novel, he wrote: "Deep in my heart, there is
still faith." But then, there is much material in his *Journal*,
both on religion and *Epaves,* and some of it is contradictory.
It seems safer to keep away from the author's own judgments.
In general, there is something disquieting in a willful insertion of an autonomous work into a system which is controlled
by elements taken from outside. In the last analysis, the novel
itself must be shown to belong in the system by reason of its
individual and intrinsic structures, and not because of extraneous relations. The initial indications may serve as a hypothesis, but conclusions will depend on an independent study
of *Epaves.*

III

Contrary to what the title announces and what critics have
repeated after Green's comments in the *Journal,* the basic
structure of *Epaves* (i.e., "shipwrecks," but translated as *The
Strange River*) is *not* the flow of life downstream, symbolized
by the Seine. Within the confines of the novel, the characters
are not drifting but, as we shall see, falling and sinking (which
could also fit the title); the movement of the water is not
emphasized as a horizontal and outgoing flow that carries
one away, as in the opening pages of *L'Education sentimen-
tale*; on the contrary, it is seen by motionless witnesses, their
eyes do not follow it, and its appeal or relation to the be-

holder, whether Philippe or the writer, is that of a continuum which does not essentially change its nature or position. Green may have intended to give the Seine a deep philosophical significance; within the boundaries of the gloomy city and low clouds it does hold some freedom and mystery which correspond to the role of the sky as an avenue of escape in other novels; but its actual structural function appears to provide a bottomless mirror in which the troubled self perceives certain truths. In short, it is a stable and solid point of reference rather than a symbol of action.

In fact, the novel actually opens with a brutal interruption of what could be called drifting, since the initial event that shapes its structure results from an impulsive departure from routine: if Philippe had followed his usual way home, nothing would have happened. But he did not, and the entire development of the novel was triggered by a scene that dominates the major structural networks, reverberates through the book, and, about twenty years later, is echoed by Camus. Stripped of all accompanying material, it may be summarized in one sentence: Philippe turns his back on a woman who calls for help because she is about to be thrown in the Seine. Similarly, in *La Chute,* Clamence hurries away from the outcry of a woman who jumps into the river. In both cases it is night, the characters are alone, and a certain amount of ambiguity or sense of futility offers them a margin of free choice beyond the categorical imperative or conditioned reflex which could have prevailed under clearer circumstances. (There are other similarities as well: in both cases the event is associated with ironical laughter; in both cases it is related to an earlier manifestation of cowardice; but these are extraneous matters, interesting to students of Camus' sources.) Whether conscious of his borrowing from Green, and hence better aware of the possibilities of the image, or simply luckier in his choice of title, Camus found in this fall the correlative of the novel as a whole: the body's fall in the water, Clamence's fall from an exalted social status to that of a bum, man's fall from grace into the concentric regions of hell. Green does not show his hand so clearly. But the notion of the fall dominates *Epaves* as much as it does *La Chute,* and, despite some obvious divergences, suggests the same religious overtones.

It is evident, indeed, that the fall provides the key movement for the interpretation of Philippe's and Eliane's experiences. At the outset, we are made to believe that they lead a relatively level existence in a stuffy apartment, enjoying a measure of "moral security reflected in the well-drawn curtains" (p. 15). Eliane loves her brother-in-law, but rather platonically and with resignation, compensating for her nostalgia with the management of the household; and Philippe suspects her love, but it neither bothers nor moves him. The first Seine episode, "something which seemed so minute when viewed in the perspective of all these past years, a trifle, brought down this intricate equilibrium" (p. 42). A series of successive revelations tumble both characters from their stable accommodation with life and their confidence derived from a number of illusions, to the ultimate confrontation with their true nature and the resulting acquiescence in their downfall. Assuredly, it is not a fall from grace, but the final destination is a personal hell that mirrors the surrounding infernal landscape. Viewed from that angle, the structure of the plot reveals two descending lines which, like graphs of a bearish market, drop from level to level at each new report of activities. Philippe's graph begins its downward movement with a first intimation of cowardice when he fails to answer the call for help; the second Seine episode causes a second drop: faced with a new and more decisive test in the form of a direct threat by a young delinquent, Philippe must acknowledge that he is a coward, though he still hopes to keep it from the others. Thereafter, most events in his life bring about a further depreciation in his self-appraisal and his relations with both family and strangers: old pictures and an ill-fitting jacket plunge him into the melancholic awareness of middle age; the cellar scene makes him realize his loneliness and moral deterioration; a walk among a festive crowd exposes his humanitarian illusions; the discovery of his wife's affair serves to demonstrate his indifference and loss of pride; fi-

nally, he stoops to enticing Eliane through an appeal to her
carnal imagination and, when she forces him to confess his
cowardice, he gives up all resistance and passively submits as
she drags him down to the bottom of the pit. Between these
major steps, intermediary tumbles contribute to a more gradual slope: admission of his failure as a businessman, various
manifestations of lack of feelings, etc. Viewed one after the
other, and with the exception of the first and the last, all
these partial falls are arranged in a way to assure a relatively
smooth movement, which may explain the impression of drifting; however, as there is almost nothing that checks the downward trend, the commanding image, both in each episode and
in the general structure, is that of a steady fall.

A parallel graph may be drawn for Eliane, though her
downward movement is less regular, starts slowly and almost
imperceptibly, and is interrupted by at least one serious attempt at reversing the direction: her escape to the Moroso
pension and the letter she writes to Philippe; however, this
is immediately followed by a compensating dream which drags
her back below, after which she rolls downhill with increasing momentum, till she overtakes Philippe and pulls him
down to the ultimate fall. The two graphs thus merge into
one, and their combination reinforces the dramatic impact:
the almost perpendicular drop in Philippe's line at the beginning of the novel is repeated and recalled by an equally sharp
slope of Eliane's line at the end, as the center of gravity
moves from one to the other. Furthermore, the entwining of
the two lines offers the possibility of attributing a fuller
meaning to the fall, since each character considered separately
yields only a partial significance. Philippe's downfall is basically psychological: from security he slides to insecurity and
then to debasement. Eliane adds the moral touch: as she
frees herself from the illusions of goodness, she becomes
driven by lust. The minor sin that unites them at the end
receives its importance from this combination: apathy and
carnality, weakness and power-hunger. A single fate could
not have exemplified these contradictory notions.

IV

If the commanding concept of the fall and its implicit and explicit connotations obviously are a part of Catholic imagery, the use of the same concept by Camus, whose religiosity is more than questionable, provides a warning against drawing definite conclusions from one controlling structure only, especially when it principally affects the main outline of the plot. On the other hand, since it confirms the earlier indications, it may be expected to inspire, and relate to, a certain number of secondary networks of more intimate structures, i.e., expressing the often unconscious creative processes of the writer's imagination. Carried out in this spirit, a second reading of *Épaves* yields four striking structural schemes which are closely interrelated and tied to the concepts of fall and hell. All four appear in the same basic form of two opposite poles: movement up and down, light and obscurity, childhood and middle age, poverty and wealth. To a certain degree they can be detected in the use of specific images and words, but they are most significant in that they situate the major characters in distinct positions along the scale stretching between the two poles. Each of these systems is interwoven with the others, but it will be best to examine them separately, showing their mutual dependence as they take shape.

The downward movement is obviously associated with the key image of a body falling into the Seine. However, it also accompanies some other important episodes of the novel, especially those which lead the characters to the realization of their true nature. When Philippe first varies his routine, he takes a street that "runs down" to the river and ends with a triple flight of one hundred steps, descending to "a sort of abyss," a "shadowy cavity," a "hollowness"—i.e., the river bank, which is actually only twelve meters "deep" below the street level (pp. 1–2). From this pit, "voices rise up to him" (p. 2). Philippe goes down one flight of stairs, goes back to

the street level, goes down again, and, after some lateral
progress on the intermediate level, leans over in time to receive from the bottom level the pathetic call for help. During
this first episode, still inconclusive in terms of the realization
of cowardice, the downward movement is thus interrupted.
The second Seine episode, however, brings Philippe all the
way down to the river, despite an intuition that "it was ab-
surd to go down" (p. 38): it is on this basic level that the
decisive revelation takes place. In general, the entire first part
of the novel is built on a contrast between two levels: the
river banks where Philippe descends to learn new truths, and
the apartment to which he ascends to recapture a feeling of
security. In Part II, where the second sentence already echoes
the up-and-down polarity in its description of the house that
"rose" on a street that "was running down the hill" (p. 63),
the most important downward movement occurs when Philippe and his son go down to the wine cellar. Here, too, the
descent is divided into several stages: first, the dark court-
yard smothered under a cloudy sky, then the even darker
cellar, and, finally, the total obscurity of the gallery where
Robert alone disappears, "sinking into the shadow" (p. 99),
and from which, repeating the pattern of the first Seine episode, he calls for help. On this occasion Philippe does answer
but, at the same time, realizes he is essentially alone. The
parallel between this experience and a descent to hell, suggested by the description of the janitor's "grotto," the combination of black and red colors, and the quasi-ritual incan-
tation: "Open the third door at the end of the passage. Turn
the key twice in the lock, and put four bottles in the basket"
(p. 99), assures a transition to the evocation of the coalfields
in the North, where miners "descend into the coal hell, like
black gods threatened by the fury of fire" (p. 124). A few
moments later Philippe decides to give up his career as a
businessman. A third downward movement takes place within
the movie which serves as a symbolic representation of reality: after Philippe's identification of a part of the setting with
his own apartment—"his heart beat faster, as if in the midst
of a coarse fiction he suddenly found a part of himself" (p.

164)—and the reader's identification of the triangle on the
screen with Philippe's situation, it is the lovers' descent into
a cellar that brings about the husband's discovery of his mis-
fortune and, simultaneously, Philippe's discovery of his lack
of real feelings. Part III presents several minor up-and-down
moves, but the downward direction is particularly stressed
in two episodes placed at the end of the novel as if to balance
the two Seine episodes at the beginning. In the crucial scene
depicting the final fall, Eliane and Philippe are on the same
level, sitting on a sofa; yet the moment of truth introduces
a vertical dichotomy in their positions: Philippe's "eyes slowly
rose up to Eliane's," immediately compared to a threatening
sky; "his body sank down into the sofa"; Eliane "leaned
over him," etc.; when she finally crushes his lips, the visual
suggestion is that of two bodies toppling down (p. 278).
The last chapter shows Philippe reaching the bottom of his
degradation as he gives up any glimmer of revolt, and this
act of total resignation takes place even below the bank of
the river, as Philippe goes down four small steps to the actual
level of the water. This image is at once contrasted with its
ultimate opposite: "Above their heads something was shining in the fog, a vast copper colored spot, the sun" (p. 286).

The implications of the downward movement become indeed
clearer when it is matched by a converse upward movement.
As in the case of the other structural schemes, the up-and-
down polarity operates in a distinct manner for each individual, so that some characters gravitate toward one pole and
some toward the other. None of them can be absolutely identified with one extremity of the scale, and even the most systematic moves in one direction allow for some contrary indications.
This restriction does not, however, affect the general picture
which emerges from an attentive examination of the major
characters. Since Philippe and Eliane tend to move toward
the lower pole, it may be expected that Henriette will exem-
plify the upward trend. But even Philippe and Eliane occasionally are shown attempting to move up, though with a
lack of success which is revealing in itself.

The symbolic meaning of the upward movement, contrast-

ing with the image of hell as the representation of the opposite swing downward, could be derived from a minor "epiphany" placed at the beginning of the novel. Philippe recalls
his mother's efforts to lift a statue from the mantelpiece:

> Too small to reach it without raising her arms, she seemed in this posture
> as a suppliant in front of an altar. This recollection was unpleasant; he
> felt that the vigilance and the fears of his mother succeeded in incarnat-
> ing something mysterious and inalterable in that block of clay" [p. 14].

Similarly, but with reference to her own gestures, Henriette
identifies her happy childhood with her joy when, climbing
on a chair and stretching up her arms, she managed to touch
the ceiling, and with the recollection of the corner of her rug
which "always would curl up," however one tried to weigh
it down (p. 139). Among her current activities, the most
meaningful by far is her affair with the impecunious and ugly
Victor, and, less paradoxically than it may at first sight seem,
this action also is associated with the upward movement.
Her quick decision made during the street encounter is translated by a concise "They went up" (p. 114), reinforced by
the stress on the noise produced by Henriette's shoes as she
climbs the staircase. Afterwards, Victor never appears outside his room, to which a new ascent must always lead. In
general, with the exception of transits between the two apart-
ments, her husband's and her lover's, Henriette is never seen
on the neutral level of the street. In fact, whereas Philippe
must go much lower to experience his truth, his wife's "down"
stops precisely on that level, viewed from the window as the
place of horrible fascination. But this is an exceptional attitude in the case of Henriette. Just so Philippe's few ascend-
ing movements do not compensate for his general orientation:
he looks in vain for reassurance from the police on the upper
level of the river banks; it is a fleeting feeling of solidarity
that links him with Robert after "climbing up" to the Passy
bridge (p. 231); and he fails to experience the suffering for
which he hoped when, following Henriette, he climbs the
flights of steps leading to Victor's apartment. In the same

spirit, Eliane's nightmare brings her to the edge of a gulf, after an unsuccessful attempt to ascend a steep hill representing the solution of her problems.

Despite the prevalence of downward movements as carried out by the major characters, the spatial coordinates of the novel seem rather fairly determined by an equal stress on high and low. Terms such as "abyss," "gulf," "pit," "depth," "sink," "fall," "descend," and their manifold synonyms occur at an extremely high rate of frequency, even discounting idioms and clichés such as "il tomba dans le gouffre" (he fell into the abyss) for "he fell asleep" (p. 62). On the other hand, there is an equally striking multiplicity of direct or indirect references to the ultimate goal of the upward movement—i.e., "le ciel," with its double meaning of sky and heaven. Whether Green speaks of clouds, or smoke, or branches playing under grey ceilings over the city, or skylines, or the absence of stars, or even, though rarely, the sun and its rays, he does not miss an occasion to set an upper limit of space in opposition to the lower limit. However, there is a significant difference in the nature of the two poles. While the lower regions open into mysterious depths, dark waters, endless pits, gloomy recesses that cannot be fathomed and, therefore, suggest a continuous movement downward, the upper region, on the contrary, is traced firmly as an opaque barrier that does not allow for further progress: the sky hangs low over the buildings, and its usual mixture of clouds, smoke, and mist creates the impression of a lid beyond which it is difficult to see.

One of the ways in which this contrast is achieved derives from the effects of the second structural scheme: opposition between light and obscurity. It does not always dovetail with the first scheme—after all, *Epaves* is a novel and not a geometrical design—but the points of contact are too numerous and too meaningful to result from simple coincidences. In fact, some major manifestations of the light–obscurity pattern will involve a number of key episodes already mentioned, providing additional clarifications.

In that sense it may bear repeating that the most significant

downward movements are accompanied by a particular stress
on obscurity. The first Seine episode takes place in good
weather, on a late autumn afternoon; yet Green speaks of
"vast black buildings which raised their lugubrious façades
against a blind sky"; underneath, "a thick shadow hid the
banks of the river" and "the deserted and poorly lit harbor
was sinister"; strangely enough, even the light of a café
seems to "swallow up" the passers-by (pp. 3–4). When Philippe leaves his apartment for the second episode, he sees "a
sky without stars, the river flowing in darkness . . . a blind
warrior on his pedestal . . . the doubtful light of streetlamps," which create an eery atmosphere where the more
luminous spots shine with a "funereal brightness" (p. 21).
The same effect is repeated in the cellar scene, when the can-
dle goes out; at the board of directors meeting when Philippe
"felt as if the night was falling down on him . . . and the
chandelier was growing dark" (p. 127); in the gloomy theater with its black and grey pictures; during the final truth
scene through the recreation of the first Seine episode with a
stress on obscurity, through Eliane's preoccupation with the
darkness of night, and through images of fog, shadows,
stormy skies; and finally during the last Seine episode which
takes place in the morning but in the midst of a thick fog.
Similarly, Eliane's psychological degradations generally occur
at night, after she turns off the light in her room; her self-
revealing dream depicts her as wandering in total obscurity;
and her last appearance, after the sin, shows her again in
darkness, sitting in her room, engulfed by the night. On the
other hand, while this prevalence of obscurity during objective or subjective downfalls is evident, it may be objected that
the entire novel testifies to the dominance of darkness over
light, and that all the coincidences observed above derive
from a more general orientation. But this general pattern in
its turn yields conclusions which fit the coincidences.

After eliminating a few "tell" passages, and discounting a
couple of very short "show" scenes inserted in them as flashbacks, we find that the novel contains twenty-five time-periods
of varying length and homogeneity but clearly set apart one

from another. In this total number, about one-half, i.e., twelve, take place late in the evening or at nighttime, including the first three and the last three but one, thus providing the general mood at the outset and outcome of the novel. Furthermore, among the remaining units one is situated in the obscurity of a cellar, and five others describe the transition between the early and late afternoon with explicit indications such as: "street lights went on . . . night was already there," "daylight was failing" (twice), "the day was over." Finally, the last scene, though taking place in daytime, is obscured by a heavy fog, offering an ambiguous "darkness at noon" effect. The remaining six units are clearly morning or early afternoon scenes. The objective ratio between obscurity and light is thus 3:1. Within the greatly larger number of dark units it is indeed impossible to operate a further differentiation; all characters are involved at one time or another, and many unimportant events related. A closer examination of the light units, however, discloses a certain degree of consistency that points to a meaningful structural organization.

It must first be noted that two of these six scenes occur at the Moroso *pension*. In the graph of Eliane's fall, the Moroso episode stands for her only earnest attempt at checking the downward movement by escaping both her own wish for degradation, and the situation which fans it. The episode is located at the exact center of the novel, and contains four units. The first one narrates Eliane's arrival at the *pension* at noon: it is definitely bright. The second is devoted to her nightmare, i.e., reveals her unconscious desire to go back to Philippe; and it is dark. The third relates Philippe's visit in the evening: the asylum is breached and Eliane is faced again with the situation she tried to flee; dark tonality again. The fourth unit re-creates the setting of the first one: Eliane alone at noon. When viewed as a whole, the Moroso episode appears thus essentially as a luminous spot, opening and closing with light scenes that correspond exactly to its structural meaning: Eliane's withdrawal from the situation, i.e., an interruption in her descending line. The two dark scenes account for the failure of this movement, showing from the inside why it could not succeed; but the two bright scenes are clearly associated with the upper pole in the up–down scheme.

The other four bright units are more diversified in content but have one striking factor in common: they all include Robert and Philippe, alone or with other characters. It is true that the Robert–Philippe combination also occurs in three dark scenes, but one is lost in the ambiguous morning-fog dimness which could be interpreted either way, a second mentions Robert only at the onset as he falls asleep and, therefore, practically ceases to exist as an active element, and the third, the cellar episode, actually is an insertion in one of the bright time units. With some structural twisting, it could be argued that Robert and Philippe are always associated with light. However, there is no need for such a sweeping generalization. Since we know that Philippe himself tends elsewhere to be linked with obscurity, the hypothesis may be made that the luminosity is brought to the four scenes in question as the exclusive result of Robert's presence. (The next structural scheme will help to explain this conjecture, locating the child near the positive pole of the youth–middle age scale.) Within that perspective, these four bright scenes would thus refer to brief moments of interruption in Philippe's downfall, checked by the uplifting relations with his son.

A more detailed analysis of the light–obscurity scheme as evidenced by each character in specific situations cutting across the time units lends further precision to these findings. Philippe's apartment, though redecorated with an eye to pleasant color patterns, is described as basically dark, with "a few miserly oblique rays of light for 30 minutes before lunchtime" (p. 13). When electric lighting brings a sudden luminosity to the room, Philippe draws back the curtains to let in the darkness of night; at other times, they are tightly closed. In general, his attitude toward light is mainly negative. If he happens to appreciate the increased though still relative luminosity of his apartment after its remodeling, he "feels guilty about it so that his pleasure is spoiled and sometimes changed into a violent and sudden anger" (p. 64). He acts

himself as a darkening agent, or reagent—depending upon
whether he or Green is at the source of descriptions: upon
entering the board meeting, he sees a room where "the chandelier diffused a funereal light" and "the ceiling remained in
the dark, too high to profit from it" (p. 121); a few lines
further on, he notices a "violent and pallid light" (p. 122),
implying a notion of dimness despite the internal contradiction of terms. A similar attenuation is carried out, by means
of the same indistinct idea of "pallidness," in the luminosity
of afternoon skies (p. 159). Philippe has black hair, and
much is made of his handsome dark looks. Significantly, the
other dark-haired character in the novel is his sister-in-law
who displays the same affinity toward obscurity. Eliane's
room appears in the novel almost always in total darkness,
except for the intermittent artificial light projected through
the window by a yellow electric sign: "a yellow ray that tore
away from Eliane's face the shadow which protected her like
a mask; the blemishes stood up on her flesh" (p. 17). Although somewhat suspect by its coloration and artificial nature, this yellow light has an obviously negative function with
respect to Eliane. Not only does it show the deterioration of
her appearance but, in an image recalling Hugo's symbol of
conscience, it also exposes her moral failings: "It was like a
big yellow eye watching over Eliane, pretending to fall asleep,
then opening suddenly to catch her unaware" (p. 18). In
that sense, it is the bearer of a certain truth opposed to the
dark truth reached in obscurity. As Eliane sinks deeper into
her passion, the yellow light makes rarer appearances, till the
last scene in her room, after the "sin," when it exposes her
for a last time: "Eliane shuddered, despite herself. There was
no joy on her face. . . . Then, all around her, night drew
tight again" (p. 279). At that point, she has joined Philippe.
But her choice was already made before, and expressed
through numerous allusions ranging from simple use of ad-
jectives with dark connotations to more elaborate scenes
stressing the contrast between obscurity and light. Thus, in
one of the last morning units, entering a room where Henriette is looking through the window, "she remained in the

shadow of the door, admiring despite herself this devastating light"; but she loses no time admonishing her sister: "Come on, let me close the shutters. . . . My beautiful drawing-room will fade" (pp. 240–242).

Here, as elsewhere, the light–obscurity scheme is explicitly used to underline the contrast between the two sisters. Within the structural framework of luminosity Henriette unquestionably tends toward the bright side. She occasionally appears in dark scenes, and her memory recalls dark settings, but therein she singles out the brightest elements and usually is associated rather with light images and colors. Her introduction is very characteristic in that respect: coming home at nighttime, she remains invisible till "suddenly the light is switched on" (p. 48), revealing her white silk dress (Eliane's was black satin that evening) and blonde hair. The description continues to stress "her white shoulder where the light was reflected" (p. 50), "cheeks white as marble," and, when she falls asleep half-naked, "a pale and firm flesh that shone like a polished stone" (p. 52)—a luminous effect all the more remarkable because it is achieved only with a small nightlight. As the novel progresses, this type of notation provides a steady accumulation of bright pictures of varying degrees of intensity. Among the least important, and yet not meaningless, are brief snapshots which show, for example, in a room dominated by dark colors, Henriette moving toward a white lilac bouquet and bending her face over its snowy buds. Among the most meaningful, because of their relation to other structural schemes, are reminiscences centered on some luminous spot in her past: in the dingy apartment of her parents, she best remembers the sun that brightened the red color of the curling rug, warmed up her feet, and entered into her happy games; and the habitually bleak Paris landscape suddenly changes into a display of "luminous mist where the Seine was sparkling" just as Henriette's reverie brings her back to her childhood (p. 250). This and other indications of the same nature must be weighed in contrast with the treatment of similar themes within the perspective of the other characters. When Philippe or Eliane walks through

Paris at night, the manifestations of light tend toward yellowish, red, pallid, bluish colorations, all devoid of any particular brilliance; when Henriette is out, she sees pink streetlamps and, in the background, a "web of sparkles and flashes" (p. 108). Yet this relationship with light is not completely unequivocal. On the one hand, she obviously thrives on it, could be called "a daughter of light," and has no trouble, for instance, in falling asleep "under the dazzling light of the chandelier" (p. 223). On the other hand, the same light sometimes exerts on her a hypnotic power which threatens to drag her downward: she almost falls under a car, fascinated by its beams which she sees as "white flames," "vibrant light," "a sun bordered with black" (p. 204); on another occasion, she leans dangerously out of the window as if to answer the call of a high noon sun. Although the fall is checked each time by a third person's intervention, and the second incident emphasizes Henriette's luminous appearance and elevated position as much as the danger, the light clearly plays in these episodes a role parallel to that of the yellow sign in Eliane's room: it discloses a basic truth about the woman; in this case, a deeply rooted propensity toward falling, matching, in an unstable balance, the dominant upward trend. This apparent ambiguity will be resolved by the last structural scheme.

We have already noted the high rate of coincidence between light episodes and Robert's appearances. It may be added that he displays a constant aversion to dark places, only natural at his age. On the other hand, very few indications refer to his looks and, more specifically, to his coloring. We know that his cheeks are rosy, "almost too rosy" as Eliane states (p. 95), his hands and his wrists pink, i.e., on the bright side of the spectrum. His hair is silky and brown, which places him closer to Philippe than to Henriette. But his eyes, his most remarkable feature, are first described as black (p. 79), then as blue (p. 96). The second description occurs in the same context which stresses the rosy tonality and prepares one of Philippe's generous impulses toward his son. In that sense it suggests a certain value attached to light colors. But it does not suffice to explain the evident indetermination of Robert's position on the luminosity scale. Green's confusion about the color of his eyes reflects an objective ambiguity which also will have to be clarified.

The third structural scheme, based on the opposition between youth and age, will provide some partial answers while raising some more questions, but will mainly serve to emphasize the growing dichotomy we have observed between, on the one hand, Henriette (and Robert to a certain extent), and, on the other, Philippe and Eliane. Within the second group, it will also permit us the better to differentiate the two dark characters.

As in the case of the two other structures, the youth–age scheme takes shape amid a striking accumulation of concepts, images, and words oriented toward its two poles. A statistical analysis could establish scientific evidence of the frequency of these manifestations. On the other hand, the importance of the scheme does not depend only on the number of times that "youth," "young," "childhood," "early memories," or reminiscences thereof appear in the text in an antithetic relation to "age," "old age," "wrinkles," etc., but on the intensity and relevance of these references to the basic structure of the novel, to other schemes, and to the design of characters. A first and capital clue is offered by the peculiar contradiction between the objective position and the subjective presentation of the three major characters on the age scale.

At the inception of the novel Philippe is thirty-one years old, Eliane a few months older but still thirty-one, and Henriette twenty-eight. The difference is minimal from a chronological viewpoint. Objectively the three characters should belong in the same age group, with similar attitudes toward their age. Yet even a superficial reading of the novel leaves the impression of a tremendous generation-gap between Henriette (quite close to the nine-year-old Robert), Philippe, and Eliane. It may be that this impression is partly created by the traditional division between under- and over-thirty, the limit age between youth and middle-age, purposefully left blank. It is possible that the equally traditional belief in women's maturing earlier or aging faster than men partly accounts for an unconscious differentiation between Philippe and Eliane. But the exact choice of figures with their implications only adds to an effect that the novelist is obviously trying to produce with much more complex means, i.e., setting up a clearly young character—Henriette; a clearly aging character—Eliane; and a character caught in the dangerous process of transition from youth to middle-age—Philippe. Physical appearance, behavior, preoccupation with age, and nature of attitude toward childhood memories—all contribute to this goal.

A second look at the first appearance of Henriette is in order: She comes up all in white at 1:00 A.M., calls for the light, laughs and flops in an armchair, turning "toward her sister a face which still looked youthful despite nights on the town. Although she was almost thirty, she could easily look six years younger" (p. 49). Next comes a series of short notations which, in concert with the luminous aspect, insist on her physical (and innocent) youth: "hard and lissome forehead," "innocent posture of the body," "fresh and supple body," "pure lines that years did not alter," and so forth (pp. 49–51). When she falls asleep, Eliane belabors the point: "She sleeps like a little girl," picks her up as she did "a five-year-old Henriette," and puts her to bed; then she looks "in vain for the sign of some wrinkles on the tight texture of this mat skin; the features, overcoming tiredness, exhaled the freshness of childhood" (pp. 52–53). The general picture is that of an adolescent rather than a woman approaching thirty. Only when the features harden up under the influence of an "avid" dream, "the little innocent girl of a while ago changed into a conceited and stubborn woman" (p. 52). But she is a young woman, even then, and a smiling woman. *Young and beautiful,* as Eliane repeats aloud several times. Besides, in this youthful body lives a childish personality which manifests itself in most of Henriette's behavior.

Again, the first encounter gives the keynote: Henriette has lost her purse, but does nothing about it. Soon it becomes evident that with the same indifference she turns over the household responsibilities to her sister, and the raising of her

son to educational institutions; furthermore, since the birth
of Robert nine years before, she has had no sexual relations
with her husband. Her role as an adult woman is thus whittled
down to a single expression: the affair with Victor which, as
we shall see, is quite equivocal; for the rest, she is not a housekeeper, she is not a mother, she is not a wife, and she has no
other serious interests. Her activities take the childish character of games: innocent parties on the town or ritual cross-
ing of streets and counting of trees. Even her cunning lacks
maturity: it recalls the calculations of a child who wants to
have his cake and eat it, and saddles others with the responsibility of getting it for him. The whole marriage is a case in
point, and her financial dealing with Victor a perfect illustration.

What is, then, the meaning of her affair with Victor? In a
somewhat paradoxical manner, it actually contributes to, and
clarifies, the implications of this functional reduction of a
woman to the level of a child. In the first place, it has little to
do with sensuality. Despite the appeal of her adult—but young
—body, "serenely immodest in its confidence of perfection" (p.
73), Henriette shows no interest in it herself, nor in its fulfillment by others. Philippe's impotence on the wedding night only
evoked laughter and fear of his reactions, and his nine-year-
long neglect does not seem to have caused any physical frustration. Certainly she is not sensually attached to Victor; as a
matter of fact, "she abhors his kisses" (p. 117) and in general
finds him ugly, aging, repulsive. Nor is it a case of romantic
passion, idealistic self-dedication, worshipful admiration, a
meeting of the souls: although sexually she remains faithful
to Victor, since she experiences no other temptations, she deceives him in all other ways, ranging from petty money lies
to the fundamental lie of love. In short, she does not love him,
either physically or emotionally. The two-year-old affair proves
her maturity no more than does her marriage; she does not
even function as a lover. Again she plays a game, although in
this occurrence it has a basic significance both for her and for
the structure of the novel. For the love game for Henriette
is but a way to recapture her childhood.

Green is quite explicit on this point. Through Victor, and indeed through the entire set-up of her affair, all Henriette was trying to secure, we are told, "was only a setting where her imagination would permit her to reach back to her childhood and the most happy years of her youth" (p. 147). The very ugliness of the surroundings recalls for her the drab apartment of her father; the poverty echoes the poverty of her parents; when she notices Victor's falling hair, she suddenly has the impression that she is becoming a "real" woman, a continuation of the real adolescent that she used to be, and that she is entrapping a "truth" that she knew in the past but from which her marriage had cut her off, forcing her into a "fictitious" existence. The affair with Victor, the only independent action carried out by Henriette, thus constitutes the most radical rejection of her adulthood: a willful withdrawal to a happy youth whose appearance she still wears. The ambiguity in Henriette's presentation, and more particularly the coexistence of two types of truth, one pulling her down and the other lifting her up, is compounded but also clarified by this new duality between the reality of an existence lived outwardly and the aspiration to an internal innocence. In a strangely inverted image, the two natures of Henriette are illustrated in her last description: "Behind this smooth and pure face where childhood was still playing peeked a soul worn out by age and the experience of evil" (p. 215).

Using similar techniques, Green moves Eliane toward the other end of the age scale. Here again the tone is set by early notations which create the picture of an aging woman: "a withering complexion," a "yellow neck" (echoing the yellow sign: color of autumn), a "multiplicity of small wrinkles around her eyes and lips" (pp. 6, 17). It is clearly established that Eliane is not really ugly, that she could appear pretty; but when first contrasted with Henriette she is shown unkempt, dishevelled, clad in a robe, and in the role not so much of an older sister as of a mother who waits at nighttime for the wayward child. In addition, Eliane realizes that she is aging, worries about it, and her thoughts reflect this preoccupation. Age for her becomes the prime explanation of her lack of appeal as a woman; when looking with envy at Henriette's sleeping body, she quickly and pathetically admonishes herself that "after all it is not her fault that I am three years older than she" (p. 51). One has the impression that there are twenty years of difference. It is also interesting to note that terms expressing youth are associated with Éliane only in connection with these resigned comments, and are even then extremely rare. At one juncture she sighs: "If I only were younger" (p. 17); but elsewhere, to convey the hope that smiling could take some years away from her face, she uses words which avoid any mention of youth, and actually emphasize her age: "It is the degree of joy in the eyes which gives its age to a face. Now all my wrinkles are in order" (p. 82). After mentioning that eleven years before "Éliane was young and fresh, her skin beautiful," Green hastens to specify that now she has become "a poor woman" (pp. 106–107). As the novel progresses, the generic "old maid" tends to replace the first name "Éliane," just as "young woman" is used in preference to "Henriette."

There is only one reminiscence of Éliane's childhood, and a very short one at that: a quick glimpse of a little girl playing happily in a garden. Contrary to the other characters, Éliane does not welcome this memory; it hurts her, she tries to suppress it, and easily succeeds in doing so. No further allusions of this sort occur, except for a few words about "a senior" Éliane who used to carry in her arms a small Henriette (and we note again the avoidance of terms associated with youth); in her next chronological appearance she steps into the spinster role and promotes her sister's marriage. In her affective relation to her own youth Éliane represents thus the counterpart of Henriette's attempt at recapturing childhood. The glimpse of a lost paradise is pushed as far back in time as possible. The woman who emerges from a long period of opaque silence has accepted her age, refuses to look back, and embraces the attitudes of an older person. She rules the family, mothers Henriette, views Philippe as a little boy although they are contemporaries, and in general feels that she belongs to a more mature generation which bears the responsibility for these "small children" (pp. 131, 141). Even her passion for her brother-in-law rapidly sheds any trace of innocence and turns into the physical obsession of an old maid who is haunted by sensual dreams and eventually satisfies her body by forsaking any genuine love. The picture is clear but one element is still missing. The justification for Eliane's artificial aging visibly lies in the dark intermission between her fleeting image as a little girl and her reappearance as an old maid who denies any continuity with that image: the extreme distance between the two situations emphasizes their contrast. We shall need another structural scheme to account for this initial, and forgotten, fall from grace.

Philippe's position on the age scale is located halfway between the two women's, and is the only one that moves, from apparent youth to accepted middle age. The evolution is conveyed by both physical and psychological changes. The first half of the novel abounds in complimentary descriptions of Philippe's youthful figure and features, watched and admired by himself and Eliane. His narcissistic preoccupation with his body, and pride in its formal perfection, are definitely those of a young man barely out of adolescence. The first Seine episode triggers the first awareness of the fragility of this basis for satisfaction. Perhaps because he suddenly experiences "a need to harm himself," Philippe begins to feel the weight of years: "He was thirty-one last week. What has he done with this strength of which he was so proud? . . . Usually this type of question did not torment him at all" (pp. 13–14). The second Seine episode carries the aging process a step further by setting up a confrontation with a younger man. It is interesting to note that the description of Philippe's antagonist echoes the characterization of Henriette: a "white skin," "an innocent mouth," and a laughter reminiscent of the young woman's laughter during the wedding night and after. Automatically the gap between husband and wife widens as a result of this association. By the end of the first part, Philippe is shaken; his last thoughts are a desperate call to "my body . . . my body" (p. 62). Part II continues the movement through two new confrontations with youth: the arrival of his son whose youthful reactions show up the fears of an aging father realizing that "these laughing eyes were looking at a world that was no longer his" (p. 97), and a long meditation in front of his photographs which portray an earlier self. Soon afterwards occurs a concrete manifestation of age: he is gaining weight, his jacket strangles him, his chin grows, and his worries enter an acute stage: "What were his internal problems in comparison with a humiliation of this nature!" (p. 103). The psychological reaction leaves little doubt about the basic source of his apprehensions: he pulls his son toward him, and kisses him, "as if trying to quench a thirst" (p. 104). This realization of the loss of youth is tantamount to the acknowledgment of middle age. Another step is made in that direction when Philippe for the first time feels uncomfortable about his childhood memories. From a cautious "Today . . . it was better not to think about them any more" (p. 118) to the final decision to "close the door" on his past, giving up forever the dream of "the man that he might have become . . . because this man did not exist" (p. 282), the evolution shifts the perspective from looking backward to looking forward, i.e., to an acceptance of aging. But this very acceptance cuts itself off from the dynamic impulses of youth. It is a resigned maturity, denying hope in "a dawn which calls beyond the night of the present but never comes" (p. 282), conscious of the approaching death and its peaceful "horizon without light" (p. 284), steeped in boredom and yet too passive to end a mediocre existence. Philippe has reached the quicksands of middle age, and he will sink in them with his eyes looking downward.

His relationship to his childhood thus changes from reminiscence to denial, from Henriette's to Eliane's attitude (parallel to his own move from the former to the latter), but without the extreme manifestations shown by the two women. It is possible that this relative moderation derives from a less clearly delineated emotional content of the early memories. For Philippe's childhood is not depicted as basically happy. He thinks with nostalgia about his intellectual promise, his confidence in the future, his beauty as a child, even his sensitive response to music; but an equal number of flashbacks compose a different and gloomier picture. The threatening figure of his father towers over the small Philippe, a God-like image of an "eternally disapproving" judge to whom he still defers (p. 65); a prison-like apartment with dark red velvet curtains which did not let in any light even on the nicest days; the grim school buildings where he entered each day with a "child's sorrow that persisted till nighttime" (p. 118). As far back as he can remember, he was afraid and suspicious of the world and of people, the "frowning deities" above him, the maid who saw life as a purgatory (p. 119). The gradual estrangement from his youth is affected by the ambiguous nature of that youth. It is a painful experience insofar as he must renounce a certain reassuring image of himself, but it is made easier by a contingent liberation from external constrictions. Assuredly, the resulting evolution is degrading; it is not, however, as for Eliane, a fall from grace, a loss of a happy innocence, but rather a tumble from a state of mixed blessings to desolate despair. The question is: Why this difference? Why no paradise in Philippe's background?

There is no need to demonstrate that Robert occupies a position close to the youth end of the age scale: he is about nine years old, and physical descriptions stress his childish appearance. A few observations, however, must be made inasmuch as they establish interesting relations between his function in that scheme and that of the other characters. In that sense, a most revealing oddity is the forced parallelism between Robert and Henriette. In the first place, we find almost no trace of their mother–son relationship. While Philippe and Robert are identified and address each other, more often than not, as "father" and "son," there are only five examples of similar use of "mother" and "son." One occurs when Robert is located at the table between *father, mother,* and *aunt*; another is placed after Philippe's admonition to his son not to speak of a walk to his *aunt* or *mother*; in both cases the incriminating word is visibly dictated by others. The three remaining occurrences are grouped in a single scene where Robert prevents Henriette from falling from the window, i.e., the very scene where she is exceptionally shown to be tempted by a fall—in other terms, where she acts out of character. In all other scenes the first name is used. Similarly, no reference is made to a possible biological or psychological maternal influence: twice the question is asked whom Robert resembles, and each time the only candidate suggested is his father, even when he denies it. If any relation does exist between Henriette and her son, it is that of an unconscious solidarity stemming from an equally juvenile attitude. Robert's feminine voice, "girlish" looks, and easy laughter contribute to this identity. On the other hand, his childhood, such as it is presented, does not correspond to Henriette's memories of hers. They share a good deal of innocence, but Robert is not entirely happy. A certain shadow darkens his days: loneliness, awkwardness, stress, lack of love, etc. It is not quite the frightened and tense childhood of his father, but something akin to it, and which explains the growing understanding between them. The actual causes may differ, but both wear a melancholic aura over their fundamental dispositions. There are two scenes in the novel in which Philippe and Robert come together in dark surroundings, after the cellar episode and after the last Seine episode, and both scenes end with the sad sound of a tug-boat's fog horn. It is the concluding image of the book. Why this "adult" corruption of Robert's childhood?

Most of the questions raised by our examination of the first three structures will be answered within the framework of a fourth scheme which plays a relatively minor role in the total organization of the novel but fulfills a significant function in relation to the other schemes. The opposition poverty–wealth does not manifest itself through constant use of words or images related to these concepts; they do occur, and frequently, but are grouped in passages directly concerned with this issue. Yet the contrast between the two extremes is very clearly marked, in particular through the elimination of a middle term. Individuals and groups in *Epaves* are either poor or rich, or at least presented in that way, and the only unquestionable representative of the petty bourgeoisie is Miss Moroso who, as we observed, is somehow placed outside the novel. As a result, with a few significant exceptions, there is no ambiguity about the position of the characters on this scale, whether in terms of their past or present situation, or of their choice of loyalty.

Thus all four major *dramatis personae* obviously are quite well off during the objective time of the novel. Whatever future may be predicted on the basis of elements provided by the plot, psychological analysis, and structural indications, nothing seems to announce any changes in that situation. Conversely, with the few exceptions mentioned above, all the minor characters with whom the major ones are faced, and who, for one reason or another, serve as antitheses or touchstones, are placed at the other end of the scale: they are workers, servants, failures, bums, ranging from the unhappy Victor to the old beggar asking for alms. The relationship between the poor and the rich is never indifferent or located on the plane of equality. On the contrary, it takes on the nature of a confrontation which involves an important decision or commitment on the part of the major character. Whenever Philippe is tested from the outside as to courage, charity, or human feelings, his failure is expressed through a strong emotional rejection of one or several of these minor characters. It does not matter from this angle whether fear, or distrust, or alienation occasions this reaction; structurally, each of these successive revelations or falls corresponds to the introduction of a distance between wealth and poverty. Similarly, but with opposite results, Henriette's movement toward Victor signifies an emotional movement toward poverty. To a certain extent even Eliane's attempt at escaping may be viewed as a renouncement of wealthy surroundings and a flight toward poorer conditions. It is true that the Moroso *pension* does not represent misery, but it definitely clashes with the comfort of Philippe's household; and if the distance thus covered on the wealth scale does not seem very impressive, it may be because Eliane's determination to flee is not very overwhelming either. At any rate, she loses little time in jumping back to her initial position.

The three apparent exceptions to this dichotomy are Philippe's friend Diederich, the detective, and the collective board of trustees. Diederich is rich, or so one assumes; but he comes to ask for money and therefore places himself on a lower level of the wealth scale in relation to Philippe. The detective looks and behaves like a bourgeois, but again his relation to Philippe is that of an employee paid to perform a rather dirty task, and thus relegated to a menial category. Besides, both these characters play a very small part in the structure of the novel, and their function may be reduced to showing up Henriette's duality: on the one hand she distrusts Diederich because of his low financial status and thereby betrays a negative attitude toward poverty; on the other, she is saved by the detective from falling under a car, whereby a positive association with poverty is suggested. The presence of a detective may have a different function; he reveals Philippe's suspicion of his wife; but he is never seen together with his employer and, furthermore, this role is superfluous since Henriette leaves letters from her lover lying open around the apartment.

The episode of the board of trustees is both more significant and complex. It should be approached from two angles, corresponding to its double function as a symbolic representation of life and as a landmark in Philippe's evolution. In the first sense, it is rapidly assimilated to an infernal assembly embodying a general view of the world as hell. However, within the framework of this picture, the poverty–wealth scheme plays a special role because there are actually two different and contrasting images of hell which combine in Philippe's mind: the concrete areopagus of financial wizards gathered like evil spirits in an unnatural light, and the imaginary nether regions of coal-mining where workers descend to face darkness and fire. The two representations depend upon each other, but they occupy extreme positions at the opposite ends of the wealth scale. Their unity rests on a dichotomy corresponding to the dichotomy observed among the characters of the novel: even in hell there is no middle term. The social or ethical implications of this relationship are irrelevant in this context. But it is interesting to note that the structure of Philippe's imagination in this instance at least reproduces Green's own reflexes.

The second function of the episode serves to clarify Philippe's past and present attitude toward wealth. While the current financial status of major characters is stable and shows few practical differences as they all live together and share in the same comfort, variations appear when their past history is taken into account and examined in terms of individual choices of attitude. In the case of Philippe, wealth has always been an integral part of his horizon, inherited from and associated with the dominant father who shaped his son's idea of a successful life as a combination of external security and internal strength. The board of directors carries on this influence: the rich old men are surrogates for the dead father, and it is to conform to the latter's ideal image of his son that Philippe attends the meetings. His sudden rebellion may be brought about by the realization that this image is false as a whole, that he is a weakling inside, and that there is no point therefore in keeping up the façade of a money-maker. Or else Philippe resigns from the company as a result of a more direct revelation of his failure as a money-maker. In either case he puts an end to an actively positive attitude toward wealth which was a part of his youth. On the other hand, this decision does not entail any objective or subjective movement toward poverty. From an involved millionaire Philippe turns into an indifferent millionaire, perhaps because he has never been conscious of the possibility of another choice. The structure of his relation to wealth parallels in that sense the structure of his attitude toward his childhood: an eventual denial which fails to lead to the affirmation of the opposite.

This remarkable parallelism is repeated in Robert's case. His position on the wealth scale roughly corresponds to that of Philippe at his age, but without the strong affective valuation imposed by the father. Robert profits from the inherited money though in a somewhat less comfortable way, and there is no indication that he has, or will have, a specific attitude toward it. In short, if we were to view him with hindsight, his childhood would come out as a considerably toned-down version of Philippe's insofar as the wealth scheme is con-

cerned. On the other hand, we also saw that his childhood
is not particularly happy and, in many respects, similar to
Philippe's recollections of his own, but less dark on the whole.
Both structural schemes thus establish a striking identity
between father and son, with the same downgrading in intensity in each system. Taking into consideration that for
each separate character these two schemes also present an
identical structure, it is possible to formulate the hypothesis
that a fundamental relation exists between, on the one hand,
poverty, a positive attitude toward childhood, and even the
nature of childhood as a paradise, and, on the other hand,
wealth, a negative attitude, and childhood as a limbo. A closer
look at Eliane and Henriette not only confirms this hypothesis
but suggests the extension of this relationship to the other
structural schemes as well.

In the first place, we know that the two sisters were poor
in their early years, and also that their childhood was a happy
one, appearing in bright colors in their memory. Then, at the
time of Henriette's marriage, their lines diverge. Objectively,
the marriage brings simultaneously a measure of discontent
and financial security to both of them, and from that moment
on they remain near the top of the wealth scale. Subjectively,
however, their attitudes toward wealth follow opposite di-
rections, again reflected in their attitudes toward childhood.
For Eliane, whatever her initial sentimental reasons for
bringing Philippe and her sister together, the marriage project
rapidly becomes synonymous with an escape from poverty;
she grows money-conscious and schemes to lend Henriette a
false air of material affluence. In the success of her designs she
sees the confirmation of the power of wealth. Afterwards
she takes it upon herself to play the role of the financial expert in the family, worrying about Philippe's ruin or trying
to promote profitable deals. Her freedom of choice is intact
in theory since she knows the alternative; at one time she
even dreams of poverty shared with her brother-in-law, though
the fleeting image does not appeal to her in its material aspect;
but practically speaking Eliane's attitude is set: she has rejected poverty once and for all, just as she has rejected her

childhood. Both decisions occur during the same period of her
life, emerging at the time of marriage but obviously nurtured
and shaped in the dark interval between childhood and maturity. The original choice was made during these years, gradually or all at once, by a still *young* Eliane, but Green leaves
this episode in obscurity. It would have disturbed the structure
of the novel by setting up a first fall before the combined fall
of Eliane and Philippe. Yet it was necessary to justify the
dark character of Eliane at the outset of the book.

Henriette's situation is more ambiguous, reflecting and finally clarifying her ambivalent position within the framework
of the other structural schemes. On the one hand, we have
already noted how much she is attracted to poverty which
has "for her the same fascination as wealth has for other
women" (p. 113); in her daydreams in Victor's apartment
she pictures herself as a "poor" woman, believing that only
in this role can she reach toward a "true" life. On the other
hand, she has no real intention of giving up the comfort and
luxury of her existence with Philippe, however illusory, futile,
and fictitious it may seem to her; and in her real dreams, or
relaxed moments, her face takes on a clear expression of
"avidity," of hardening-up. Neither of the two attitudes can
be said to be more basic than the other; they coexist and supplement each other: "half-poor and half-rich, she believed that
she was more or less happy" (p. 114). Her childhood is
associated with poverty, and she tries to recapture it; her
marriage and adult life are associated with wealth, and she
tries to deny them; her positive actions are mainly controlled
by the image of a lost paradise which contained innocent and
fundamental truths, bathed in light and moving her upwards.
But her objective acceptance of her situations and the daily
renewal of this choice reveal another truth, a darker one that
pulls her downward.

v

If we lay side by side the four structural schemes and compare
the positions of the major characters within their frameworks,

the general picture shows a highly integrated system of references pointing toward a unique structure marked, like each of its components, by a tension between two opposite poles. On the one end we find poverty, youth, light, and upward movement; on the other wealth, age, darkness, and downward movement. Two characters are consistently associated with the latter: Philippe and Eliane. Two others tend toward the second pole: Henriette and Robert, but cannot reach it for various reasons which can be explained in terms of the partial schemes. Furthermore, as we have seen, the two dark characters serve to carry out the dominant design of the novel which is that of a Fall, while the two lighter characters are repeatedly related to the concept of innocence, even if they do not embody it fully. Finally, the key static image is that of an infernal region into which the dark characters not only fit but sink ever deeper; the lighter characters either look for some escape or have to learn to belong. It would be possible to enrich this general organization with additional elements, to operate further distinctions, or to multiply various significant relationships obtaining between the structural schemes already outlined. It could be shown, for example, that the dark characters are subjectively and objectively more important than the lighter ones, which justifies the choice of hell as a controlling image, and so forth. But there is no need to do so. On the contrary, after an analytical breakdown of the pattern of the novel into its major components reduced to their simplest structural function, it is advisable to proceed to a further reduction yielding the most fundamental structure. On a purely descriptive plane, there is little doubt that the abstract notion of polarity, controlling each element of construction, is the ultimate result of such a reduction. Green's imagination obviously works according to a binary system. On the other hand, there also exists a single concrete structural scheme which expresses this polarity and, at the same time, provides a meaningful synthesis for all the partial schemes: the opposition between salvation and damnation.

Indeed, if the idea of salvation and damnation is nowhere expressed or even suggested in *Epaves,* it constitutes perhaps the only correlative which accounts for all structural networks, for their interdependence, and for variations within each one. It links the various elements by a logical pattern of causality, establishing causes and effects to explain the associations: It is because one is poor and retains the innocence of a child that one will move upwards to the lighter circles of paradise; conversely the loss of innocence and worship of money plunges one down to the darkest regions of hell. Each individual character, with his ups and downs, his aspiration toward salvation and propensities toward perdition, illustrates this causality in terms of his exact situation in the novel. Furthermore, an ethical coloring is introduced and justified as a reflection of the correlative pattern. The relatively minor "sins" of the characters hardly corresponded to the abysmal falls they exemplified; but their significance transcends their concrete nature when it is viewed as an expression of damnation. Everything falls in place. By the same token, the pessimistic bent of Green's world view can be formulated in religious terms. If the structural geography of *Epaves* appears indeed to be patterned after Dante's vision, the stress on its different parts modifies its theoretical balance between evil and good. Paradise appears only in glimpses, as something unattainable or renounced, or even hidden from the conscience; purgatory is practically eliminated; and hell is the dominant place of the novel. Like Milton's angels, Green's major characters have their original fall behind them; they were born to be damned or damned themselves in the past; their further descent into darkness or hovering at its edge with eyes raised but soul pulling downward becomes a matter merely of degree of damnation. There is no hope left for salvation, no way out of hell.

The alleged "dread of finding oneself in this world," brought up by Green as a proof of the religious nature of his books, appears both superficial and superfluous. It is the dread of finding themselves in hell that his characters experience—i.e., being forsaken by God. In that sense *Epaves* fits indeed the vision attributed to Green's earlier novels: a vision of the damned to whom grace has been denied. But this general interpretation only conceptualizes in theological terms a much more intimate and meaningful feature of the writer's imagination: the religious nature of its fundamental structures. *Epaves* may not contain a single explicit reference to Christian ideas, but its entire construction is inspired by these ideas and inspires them in turn. Whether this observation is valid for the other novels of this period remains to be shown (and various indications seem to point to the success of such an undertaking), but *Epaves* provides sufficient evidence that even in the least obviously "Catholic" of his writings Green is indeed a basically Catholic writer, stamped by the structures of Christian belief.

Note

1. In view of the special nature of this study, I have used the original text in French. All quotations are from Julien Green, *Epaves* (Paris: Plon, 1932). References to pages are between parentheses. I have attempted to give the most faithful translation possible of the original text, without much consideration for the literary value in English. The Peyre quotation is from Henri Peyre, *French Novelists of Today* (New York: Oxford University Press, 1967), p. 200.

The Christian Surrealism of Elisabeth Langgässer

R. K. Angress · *University of Kansas*

During the years of the Hitler regime, a small number of great novels were written in the German language by authors who, in spite of being distinctly different in idiom, outlook, and artistic purpose, yet had a bond of kinship imposed on them by a shared predicament. These novels are mainly Thomas Mann's *Dr. Faustus,* the second part of Robert Musil's *The Man Without Qualities,* Hermann Broch's *Death of Virgil,* and, as a poorer cousin, Franz Werfel's *Star of the Unborn.* The shared predicament was, of course, that of exile. The authors of all these works were out of touch with their public and had no clear idea if and when their books would reach a large body of native speakers of their language. For these writers, then, alienation from an audience was not so much an intellectual problem as a political reality. To be forced to write in a vacuum was a fact of life. But paradoxically, this situation may actually have furthered some of the common traits in these works that make for their greatness: in theme, a sense of doom and isolation; in form, a highly complex structure and a style that is not easily penetrable—hallmarks of works written for an ideal reader, not for a large and readily available public.

Only one such novel was written within the borders of the Third Reich. It is *The Indelible Seal* (*Das unauslöschliche Siegel*), one of the two major works of Elisabeth Langgässer, and it distinctly belongs to the family of the great novels of exile.[1]

Elisabeth Langgässer was born and reared as a Catholic, but her father came from "those totally assimilated Jews who rather tended to overstate their national affiliation" (*Letters,* p. 204), a background probably not unlike that which she gave to the hero of her novel. As a result, she was considered a "half Jew," her books were banned, her oldest daughter was deported, she herself was forced to work in a munitions factory which almost wrecked her health, and, as a final irony, she even had difficulty obtaining sufficient writing paper to compose her novel. Yet in spite of all this, and in the teeth of a cultural situation that led to literary sterility on the part of most authors and literary starvation on the part of the public, *The Indelible Seal* was not only finished during the war years, but is such an advance over Langgässer's earlier works that one cannot help but wonder whether the isolation in which she found herself did not lead to a breakthrough which perhaps could not so easily have been achieved in the give-and-take of an open literary marketplace with its demands, fashions, rivalries of competing schools and styles.

Her two early novels, *Proserpina* and *Walk through the Reed* (*Gang durch das Ried*), show her in possession of a fully developed style, unmistakably her own and impressively capable of accommodating a wide range of symbolic meaning; yet they are far from the revolutionary techniques and the sheer massive greatness of the later work. The first is a tale of childhood in the Rhineland, the author's own home country, dealing with a little girl who grows up along the old Roman road and develops a close sense of kinship with the natural forces that enter her dream world in the guise of Roman deities. The second is a tale that is already distinctly Christian in outlook; at the same time it embodies certain melodramatic plot elements, chief among them the hero's total amnesia, which disappears once he is willing to take on himself the sins of others. Both books contain themes that will return in the later work. The representation of archetypal forces in the shape of ancient mythology within a modern setting as well as the twin theme of memory and atonement with the concomitant inability (or unwillingness) to remember and to repent are among the besetting concerns of both *The Indelible Seal* and its successor, *The Quest*.

But even though there is a degree of continuity in style and substance between the earlier and the later work, there can be no doubt that *The Indelible Seal* marks a radical departure from what preceded it. The first two novels were written for a sophisticated book-buying public, while the dedication of the third one reads "Commystis committo," implying an esoteric selectiveness to which the other two could lay no claim.

Published in 1946, after nine years of labor, the book was greeted by a storm of applause mixed with a strong dose of abuse. Negative opinion ranged from boredom and puzzlement over the absence of a conventional narrative cohesiveness to indignation because of the peculiarly concrete disgust with which Langgässer tends to treat various forms of depravity. She has been called "Sancta Pornographia," and her theological soundness seemed so questionable to the Catholic Church that her book came close to being put on the Index. At the same time, Hermann Broch, who was deeply moved by it, wrote that it could give an understanding "of the metaphysical background of the present-day world crisis" (*Letters,* p. 153), and called it the first surrealistic novel to deserve that name.[2] Critics like Heinz Politzer have not hesitated to link its hero with those of Kafka's works, Proust's Swann, Joyce's Bloom.[3] There are many who would agree that Elisabeth Langgässer has created one of the genuinely great modern novels or non-novels. But her reputation is not settled, and to many others the book seems *in toto* or in part a bag of unfair tricks.

The central character is a baptized German Jew with a French surname, Lazarus Belfontaine. The main line of the action, which takes place in Germany and France, concerns his various encounters with the Devil and satanic agents and, on the other hand, his search for divine grace. At the beginning of the first part we find him living with his wife and little daughter in domestic comfort and financial security in a small Rhenish town. Yet a general sense of malaise pervades even the first pages. There is a negative force at work, expressed in a peculiar sluggishness that affects most of what takes place. In human beings this takes the form of the sin of sloth, in nature it is represented by stagnant water. Very early in the narrative Belfontaine's little daughter exclaims: "Ich habe keine Lust mehr!" ("I don't feel like going on!"). The context is innocent enough: it is a child's plaintive refusal to continue with her knitting lesson. But her father knows that it is his own unregenerate nature that responds wholeheartedly to this invocation of emptiness (p. 13). "Ich habe keine Lust mehr" becomes a leitmotif in an atmosphere of men and women drifting to perdition.

Yet there is a counterforce. Belfontaine is a Christian, who has been wearing the "indelible seal" of his baptism for the past seven years. Although his conversion did not come from conviction but was the result of a desire to marry a Catholic girl—his present wife, whom he will soon abandon—the force of baptism is nevertheless at work in him and has put him into a position in which he is capable of turning either to God or to Satan but cannot remain neutral in the long run. Intermittently he longs for faith: he anxiously expects the arrival of a blind beggar whom he associates with his baptismal anniversary and who represents blind faith to him, and he jealously attempts to gain the attention and friendship of the priest who baptized him. The dull, nagging consciousness of his Christianity makes him ready to change and leave—a stance that he shares with the other pilgrims and converts who dominate in Elisabeth Langgässer's fiction.

Throughout the first part of the novel, Belfontaine seems to meander rather aimlessly through his life, numbly aware of his soul but largely governed by the sheer inertness of matter and the satanic forces connected with material things. His movements are for the most part unmotivated by ordinary standards, and there is a lack of logical coherence in the sequence of events. Belfontaine turns to pursuing the Devil in the guise of a wine merchant with the same dogged persistence with which he pursued the representative of God, and when he finally does have a chance to speak to the priest, he rebuffs him with a denial of faith, although this is not a correct expression of his beliefs.

On one level the events are presented with cold detachment and as an incoherent jumble. The minor characters—there are a great many of them—are drawn with precision and seem to come to life as in a conventional well-written novel, but they act like strange natives performing rituals of obscure significance. The author's detached manner includes her hero, whom she pointedly and consistently calls "Herr Belfontaine," as if he were somewhat of a stranger or as if she knew him only socially. At the same time, starkly realistic descriptions of human behavior at its least appetizing are embedded in a web of crisscross references to mythology and hagiography, so that each character and event acquires another dimension and an archetypal significance. For example, the food for a gourmet club is cooked in a downstairs kitchen that has certain features of the underworld. The clinical detachment of the scientist observing mad animals in a laboratory[4] is tightly interwoven with a poetic level of discourse, expressive of symbolic, metaphoric, associative meaning. In the case at hand, it is this level that allows us to recognize the sin of gluttony in the eaters' ruthless pursuit of pleasure. Finally there is a third level of discourse, that of a running moral and theological commentary. The following quotation forms a climax to several pages of detailed, sensuous description of food and men struggling to gain enjoyment from eating. Now they are shown in monstrous isolation:

These people: were they newly fallen or had they been damned already? Their silence—a type of stillness that consisted of their inability to have any feeling or emotional perception of one another, so that they seemed to be incapable of either love or hatred: their silence lent support to the frightening view that here was neither limbo nor Orcus but simply the table of the damned [pp. 72–73].

To the reader of modern literature such a running commentary will seem strange and perhaps unacceptable. The reader of medieval literature will be familiar with it and will not be surprised to find some of the most powerful writing in the novel contained in such explicit interpretation. In any case, it is an integral part of Elisabeth Langgässer's style and certainly a significant aspect of her experimentation with the novel as a form. At worst it may be seen as an experiment that fails; but it must not be confused with an inability to express meaning in realistic or symbolic terms. There is more than ample evidence that the author is quite competent to do both.

Belfontaine partakes of the feast only to the extent of eating an omelet, because it is Friday and he is abstaining. This is a good minor example of the manner in which he is and is not part of the circle of sinners. He leaves early to find his priest; for, like a baroque stage, the scene on earth borders not only on hell (the kitchen) but also on heaven. A Wandering Jew, seeking redemption but incapable of turning fully towards God of his own volition, in need of divine help and only partially aware of his need, Belfontaine walks through the sins and amusements of his contemporaries, sharing and rejecting them in turn, restless and on the verge of departure. Till the end of Part I it is uncertain which way he will turn. The time is the summer of 1914. Like Europe, Belfontaine stands at a crossroads. The ignorant, semivicious half-blindness with which he finally allows the Devil to abduct him, points beyond the fictional character to an historical moment.

In several statements, Elisabeth Langgässer has made it quite clear that there is only one type of plot which ultimately makes sense, and that is the plot of the "Heilsgeschichte," the story of salvation; and only one type of conflict worth taking seriously, namely the struggle between God and Satan. But Satan has such an iron grip on the world that God can win only through direct intervention, which is always undeserved and unexpected.

What is unexpected and unannounced cannot accurately be described in terms of the conventional chronology of a man's life. Spiritual progress is marked by leaps and bounds, backslidings and terrible falls, for the simple reason that Satan is always present and man has nothing to contribute to the advent of grace except his readiness to receive it when it should come. It would seem that Langgässer has tried to give literary shape to this state of affairs in the structure of her book. In other words, this structure is neither arbitrary nor a loose bundle of symbols that could be tied together in any other way as well. Rather, there is a purposeful surface of meaninglessness on a realistic and even a psychological level to show up the actual inexplicability of human events in terms of mere reason. But, seen another way, "sub specie aeternitatis," as world theater, the same events reveal a hidden meaning, analogous to the mysterious plan of the world.

For example, a clear misunderstanding on the surface may reveal a profound understanding below the surface. Thus, the child Elfriede is puzzled by the word "providence," and through a series of faulty associations comes to connect it with a lottery ticket which her father has bought and hidden in a glass ball, a pervasive symbol of nothingness. However, by confusing fortune and providence, Elfriede has touched on a real problem, and ultimately it turns out that she was unwittingly right, for the lottery ticket comes to play a certain role in her father's departure and ultimate salvation. Another example: the priest Mathias mistakes an enormous display of fireworks for part of an enemy attack. His terror is quite ludicrous for the present, but a few months later his vision of an impending holocaust will turn out to have been correct.

For the same reason, the various parts of the novel mirror one another, and the story of one character can be made to substitute for that of another. This happens most notably in Part II, which seems to present us with an entirely new novel. It takes place in a small French town and deals for the most part with the story of Hortense de Chamant, a woman of about thirty whom her fiancé left years ago to enter the priesthood and become a missionary. Hortense seduces a young girl, Suzette, the daughter of a neighbor. Suzette's father arranges for an elaborate and sadistic revenge which finally drives Hortense to despair and suicide. Throughout this section of about 170 pages, not one of the characters has any connection with any character of the first part.

In Part III Belfontaine has reappeared and has married Suzette with whom he lives in bigamy. Gradually the complementary nature of the French and the German sections reveals itself, though the link is never of an obvious, realistic kind. To take a striking example: Lucien, the missionary who was Hortense's beloved and the cause of her life's disappointment, returns, himself a worn, disappointed, and dying man. In his last prayer he asks God to create another blind beggar to take the place of one who has died and who was the incarnation of blind faith. This prayer is answered, and it is Lazarus Belfontaine who is chosen to be this person. Thus, the man who was the indirect cause of the corruption of Belfontaine's second wife is also the instrument of Belfontaine's own salvation. The last pages of the book, where Lazarus has actually become the beggar, tie in with the first ones, where he frantically searched for one like him. The story has come full circle, through the convolutions of an apparently incoherent plot.

The Lazarus who finally meets grace lives in a petrified hothouse world. It is the time between the two wars. He does not think of his past and lives without memory and without his previous sense of guilt and urgency in a perpetual aestheticized present. He plants cacti, writes elaborate sonnets, eats in isolation, and makes love with detached refinement. He is spiritually dead, Lazarus in the tomb. In a revealing letter Elisabeth Langgässer once described her own horror of the aesthetic temptation. There she speaks of her recurrent "terrible fear" (*"entsetzliche Furcht"*) that she might be tempted to put art above life and desire to become "blessed" through the artistic form and the aesthetic ecstasy—instead of, conversely, to derive the aesthetic form from the (Christian) substance (*Letters*, p. 200).

The conversion scene is a piece of extremely ambitious writing, giving, on the one hand, a very precise account of a thunderstorm and the physical sensations of the person who finds himself caught up in it, coupled, on the other hand, with a description of the sensation of grace descending on the sinner. The same vehemence and directness informs the telling of both aspects of the event, and the result is a curious, intense fusion of the abstract and the concrete, of a physical and a spiritual occurrence.

Lazarus has taken shelter in his hothouse, and there, in the stillness at the center of the storm, he finds his former self again and becomes receptive to a voice that calls him to come forth from his grave. Leaving behind his cacti, symbols of stunted growth, he obeys and steps into a new life.

Thereafter he fades from view. He becomes a legendary figure, a Christian Jew who survives the concentration camps, who is seen by many yet defies description, because he looks like everyone and is yet unmistakably himself. The news about him is always second- and third-hand, he has become a figure of hearsay. This ending implies, among other things, an attempt to interpret the fate of European Jewry in mystical terms.

It is probably not too much to say that the book stands and falls by the success or failure of such scenes as the conversion passage. The author's achievement lies to a large extent in her ability to present the experience of faith with the same intensity and almost violent straightforwardness with which she presents the experience of sin. The very essence of Elisabeth Langgässer's later work consists of this mixture of sensuality and spirituality, embedded in a dense symbolic context.[5] The transformation of Herr Belfontaine into Lazarus the beggar is a superb example of such writing.

Her next and last book, *The Quest* (*Märkische Argonautenfahrt*),[6] moves even further away from the traditional novel. It was finished only four weeks before the author's death at the age of 50, and was published posthumously in 1950. Portions of it seem hastily written and might have been revised had she lived. Critics have been quick to point out these flaws, and the book has received less attention than *The Indelible Seal*. Yet its achievement is far greater than its blemishes. In some ways it is an even more interesting book than its predecessor, for it attempts to strip the Christian experience down to its core, omitting as many inconsequential or mere accidental elements as possible.

In a letter to her daughter, Langgässer wrote about *The Quest*: "This novel is an attempt to give shape to the various German heresies, to present the typically *German* sins in their various destinations—on trial, as a call to repentance and as purification" (*Letters*, p. 184). The framework is provided by the journey of seven pilgrims to a convent near Berlin. They meet by a providential accident as they set out from the city. It is 1945; the war has ended. All of them are burdened by their memories, which are archetypal as well as individual. The title itself indicates the fusion of the present with the mythological past: "Prussian journey of the Argonauts" (the adjective *märkisch* refers to Mark Brandenburg). Each of them has had his or her own experience of the underworld, and each experience merges at one point with that of the others and with ancient myth and Christian legend.

Their journey is from one city to another, from one spiritual abode to its opposite. The city from which they come is the city of death, and this includes not only their memories but the actual city of Berlin. Its bombed-out façades are a backdrop for the underworld:

Tartarus had come to the surface, the realm of the underworld had become visible, with its roads and its minerals: rusty shells, tin cans, duds, all sorts of iron pieces with jagged forms; and between them, mouldy and shining, stood the sweetish water of Lethe which filled the craters [pp. 126–127].

As Berlin is a terrestrial representation of hell, so Anastasiendorf, the convent, is a terrestrial representation of the heavenly city. But the journey to God is not a scheduled trip with set arrival and departure times. Although they travel together, the path of self-recognition that leads to grace is different for each pilgrim, and the same is true of their ultimate destination. The only one of the argonauts who has had a vision of the Heavenly Jerusalem and thinks he knows his direction does not arrive at all but dies on the way; while the only other traveler who came reluctantly and without faith is destined to stay permanently. The others return to the world, to the in-between cities, after a brief and inconclusive visit.

The bulk of the novel takes place on the road and consists of memories, highly charged conversations, and a host of episodes which symbolically and directly illuminate the central problem of sin and redemption. To understand the structure of the book, it may be permissible to return for a moment to a passage in *The Indelible Seal,* where the author seems to indicate something about her narrative technique. At the beginning of Part II, two German officers climb a church tower. One of them remains on a lower level to inspect a Spanish manuscript from the local library, while the other one climbs higher and is shown the view by the sexton, who also supplies him with a brief history of the surrounding countryside. The manuscript proves to be difficult, not only because of the foreign language, but also because of its many cross-references and marginalia. It contains a vision of history, which the one officer reads, while on the upper level the other officer listens to and views a piece of that history. With each paragraph the reader has to shift from one to the other of these interlocked "levels." [7]

In *The Quest* another metaphor has been added for this type of narration, i.e., for the narrow intertwining of vision and actuality. It is the image of the palimpsest. With this suggestion of two texts upon the same sheet of paper, Langgässer intersperses a number of bracketed passages within the main text. For example, a conversation of the argonauts receives a bracketed comment through a conversation that takes place in Anastasiendorf. Sometimes a voice from the underworld of memory is thus bracketed, sometimes simply the observations of one of the pilgrims on some of the others. Elisabeth Langgässer often expressed her admiration of Claudel, particularly for his *Le Soulier de satin,* because of what she called its cosmic, three-dimensional effect (*Letters,* p. 154). In *The Quest* such an effect has certainly been achieved.

The mythological background of each character contributes,

of course, to this effect. None of them is wholly identified with
one mythological counterpart. Features of both Eurydice and
Proserpine attach to a young girl who has been a political
prisoner in a concentration camp. (The author could—and did
—apply to her oldest daughter for details.) Another one of
the pilgrims, the young wife of a missing composer, also has
some traits of Eurydice and is, moreover, in constant danger
of becoming Medea. The man who saves her, an actor who
knows a great deal about the interchangeability of masks, is
at times a Hermes figure, substituting for Orpheus, and so on.
These shifts are indicative of the transitoriness of the individual inhabiting the mask and, concurrently, of the fact that
the wearers are not slaves but pilgrims on their way to becoming Christians. This point is made very clear in the figure
of an older Jewish woman, who is Rachel mourning for her
children, but also Flora, a goddess of vegetation, and who, as
a converted Christian, is free to praise the creator in His creation, without ceasing to weep for her losses. This woman embodies a central Christian paradox, rejoicing and lamenting at
once, bound by her past, yet free to be redeemed. As early
as 1935, Langgässer had written: "The Christian church is
the legitimate heiress of the ancient world. She is the baptismal
fount of nature" (*Letters,* p. 64). Here the church redeems
the argo, the eternal quest that goes by a pagan, a classical
name, and which can redeem each of the voyagers in his turn.

For a large part of the way, the pilgrims are accompanied
by two somewhat ridiculous nuns, a very tall one and a very
short one, whom they nickname Pat and Patachon, two slap-
stick comedians of the silent movies. These nuns like to lecture
the argonauts on points of dogma, although both of them are
far less subtle and imaginative than any of the other travelers.
At the very end of the work we learn that their real names are
Dolores and Perpetua, and that they were, thus, comic representations of the external grief that is the fitting accompani-
ment of every quest.

In cases such as these, symbolism becomes simplified to the
point of allegory. Similarly, there are extensive conversations

in the book that deal with points of history and theology and have virtually no metaphoric or any other literary embellishment. Yet contemporary literature has certainly seen enough experimental fiction to be tolerant of the proposal that allegory should be considered a reasonable device in a Christian novel and that burning issues are sometimes most effectively treated when tackled directly.

Time will tell whether Elisabeth Langgässer has created a new kind of religious novel, one that can deal with mystic experience, accommodate theological problems in an intellectual way, and at the same time dispense with the conventional framework of story and character. But it is very unlikely that such a work as hers can sustain interest without at least a slight amount of sympathy with the Christian viewpoint on the part of the reader. These novels will almost certainly fail if they are seen as avant-gardistic literature pure and simple. If their Christianity is meaningless, their technical competence will not save them. For Elisabeth Langgässer's surrealism is rather like the glass bead of Friedrich am Ende, the fallen angel among the argonauts: it is a toy that could have been a symbol of the total void, if it had not originally been part of a rosary and hence rolled back to the cross from which it came.

Notes

1. Citations from Elisabeth Langgässer's works in my text are to *Gesammelte Werke*, 5 volumes (Hamburg, 1950). The letters are cited after . . . *soviel berauschende Vergänglichkeit. Briefe 1926–1950* (Hamburg: Claassen, 1954) —hereafter cited as *Letters*. All translations are my own.
2. Broch, " 'The Indelible Seal': A German Novel of the Pilgrimage of Faith," *Commentary*, X, 2 (August 1950), 170–174.
3. *"The Indelible Seal* of Elisabeth Langgässer," *Germanic Review*, XXVII, 3 (October, 1952), 200–209.
4. Bernhard Blume, "Kreatur und Element. Zur Metaphorik in Elisabeth Langgässers Roman *Das unauslöschliche Siegel"* (*Euphorion*, XLVIII [1954], 71–89), points out the extent to which animal imagery is applied to unredeemed human beings.
5. Readers interested in a detailed study of Langgässer's symbolism are referred

to Eva Augsberger, *Elisabeth Langgässer. Assoziative Reihung, Leitmotiv und Symbol in ihren Prosawerken* (Nuremberg: Carl, 1962).

6. Translated by Jane Bannard Greene (New York: Knopf, 1953).

7. For an extensive discussion of the content and source of the "tower chapter" see Anthony W. Riley, "Elisabeth Langgässer and Juan Donoso Cortés: A Source of the 'Turm-Kapitel' in *Das unauslöschliche Siegel*," *PMLA*, LXXXIII, 2 (May 1968), 357–367.

The Moral Structure of Carmen Laforet's Novels

PIERRE L. ULLMAN · *University of Wisconsin–Milwaukee*

IN THE YEAR 1944 SPAIN had hardly begun to recover from her catastrophic civil war. The conflict for which she was a proving ground had spread to neighboring lands, thence to the rest of the world, and she feared that the conflagration might pass through her again. The Spanish people were still hungry, their cities still in ruins, and their neighbors too pre-occupied with domestic struggles to give much thought to the other side of the Pyrenees. Any extraneous prosperity that might be used to Spain's benefit was thus nowhere in sight. As for her cultural life, it was not much richer than after the Napoleonic invasion. The foremost intellectuals either were dead or had emigrated; a great generation of writers had disappeared and no one seemed qualified to take their place.

Under these inauspicious circumstances a long time had to elapse before a literary regeneration could even begin. Very little that might be called "new" was happening. Spaniards were bent on rediscovering their past—to see what went wrong —by rereading Galdós, the nineteenth-century giant whom the early twentieth century had attempted to bury. To be sure, there was a new writer of promise, Camilo José Cela, who had just published his first work, a picaresque novel, thus reviving a genre born of a previous era of decay and orthodoxy. But more was needed to uncover latent talent.

Fortunately, Spain's first literary prize since the civil war was created—the Eugenio Nadal award. Soon a jury busied itself in culling a multitude of manuscripts, and not long thereafter the public was astounded by news that the award would go to an unknown young woman of twenty-two, and that the title of the novel was *Nada* (*Nothing*).

Nada is a slice-of-life novel about an eighteen-year-old girl who arrives in Barcelona from the provinces soon after the civil war, in order to stay at her grandmother's while going to the university. Andrea walks into a decaying, squalid household inhabited by a hungry, demoralized, and deranged family consisting of the grandmother, two uncles, the wife and child of one of them, a spinster aunt, an old servant, a dog, and a cat. Andrea's only relief from her nightmarish home life is the company of fellow-students, especially Enea, whose parents help the protagonist escape her lugubrious environment in order to pursue a new career in Madrid. The reader perceives, however, that Enea's affection is not totally disinterested. While befriending Andrea, she gains entrée to the dismal household to settle some old accounts with one of the uncles, Román, who years before had broken the heart of Enea's mother. Román eventually commits suicide; Enea thus fulfills her thirst for revenge and, through her betrayal of Román, asserts her seductive powers.

Some critics, notably Juan Luis Alborg, now claim that if the book had been published a few years later it would hardly have attracted any attention, because many like it have been written since. This is probably an unfair judgment. There is an intensity of atmosphere and precision of structure, in combination with a narrative matter-of-factness, which gives this novel its peculiar vibrancy. Insanity, morbidity, crime seem to be taken for granted throughout, but—and this is highly significant—without cosmological pessimism. Insights into the recesses of the mind are described as crudely as the decay surrounding the characters. In no other novel that I know of do the characters seem to be, spiritually, so much a part of the furniture. Perhaps this is because the author considers material possessions in the traditional Spanish baroque manner as ornaments of life. If human beings allow themselves to decompose spiritually along with material decay, then they give the impression of being appendages to the objects around them. Loss of spiritual values becomes more evident in such an ambience. In *Nada* even acts of kindness, like the well-to-do Enea's befriending the heroine, seem motivated by selfishness or, like the grandmother's gifts of stale bread, by animal instincts of maternal sacrifice. D. W. Foster, in a recent essay, has put forward the theory that *Nada* is, strictly speaking, a romance rather than a novel, and has thereby vindicated the excellence of its structure, which had been criticized by Carmen Laforet's detractors. Another factor can likewise be summoned to the defense of *Nada*'s structure: the highly important themes of hunger and ingratiation can be considered as structural determinants of the novel. This seems to have been overlooked even by such apologists as Foster and Eoff, which all shows perhaps how unnoticed—and thereby successful—the author's capacity is, subtly to make us take for granted the more dismal aspect of the book's ambience.

In a very broad sense, *Nada* could be called a Catholic novel. For one thing, certain notes and themes indicate the author's unconscious acceptance of her traditional education. Furthermore, the implied portrayal discussed above, of flesh-and-blood characters as adjuncts to broken objects, reminds the reader of Spanish Catholic emphasis on the analogical, metaphorical concept of idolatry; in this sense idolatry is subservience to any vice: worship of Venus, of Bacchus, and so forth. Perhaps more important is the fact that the author's outlook as revealed by this work is far from pessimistic, despite its dreary ambience. Tragic existence is not inescapable, even in the post-bellum period. To be sure, readers are free to seek a symbol of Spain itself in the family situation of *Nada,* in which two brothers who have been on opposite sides during the civil war now reside together uneasily in a shattered household. At the end Andrea departs from this house, but the house remains in spiritual and physical disarray. We are reminded here of what Sherman Eoff writes about Spain's great nine-teenth-century woman—and Catholic—writer, the Countess of Pardo Bazán: "The great God Unconscious which, as both will and idea, flows through the very veins of Zola's characters is personalized by Pardo Bazán and placed outside her own intellectual home." [1] The situation in *Nada* would have to be seen, for analogical purposes, as the other side of the coin.

Sherman Eoff, interestingly enough, has also written about *Nada*. He points out that as the protagonist plunges into pessimism the author progressively presents a mechanistic view of the universe—since *Nada* is pseudoautobiographical, the author may put before us an identification of mechanistic views with pessimism without necessarily asserting a phi-losophy of her own—but abandons this presentation when the protagonist leaves despair behind. As an illustration, Eoff quotes a pasage from the novel which brings to mind Saint Thomas' opinion concerning the powers of the stars over us: ". . . these luminous impalpable threads which come from the sidereal world worked on me with powers impossible to determine, though real." Philosophically significant statements are thus subject to the vicissitudes of the pseudoautobiogra-pher's fortunes. What, then, is Miss Laforet's own philosophy? —"Nada"? Perhaps the question should be approached dif-ferently, with the plot in mind rather than the heroine's thoughts, since action induces moral conceptions in the case of this novel. The heroine does escape a house of despair. Hence, she has been able to overcome the power of the stars, through the exercise of her free will. An observation of D. W. Foster's is also to the point, that Andrea begins to dominate the situation precisely upon perceiving the ineluctable inter-penetrability of the two worlds in which she exists: that of her decadent household on the one hand, and student life on the other. It is her acknowledgment of this situation which results eventually in the escape from a home that is moral decay incarnate.

Any conclusions we may draw from the above evidence could also be deduced partially from what Miss Laforet her-self writes about *Nada* thirteen years after its publication:

Andrea, the protagonist of this novel, seeks, among a few human beings in the atmosphere of a way of life convulsed by circumstances, something that her upbringing has given her the right to expect. She searches for truth in convictions, purity in life, and solid ideals to give her a solution to the meaning of existence. With open eyes and curiosity, but not bitterness, Andrea makes her way through the story. She leaves it empty-handed, having found nothing, . . . and moreover—I would point out—without despair! [2]

Consequently, despite its title, the work is not nihilistic. When the older, vitiated generation is left behind, the new generation is given a chance to begin anew. Since the protagonist has friends who help her escape from this decadent milieu, whatever hope there is comes from outside; it cannot arise directly from the protagonist's immediate environment.

Hope through the possibility of escape is likewise present in Miss Laforet's second novel. *La isla y los demonios* takes place on the Canary Islands during the civil war. Martha, the sixteen-year-old protagonist, is heiress to an estate owned by her insane mother, Teresa, who is confined to one room of the family's country villa. The estate is administered by José, Martha's older half-brother. The brother's wife, Pino, as well as an aunt, an uncle, and the latter's wife, live at the expense of Teresa's fortune. At the book's conclusion Martha is allowed to leave this morally unhealthy atmosphere, and it is assumed that José will gain increasing control over her heritage. Though some critics have found little difference in outlook between *La isla* and *Nada,* there is evidence, if we seek it, for the hypothesis that the author is moving toward a Catholic stance. As we have seen, Carmen Laforet states that Andrea steps out of *Nada* without despair. But lack of despair is not an affirmation; it indicates a philosophical vacuum. In *La isla y los demonios* this void is filled with hope. The presence of hope, however, is offset by another factor. Martha gets much less help from the outside than Andrea did. But, to balance this, the outside is less hostile than in *Nada.* Perhaps we should account for the latter by the difference between dismal post-bellum Barcelona and the Canary Islands. For example, Martha's first courtship takes place mostly on the beach, a beautiful setting for amorous trysts; so that, despite the mercenary motives of the boy, who seems to be mainly a dowry-hound, the scene is not repugnant. In *Nada,* on the other hand, a corresponding courtship scene, in which a fellow named Gerardo escorts Andrea through the old quarter of Barcelona, is meant to give an impression of disgust.

Moreover, unlike Andrea, Martha is not limited by the search for bare necessities. Consequently, her independence and youthful rebelliousness are more obvious, even though in *La isla* the need to revolt against the degenerate, corrupt atmosphere of an egotistic adult world is not necessarily more urgent than in *Nada.* The teenage protagonist must find herself, seek wisdom almost unguided, because the adults around her are fools. It goes without saying that their recent civil war attests their inadequacy, as a group, to cope with life. They cannot provide models. It could even be said that what puts into relief the fortitude of teenagers is the inanity, selfishness, and sadism of their elders. Martha can withstand buffeting from the adult world by relying on her inner strength and sense of good, despite—or perhaps thanks to—her heedlessness of gossip (not unlike Andrea's absentmindedness). She has her faults, of course, but Martha's basic goodness, her idealism, her superiority of character over the elders stand forth even at a moment of transgression. Her major fault is an unawareness of the hurt she can inflict on others. As José Luis Cano notes, Martha is all intuition, like adolescence itself. Hence the fault is pardonable, especially since the adults of *La isla,* unlike those in *Nada,* are not in a desperate situation. They are much more resilient, and thereby less justified in their bad behavior.

The obvious similarities between *La isla* and *Nada* have led one critic, Joaquín de Entrambasaguas, to classify Carmen Laforet's obnoxious adult characters into certain types. Others have asserted that, considering the similarities, Carmen Laforet improved on her basic material when she set about composing the second novel. Yet some of its qualities are offset by a few rather commonplace passages (e.g., p. 465). Moreover, though *La isla* contains more detached allegorical elements, such as the Jericho theme (p. 430), as a whole it does not possess the allegorical suggestiveness of *Nada*. Nevertheless, the author has begun to explore the possibilities of religious allegory.

The pagan demons of Canary folklore bear no direct relation to the Satan of Christianity, but they do hold a religiously symbolic meaning. Perhaps Miss Laforet's fascination with the symbolism inherent in this pagan lore marks the beginning of a process which culminates in her markedly affectionate understanding of Christian symbolism a few years later. It may have been an aspect in the renewal of the author's religious faith. This could possibly be what one critic, Fernández Figueroa, sensed when he stated that *La isla y los demonios* teaches without being didactic.

Hence we are unavoidably brought to the problem of morality. In *La isla,* Martha's innocent flirtation with a boy her own age, whose interest appears motivated by the girl's inheritance, brings on excessive punishment by José (who is himself envious of Martha's fortune). But the heroine sanely perceives that any feeling of guilt that the half-brother might attempt to implant in her would not be related to morals but to reputation. We should note parenthetically that the same theme of wrongfully tarnished reputation reappears in Carmen Laforet's latest novel, *La insolación,* whose hero, however, is a boy badly beaten and then disinherited by his father, under the false impression that the boy has had homosexual relations. Miss Laforet has thus undertaken to deal with a topic very dear to Spanish writers of all epochs, the theme of honor. Its manifestations in present-day Spain are reduced, in the case of girls, to vestigial adherence to the Moorish past, and, in the case of boys, to an abhorrence of this past. The author thus indicates, intentionally or not, a certain feeling that excessive concern with honor can disrupt family harmony. External pressures on the individual from an honor-directed society provoke internal quarrels that shatter family structure. Let us not forget that *La insolación* was written after the

author's "conversion," whereas *La isla* came out before this
critical moment of her life. And for a Catholic like Miss
Laforet the family is fundamental (shortly after the publication of *Nada* the author married Don Manuel Cerezales, and
by the time *La isla* appeared she had given birth to their fourth
child), so that her Catholicism turns the author against the
traditional Moorish mentality as well as its counterpart, the
fanatical reaction to things Arabic, both of which have passed
for Christian orthodoxy much too long.

In *La isla y los demonios* Martha shrugs off guilt feelings
because she knows she has done nothing wrong. Chastisement
upon guiltlessness results in loss of faith. She turns to fatalism
and superstitiously regards impending doom as Fortune's com-
pensation for moments of happiness (p. 548). This theme is
also found in *Nada,* but the cosmic forces of the earlier novel
are now the demons of pagan island folklore. Hence, in *La
isla,* fatalism is treated as a thoroughly popular attitude.
Martha will cast it off as she grows up. We must conclude,
then, that Miss Laforet associates this type of popular tradition with immaturity. At the end of the novel Martha realizes that legends about demons of the Canaries' pagan folklore should be viewed only as childhood memories. The real
demons are everywhere and penetrate the hearts of all men
(pp. 634–635). This enlightenment displaces the heroine's
obsession with the fatalistic notion that her mother's death
occurred to prevent her, Martha, from leaving the island (p.
562). Significantly, the enlightenment is precipitated by a
secret rejection of inane adult attitudes. When everyone around
her believes that Martha mourns for her mother, the girl is
really grieving over the loss of her own spiritual innocence
(p. 625).

The truth is that lamenting for Teresa, her mother, would
be merely an adult ritual. Real grief had occurred long before,
when the mother became catatonic as a result of an automobile
accident. Martha's secret is simply beyond the understanding
of the adults around her. The death of Teresa's living ghost
is but a motive for the recall of pleasant memories, memories
which help Martha recuperate an empathy for her fellow

human beings that seemed to have faded when adult hostility
forced her to retreat into her own mind. Remembrance of the
mother, in association with prayer, is fundamental:

After this childish prayer [Martha] closed her eyes, and then she was
truly able to see Teresa. She could also see herself, at the head of the
stairs, in pyjamas and barefoot, very young, perhaps not over four years
old. There were guests that night; so they had put her to bed early.
But as usual she had sneaked out of her room and tiptoed over to the
staircase, driven by curiosity, even in the knowledge that her father would
thrash her ruthlessly if he found out. The grown-up scene downstairs
proved too fascinating.

They were all laughing, especially Teresa in that peculiarly pleasant
and contagious way of hers. Now Martha could hear her still, after so
many years. She looked beautiful in low-cut gown and pearl collar. The
child saw her raise her wine glass and suddenly realized that on doing so
her mother caught sight of her. It was a wondrous instant: the mother re-
fraining from the slightest gesture that might betray the child's presence,
but sending her a tender smiling look, as though a kiss from her eyes.
And Martha had been filled with the first intensely sweet emotion she
could remember; her mother was thus a friend, an accomplice, against
the father and everyone else. . . . Her mother, she now perceived, far
from preventing the realization of Martha's wishes, would have come
to her aid.

Martha's mind was now overcome by tenderness, and, with closed
eyes, she began to weep. The dead, in truth, abandon us much less often
than the living, for they are wont to approach us so that we may speak to
them from the heart [p. 571].

Man, finding no succor around him, has the capacity to fathom
his memory for comfort and strength.

This habit of searching our own souls for love when neighbors fail us may lead to love of God. Likewise, Carmen
Laforet's interest in her characters' lonesome soul-searching
may have prompted a disposition for religious motifs later
in her career. It is noteworthy that social conflicts have not
been beheld by her as such; in her works class hatred is viewed
as a moral problem. Vicenta, the old housekeeper of the
Camino family, "abominated her husband, more than anyone
in the world, even more than the rich who own wells and keep

them for themselves, their goats and their camels, while people are dying of thirst" (p. 575). If greed is the vice of the rich, envy is that of the poor. Later, Vicenta manages to rise in station by marrying off her daughter into a relatively prosperous family. "When she brought about that marriage, the housekeeper learned about envy, the envy hidden within those humble dwellings and glaring in a hundred eyes."

To Martha, then, the author apportions solace issuing from the departed; in Vicenta's case social tensions are traditionally viewed in terms of sin. Carmen Laforet must be moving in a direction of renewed faith, though perhaps absorbing it unconsciously from the culture in which she is immersed. This is already evident in some short stories written between the appearance of *Nada* and *La isla*. Granting that, among them, "El veraneo" and "La foto" remind us of the nineteenth century, of Clarín and Maupassant, it must likewise be recognized that one of the tales, "La muerta," could only have been created after acquaintance with Graham Greene. "La muerta" does not have much scope or momentum, but Miss Laforet can compose something charming and almost profound out of a banal domestic situation. And while we are on the subject of Graham Greene, we might as well allow the almost irrefutable evidence of his influence on Carmen Laforet's longest novel. We can certainly find similarities between *La mujer nueva* and *The End of the Affair* (adultery and repentance in a wartime atmosphere), though the latter novel in a Spanish setting would be unthinkable. The Spanish public would probably find it extremely presumptuous of an adulteress, occupied as she should be in saving her own soul, to attempt the saving of others. Consequently, the author makes certain that the heroine of *La mujer nueva* does not attain sainthood, or even beatitude for that matter. Such an ending would just be too much for a Spanish audience, for we must remind ourselves that ever since the Middle Ages foreign themes and ideas have had to be radically altered for Peninsular adaptation, and the Catholic novel is no exception.

Passing from Carmen Laforet's short stories to her short novels, we may come to decide that the latter constitute, besides *Nada,* the most lasting part of her work. The criteria that might point to such a conclusion should be elucidated at this point. Some critics have felt, not without justification, that the more idealistic the author becomes (as a result of casting out pessimism), the less successful is her portrayal of human ideals, because it is easier to portray human weaknesses. It has also been noted—and of course such an assertion can be considered a corollary of the above—that some of the short novels are too sentimental. This is a moot point; by the same token we could argue that *The End of the Affair* is sentimental; in any case, when such a judgment falls upon a woman writer, it is even harder to refute. Nevertheless, in a good short novel an idealistic protagonist becomes an unforgettable character, simply because in such a genre the author cannot permit himself to dilute the hero's impact on the reader. And it must be admitted that Miss Laforet manages extremely well in this respect: witness Alicia of *Un noviazgo,* Rosa of *El piano,* Luis of *El último verano,* Luisa of *Los emplazados,* Carolina of *La niña*—especially Luis and Rosa. In the lives of her characters, Carmen Laforet can still find hope, even happy endings, by penetrating to charitable fibers through layers of war-grown callousness. This idealistic hope is attained through the triumph of an innocence heedless of post-bellum despair. In *La llamada* we witness a case of dire poverty compounded by illusions of a lost middle-class respectability. In Spain, where shabby genteelness is bolstered by aristocratic pride, this is a pregnant theme. Pride, as we might deduce from this tale, must be cast off before any individual can benefit from Grace. To discard pride is especially painful when you are sliding down the social ladder; if you are a Spaniard it is doubly so. But innocence can still win out and sometimes Grace will inspire our fellow-men to charity if, and in harsh times only if, our need is communicated by a disarming innocence that pierces the armor of their own pride. That much-vaunted Spanish pride—or honor—does have its bad side after all, and by rejecting it we stand a miraculous chance of seeing others cast it off too. The impoverished and visionary protagonist of *La llamada,* Mercedes, who, as the

critic José Luis Cano remarks, may remind us of a Maupassant character, happens to be fully informed at the end of the
novel about the chain of events that led to her stroke of good
fortune. When she gratefully walks into church, she finds her
ingenuous friend Eloísa already offering thanks for what
Eloísa believes to have been a miracle; and the author comments: "If Mercedes had explained it to Doña Eloísa, the old
lady would have assented. . . . Then she would have kept
on thanking God with equal fervor, because Doña Eloísa and
Doña Mercedes had different ideas on what constitutes a miracle; that's all" (p. 680). The real miracle is Mercedes' humble acceptance of reality.

In *El último verano* a mother offers a moment of intense
sympathy to her son Luis, a rebellious, lazy, seemingly un-
grateful boy, thus revealing her deep understanding; later
she is repaid a hundredfold through a generous sacrifice on his
part. But the tale possesses an added dimension, because
generosity likewise shows its unexpected presence in María
Pilar, a working-class girl betrothed to Lucas, Luis' brother.
This is a white-collar family attempting to put on a show of
respectability under extenuating circumstances. A foil is provided by María Pilar's family, who live in a filthy, stinking
hovel, but make more money than and have the greatest contempt for Lucas' relatives. Though hard-headed, they do not
necessarily beget hard-hearted children, however; and in the
end it is the working-class fiancée who exhibits the noble trait
of generosity, in contrast to her middle-class counterpart
Lolita, wife of Roberto, the third brother. María Pilar seems
to belong somehow to the popular Spanish tradition of proud,
ascetic generosity that provides the "cultural plateau" from
which Luis' eminent sacrifice will rise. The beneficiary of María
Pilar's selflessness is the middle-class mother, stricken with an
incurable disease, whose last wish is to pass a summer at a
seaside resort. The mother does not like her future daughter-
in-law. "When Doña Pepita met this María Pilar for the first
time, after Mass, she took an immediate dislike to her. It was
obvious that she wasn't what one would call 'a young lady,'
like Lolita for example" (p. 726). And then the mother has

to suffer in silence various remarks comparing her looks with the girl's. It is not abnormal, of course, for a man to be physically attracted to a woman who looks like his mother, but falling in love is one thing and staying in love another. Every one of Lucas' relatives probably asks himself secretly why love persists between people from such different backgrounds. And now the mother, having been the most adverse of all to this union, is the first to comprehend the reason, which consists in the pervading charity of María Pilar's character. "Tell your fiancée," she says to Lucas, "that she does not resemble me as much as all of you would have it. . . . Tell her that at her age I wouldn't have given all my savings for the summer vacation of a future mother-in-law I'd scarcely met. That's the truth and I've got to admit it. I wouldn't have contributed them" (p. 729). Be it called generosity, liberality, or charity, this is the stuff which Carmen Laforet has used here, as in other works, to join what was asunder.

Her next piece, *Un noviazgo,* depicts an old tycoon who decides to marry his fifty-year-old secretary, who has been loyal to and unconsciously enamored of him for thirty years. But this Spanish heroine has survived on pent-up pride for too long. It comes to the surface at a most decisive moment, and she sacrifices her future happiness, as well as her aged mother's, by haughtily refusing to marry on the tycoon's terms. *Un noviazgo* is the favorite of Juan Luis Alborg. One of Miss Laforet's harshest critics, he deems her male characters unconvincing except for De Arco, the tycoon. But Alborg's opinion is not shared by all his colleagues. Among the author's short novels, *Un noviazgo* seems to have the least ideological content. It may remind us of a nineteenth-century short story, but drawn out and extenuated. It is through this kind of story that, after several decades, the creation of male characters of De Arco's type became accepted. De Arco is a wealthy *macho* with little understanding of women's feelings. Set over against this type is Alicia, the excellently portrayed female protagonist, more interesting because of her complexity, a mélange of devotion, pride, sense of honor,

dreams of glory, and complicated reasoning necessitated by
her rationalizations—in sum, as José Luis Cano puts it, "a
sentimental and grotesque product of [her] society. Now we
pity her, now we are irritated by her stupidity." Alicia's "traditional" Spanish virtues are no match for the insensitive
egotism that unmindfully exploits them. Hatred makes itself
felt at last, the odium of wounded pride.

There is one aspect of the tale that should be brought to
the fore in order the better to evaluate the author's ideas. It
is the wry pathos with which Miss Laforet exposes the exaggerated sense of honor of her somewhat ridiculous heroine.
This is sharply brought out in the last scene:

> "Well then, Mr. De Arco, I have the pleasure to inform you that I
> am turning you down . . . the immense satisfaction to tell you I reject
> you . . . the honor to refuse to be your wife. . . . Do you understand?
> I won't marry you!" Alicia was theatrical, magnificent; oblivious of
> everything else and elated. Her joy was short-lived but splendid. De
> Arco, in spite of his stature, seemed smaller than she, and as if she were
> slapping him.

All this, I might add, goes on with Alicia's old and needy
mother standing by helpless. Only a traditionally oriented
Christian writer can ridicule Spanish honor so mercilessly! In
pointing up its insubstantiality, its vanity, Carmen Laforet
shows herself to be a spiritual heir of Quevedo ("for honor's
sake, without knowing what is a man nor what is pleasure,
the maid spends thirty years married to herself. . . ." ["Vision of Hell"—1608]).

El piano is the most obviously Christian of Miss Laforet's
works before the appearance of *La mujer nueva*. It is a
beautifully written tale of a young woman who comes to feel
that her unconcern for material possessions places her among
the blessed, the poor in spirit. For one thing, she has already
lost out on an inheritance because of sheer disinterestedness.
Rosa is the quintessence of the best in the heroines of *Nada*
and *La isla y los demonios*. All three elude despair, Andrea
by partial oblivion to hunger, Martha by indifference to public

opinion, and Rosa by easy resignation to the loss of her prize possession, a piano. The instrument has given her "class," social status within the tenement block where she lives with her husband and child; her flat soon becomes a gathering place for musically inclined friends; a certain joyful well-being enters into a dull existence. Then one day, because of her husband's illness and ensuing financial straits, the piano must go. Nevertheless, she sells it without a sorrowful heart. The piano is a material possession and she, poor in spirit.

La niña, a tale of adoption, would be merely sentimental were it not for a clever development originated by the author. Here, as in Unamuno's *La tía Tula,* a spinster marries her widowed brother-in-law from a sense of duty to her sister's children. But our author goes further than Unamuno. The aunt's sense of duty, being sincere, is founded on charity, and from the depths of her being will unavoidably reach beyond her sister's family because, from the first, the love she offers is not to her own brood. In spite of her many wards, the aunt one day brings home an orphan, thereby remaining true to a promise made to the child's dying mother. The author has thus taken the best from the Unamunian spirit and brought it into the Catholic ethos.

Los emplazados, an inspiring short novel of compassion, takes place at a time when that virtue is rather scarce—the last Spanish Civil War. There is much extraneous material here, at the beginning and end, forming a sort of elusive frame for the story; and in this frame, moreover, the Devil is introduced as a symbol. Somehow the fanciful structure calls to mind Pedro Salinas' fiction. *Los emplazados* is a love story; it also deals with a capital crime committed under martial law, that of hiding a Republican; but within the tale the crime can be forgiven. All this indicates perhaps a Christian approach to the cleavage in Spanish society, an intuition of reconciliation through charity.

To write an appealing Catholic novel about the Spanish middle class is a laborious enterprise, especially if the protagonist is to be a woman. The unavoidable difficulty was already encountered in the last century by another famous Catholic

novelist, the Countess of Pardo Bazán, who commented on
it. It consists in limitations imposed on the fair sex and lack of
variety among its members in comparison to the rest of Europe.
To be sure, some opportunities did open up to Spanish women
in the twentieth century, and it is significant that the heroine
of the novel in question, *La mujer nueva,* happens to be a
science and mathematics teacher. I say "happens to be"
because herein lies the novel's main flaw, related to what the
Jesuit critic Rafael M.ª de Hornedo sees as inconsistency in
the protagonist's character. Although Fr. Hornedo does not
point specifically to this aspect, it should be noted that the
author failed to take advantage of the excellent opportunity
to portray the professional side of the heroine, to depict her
in scientific cogitation for example. Paulina is treated mainly
qua woman. Her work seems to bear little spiritual relation to
her life, and hence her profession appears merely topical.

Be that as it may, her profession as well as her independence
does make the heroine, in the worldly sense, a new woman.
But the book's title has a deeper meaning; Paulina must become a new woman in the way indicated by the epigraph from
Galatians 6:15: "For neither circumcision counts for anything,
nor uncircumcision, but the new man. . . ." Perhaps Carmen
Laforet insinuates by means of this epigraph that, to be saved,
one must be more than a nominal Catholic. The new prologue
written two years after the novel's first edition corroborates
this assumption: "The human event that inspired the theme of
this novel was my own conversion, in December of 1951, to
the Catholic faith . . . a faith which one might have taken
for granted to be natural in me, since I was baptized at birth;
but that I never bothered about after childhood and whose
practices I had totally abandoned, deeming them outmoded
and meaningless" (p. 1018). The author emphatically adds,
however, that *La mujer nueva* is not autobiographical.

The significance of the title, then, is quite acceptable. On the
other hand, the reader might balk at other connotations. The
heroine's conversion begins with a mystical illumination of
the soul (pp. 1135ff.) and her name is Paulina, which may
lead us to expect an allegory with the life of Saint Paul. Now,

in the saint's life the most moving aspect from a purely human point of view—putting aside for the moment its religious significance—is the theme of the persecutor who suddenly and willingly decides to join the persecuted. The story of Paulina, however, seen in such a light, in no wise resembles that of Paul. On the contrary, Paulina was always to be counted among the persecuted. In fact, at one time, long before her conversion, she was jailed unjustly, and by the Church-sympathizing party at that. After her conversion, on the other hand, the forces of society cause her no trouble. If anything can be considered martyrdom, it occurred before the conversion, so that to establish a parallel with the life of Saint Paul would be utterly false. Any implied allegory must therefore exist solely on the plane of ecclesiastical symbolism, and thus lacks a persuasive human dimension. Unfortunately, the heroine's inappropriate symbolic name is not the only irrelevant note which almost spoils this fine novel. One of these tendentious details is the author's advocacy of the most primitive views on family planning. A neighbor of Paulina's, an overburdened mother to whom the protagonist had ventured to give a bit of advice, retorts, "I don't believe only in what suits me and then stop believing whenever it doesn't, and I'll never avoid having the children God ordains. . . . How did you ever think I could do such a thing!" And the author goes on to note: "Paulina had been stunned, partly with admiration, partly with horror, at the sight of such a bullheaded woman. But suddenly she heard the children cry and realized that Luisa understood the truth. Burdened by her cross, doubtlessly heavy, like so many men and women who knew perfectly well what they were doing" (p. 1262). In another passage, Paulina sees two young women taking a group of children on the train for a weekend vacation in the country; a priest comments that they belong to Catholic Action and goes on to praise their philanthropy (p. 1325). There is also a chapter whose climax consists in the surprising discovery that an order of nuns who run a retreat do not wear religious garb (p. 1154). If all these touches had been inserted matter-of-factly, they would now seem less dated, and the novel less patently tendentious. A dearth of subtlety consequently takes away from the universality of what could have become a minor classic of Christian fiction. Despite its preoccupation with an exclusively Spanish problem, *La mujer nueva* might have attained more than a Spanish audience, for it is not the nature of a problem which gives a work universality, but rather the artistic treatment of the human predicament that the problem creates. After all, our understanding of the artistic treatment of a social issue, if such a treatment possesses ethical, human significance, can transcend societal limits.

In any case, the nature of the problem in *La mujer nueva* must first be explained, and we shall have to begin with a plot summary. Paulina, daughter of a tyrannical and dissolute mining engineer, elopes with a young Loyalist neighbor, Eulogio, after her father is killed by the miners. Eulogio's father, on the other hand, has been shot by the Nationalists. The two young people are married in a civil ceremony near the front where Eulogio fights for the Republican cause. At the war's end he manages to escape abroad, and soon thereafter the Nationalists jail Paulina and her baby. Antonio, a cousin of Eulogio, intervenes with the authorities and she is released. During the difficult post-bellum period, the two inevitably fall in love. After several years Eulogio is amnestied, but upon his return Paulina realizes that her love for him, kindled in wartime frenzy, has not withstood the long separation. At this point her love for Antonio is finally consummated, though the latter is by now married, but to a woman who is about to die of an incurable disease. No divorce is allowed in Spain, to be sure; but the present Nationalist government will recognize a wartime civil marriage performed in the Republican zone only if both parties agree to confirm it. Eulogio, unaware of her love affair, urges his wife to validate the marriage by a church wedding, but Paulina is reluctant. She goes to Madrid to get away from both men, leaving her son in the care of a priest. It is on the train that she experiences a new sensation of bliss. Once in Madrid, she begins to lead an ascetic existence and is almost drawn to the religious life before she realizes that her worldliness stands in the way. Later, on learning that Antonio has become a widower, she is tempted to marry him but understands at last her moral duty to return to her civil-law husband. This ethical decision is in no wise urged on her by the Church, which does not recognize the marriage. What cannot be disregarded, however, is the Church's role in guiding her in a faith by whose sole light she can make a truly ethical decision, a decision necessitating humility and resignation.

La mujer nueva is a well-structured novel. Some of its more beautiful passages delicately allow the reader a glimpse of the processes by which a Christian may acquire wisdom. The influence of Graham Greene's *The End of the Affair* is obvious, but it is felicitous, especially in the treatment of intercessionary prayer. Many unfavorable judgments on *La mujer nueva* should be refuted. Its plot is as subtly woven as *Nada*'s. The Julián Mateos episode, which some critics consider irrelevant, points up the impossibility of keeping two worlds apart and accomplishes their inevitable fusion in the heroine's mind. The moral process is thus similar to *Nada*'s.

Carmen Laforet's latest novel, *La insolación,* is the first of a trilogy whose other two volumes, for unknown reasons, have not been published. Although it cannot be said that *La insolación* displays a particularly Christian tendency, possibly the last book of the trilogy would have offered a solution to the problem of stifled charity in the first.

It is difficult to escape the conclusion that Carmen Laforet has written much more than one piece reflecting her faith. She wrote Catholic literature long before she fully realized that she was a Catholic; and she writes better Catholic novels when she does not attempt to do so. Let us hope to enjoy more works from the pen of Carmen Laforet, who, having found her way anew as a Christian, may ever find it as a writer.

Notes

1. *The Modern Spanish Novel* (New York: New York University Press, 1961), p. 110.
2. All page references to the works of Carmen Laforet are to *Novelas,* Volume I (Barcelona: Planeta, 1957).

Giovanni Papini, or the Probabilities of Christian Egoism

WILLIAM A. SESSIONS · *Georgia State University*

THE NAME OF GIOVANNI PAPINI would seem today to belong to that catalogue of "high camp" compiled by Susan Sontag some years ago. If one adds the fact that Papini is best known for a life of Christ that in the 'twenties and 'thirties enjoyed an international vogue and had the disadvantage of being accepted piety for Catholics and Protestants alike, his relevance to the list zooms astronomically. If, further, the reader of the last third of the twentieth century should view the strange shapes of egoism stamping his work from its agnostic beginnings to the rhapsodies of the mythical Pope Celestine VI and the mystical defenses of the Devil, what else but "camp" of a very special grade could describe this forgotten Italian writer?

Yet in 1904 William James, having just met the twenty-five-year-old Papini, wrote to Schiller at Oxford:

Papini is a jewel. To think of that little Dago putting himself ahead of every one of us at a single stride. And what a writer! and what fecundity! and what courage! and what humor, and what truth.[1]

The next year James wrote an essay "Giovanni Papini and the Pragmatist Movement in Italy" in which he showed him-

self indebted to the young "Dago" for two evidences of his critical acuity, evidences that would recur in almost every line
of Papini's until his death in 1956: the brilliant image and
the insight into the possibilities of transcendence. James, for
example, appreciated Papini's explanation of Pragmatism
"like a corridor in a hotel, from which a hundred doors
open into a hundred chambers." [2] The Italian's "most original contribution to Pragmatism," [3] however, concerned—
typically—the movement of human action into transcendence. Inspired by Papini, James wrote: "man becomes a kind
of God and where are we to draw his limits? . . . The program of a man-God is surely one of the possible type-pro-
grams of philosophy." [4]

Already, therefore, Papini had evinced that power of intellect and personality that would sometimes appear like the
self-glorification of his contemporary D'Annunzio or the more
sinister swagger of Mussolini, with whom he cooperated on
the *Popolo d'Italia* in a campaign for the intervention of
Italy in the First World War. But Papini's mask of egoism—
as self-conscious as the other two—has roots more complex
and more clearly probing into the whole secret of human
action. Like Miss Sontag's Sagrada Familia in Barcelona,
Papini stands bizarre and toweringly alone in an age of com-
puter anonymity; but, similarly, he echoes other possibilities
for human existence in the last part of the twentieth century.

II

Giovanni Papini's greatest literary achievements are his biographies or, more exactly, his critical studies of human actors.
Like his contemporary Pirandello—but with entirely different
results—Papini tends to see all forms of human action
through the mask that the actor wears, or is. The personality is all-important; the achievement is the result of the passion of that personality. "My book," says Papini in his preface to his biography of Michelangelo, ". . . aims to tell
the story of Michelangelo the man, searching into his soul,

his character and his spirit. . . ." [5] His famous study of Dante is called *Dante Vivo* and "is an essay of investigation about the things in Dante which really matter to us today." [6] Similarly he admires Ignatius Loyola because he is a soldier of Christ whose *Spiritual Exercises* "are not meant to be *read* but *done*" [7] and whose genius in constructing the method of the *Exercises* was to give back what Renaissance art had lost: "familiarity by sight, hearing, almost by touch and breathing, with Christ the Son of the Living God." [8] It is Petrarch's personality that makes all his works "an intimate diary for the public, written in ten styles," [9] magnificent in its "sapphire brilliance of the right word inlaid into the right harmonies of rhythm," [10] and dominated by the passion of nostalgia "which gives consistency to Petrarch's mind." [11] Both the fictitious Pope Celestine VI and the real Pope Pius XI offer heroic solutions to their ages, solutions born of their personalities. Finally, at the end, the Devil himself becomes for Papini a passionate hero. It is as though Papini—from the beginning, even though with different terms—saw that human action as opposed to its transcendence is a mask, or that, as he might have said later, all men, even Christ (or especially Christ), in the eyes of God, are performing actors.

As one might expect, Papini's origins are important to the development of this concept of vitalism. Giovanni Papini was born on January 9, 1881, into a lower-middle-class family in Florence. His father was a furniture maker, philosophically a product of nineteenth-century Italy. He was an atheist and a patriot while, in the traditional fashion, his wife was a simple woman, a Catholic devoted to her three children. Papini's origins, then, were somewhat proletarian, but with his marriage in 1907 to Giacinta Giovagnoli, a peasant girl from Bulciano in Tuscany, Papini escapes the social force he most despises in all his work: the commercial middle class. Papini is really unique in stories of conversion in that he continues to attack this class until the very end. Neither Pope Celestine nor Papini's Devil is a product of the genteel middle class of Europe in the early twentieth century or of the technological capitalist class of the mid-century. Papini is,

in many ways, his father's son until the very end of his life
in that the established is no friend of his.

But it is Florence that primarily created the man. The ancient city reminded Papini in all his metamorphoses that human action could transcend the limits of twentieth-century
life. Papini's biographies of Dante and Michelangelo constantly recall the reader to the importance of this "holy"
city where the great egoists of spirit achieve transcendence
through the action of art. His study of Dante, says Papini in
his introduction, is "the book of an artist about an artist, of
a Catholic about a Catholic, of a Florentine about a Florentine." [12] The city taught him from the beginning that the positivism and scientific industrialism of nineteenth-century Europe were not enough. "I knew him when I was still a child,"
writes Papini in the last lines of *Michelangelo,* "walking on
the uneven cobblestones of San Miniato; his David was
among my earliest and most eloquent teachers." [13] But the
transcendental nature of Florence—its part in his redemption
from twentieth-century materialism—is evidenced most force-
fully in the last part of Papini's introduction to his biography
of Christ:

This book is written, if you will pardon the mention, by a Florentine, a
son of the only nation which ever chose Christ for its King. . . . Although changed by Cosimo, this inscription is still there; the decree was
never formally abrogated and denied, and even today after four hundred
years of usurpations, the writer of this book is proud to call himself a
subject and soldier of Christ the King.[14]

But the Florence the young Papini knew had, like Europe,
become, in the fashionable phrase, post-Christian. In his introduction to his study of the African saint, Papini cites two
early discoveries of Augustine. The impression given is somewhat like that of a modern Russian student staring at an icon
in the Hermitage or at the ghostly domes of Saint Basil's in
Red Square. Augustine existed for the young Papini not in
any religious context at all, but in a Botticelli accidentally discovered in the Uffizi and in the glimpses of frescoes at the
top of his school gymnasium, formerly a convent.[15]

It was natural, then, that the period of *Sturm und Drang* so vividly described in his early autobiography *Un Uomo Finito* should follow. Where in modern Europe was a system that could govern life by providing it with a vision large enough or stable enough to allow human action to move into transcendence as it clearly had at one time in Florence? In 1903 the remarkable journal *Leonardo* edited by Papini and Prezzolini had as its prime desire a renewal of modern life, "di rinnovarsi." [16] In the same way the early works, *24 Cervelli, Stroncature,* and *Testimonianze,* probe contemporary and past heroes of the intellect like Croce, Hegel, Bishop Berkeley, Spandini, Walt Whitman, Spencer, and Remy de Gourmont. Papini is never neutral in these studies: the negative is as much a method of finding reality as the positive. Similarly, in his editing of various journals like the futuristic *Lacerba,* his desire for true renewal led to violent attacks by "the wild man," as he was called, and ultimately to a kind of nihilism that coincided with the First World War.

The terrors of the First World War may seem remote to us today, but its devastation of modern Europe and its consequent technological horrors sparked, as much as any one social force, Giovanni Papini's conversion to Christianity as the one teaching left in the modern world capable of giving human action the dimension in which it could truly be itself —that is, in which it could transcend itself. Of course, Papini's conversion was a shock to the Italian intellectual world, as Prezzolini himself has noted.[17] But those who doubted Papini's sincerity did not understand "the will to believe" or the stages of any metamorphosis as well as Papini himself. Writing of Jacopone da Todi, he said: "The old Adam does not die in a single day, especially in those who discover Christ only in maturity";[18] and later of Augustine's conversion: "The soul alters its direction, not its nature." [19]

Immediately, there was no startling change in subject matter. Rather, as Papini might have shown from that Platonism which increasingly served him, he moved up the ladder of ascent. That is, the great individualists—the heroes of his intellect, the egoists of reality like Nietzsche, Swift, and Don

Quixote—become heroes of another type. The heroes of art remained just that, and the heroes of the intellect remained themselves or they became what was for the new Papini a higher reality, heroes of faith. This faith, however, always remained carefully circumscribed by a tough realism, either of the intellect or of the social context. In other words, there were now two great egoists for Papini: the saint and the artist. In his volume of critical studies, *Laborers in the Vineyard,* Papini defines the only true forms of individualism possible for him in the modern world (or the world at any time):

For I confess that in my view the only people one can really admire or tolerate in this world are saints and artists: those who imitate God, and those who imitate the works of God.[20]

It was inevitable, therefore, that biography should be his most successful literary form. Papini began writing at fourteen and produced no fewer than sixty-five volumes of fiction, poetry, philosophy, literary criticism, theology, and history. His poetry is quite negligible; his novel *Gog* is the only one translated into English and its primary interest is its repetition of Papini patterns and themes. Only when Papini turned to historical human action—the philosopher or artist or saint in time—did he draw upon his fullest resources as an artist himself. This human action moving into transcendence was seen, however, not by the imagination of a poet or novelist but by an exalted critical intelligence. As vivid as are the fictional cries of Pope Celestine before a world gone mad or the anguish of Jesus in His last days, they are, in the most magnificent sense, commentaries. They do not offer the immediate realities of Raskolnikov or Alyosha. In fact, the great achievement of Papini's biography of Christ is that it leads us, at every turn, back to the Gospels.

Early in the 'twenties, in the first flush of conversion, Papini wrote his greatest biography, *Storia di Cristo.* It was a tremendous success on all continents. His books, then, won him

fame, fortune, prizes, and academic positions. But the remarkable ferment of Papini did not allow stasis of any kind.
At the end of his life, in 1953, he published the result of years
of meditation, *Il Diavolo,* which shocked the Catholic world
and was promptly put on the Index. He died in his beloved
Florence on July 8, 1956.

III

If it is through his biographies that we can know Papini best,
his study of Saint Augustine (1930) would seem to offer some
understanding of his conversion. In a sense, as with so many of
his biographies, Papini seemed destined to write a study of
the African saint. For Papini's Christianity is essentially Augustinian. Indeed, it is his subtle understanding of the intellectual and sexual temptations besetting Augustine that makes
the book relevant to a twentieth-century audience. Its weakness lies, perhaps, in its chosen limits: "a story of a soul" in
which "his vast labors are but examples necessary for a better
understanding of his spiritual nature. . . ." [21] It is, like all
his biographies, however, carefully appointed in its research;
and his examination of the intellectual ferment of the day,
the heroes like Ambrose and the heresies like the Manichaean
and Pelagian, is made all the more conclusive by its restate-
ment in modern terms. Similarly, his analysis of Augustine's
sexuality may be exaggerated, but the idea of Augustine as
homosexual in one phase of his early life[22] is certainly contemporary. It thus illustrates more vividly the dramatic conflict of the ascent toward Grace, or, in Papini's terms, "the
deeper the valley, the stronger the light upon the heights." [23]
   Papini had loved Augustine before his conversion, and the
author of the *Confessions,* with their unraveling of a great
ego, further revealed to the Christian Papini the meaning and
depth of two forces associated with the great egoism of sanc-
tity: prophecy and the meaning of paradox. The first is clearly
placed within a context of Platonism, as in the Johannine gos-

pel; but the latter was a means of escaping both the monism
that he despised in positivism and in Spencer, and the dualism
so obviously fraudulent in Hegel and his Italian admirers.

Half-solutions are mediocre, but if they contain the extremes, and all of
the extremes, a synthesis is reached which is not compromise but transcendence. . . .[24] Here we are confronted with expressions divinely
exact and of profound significance, but with all the appearance of
paradox.[25]

The paradox in Papini—rare enough in any convert to any
faith—is, furthermore, always placed in an eclectic context
of Plato and Chinese philosophers like Kwang-Tze. But what
sustains the paradox and the prophetic in Papini is what he
found in Augustinian Christianity:

He referred the most transcendent problems to his own ego, made
theology a part of his being, melted pure thought in the furnace of
his heart, soared freely in the realms of ideology but always with wings
of flame. Beneath his serene universality there lurked ever a trace of
personal controversy, a shadow of autobiography.[26]

Papini's biography of Michelangelo was not published until
the very end of his life (1949), but in it he sounds very much
like the fiery critic of his youth. Acidly denouncing "contemporary Italian criticism" for its dissecting "to infinity" [27] the
work of a great man, and then ignoring the great man himself in his time and place, Papini repeats his whole theory of
biography:

We must acknowledge the fact that the life of a great artist, that is, a
man who is set apart from the herd of men and who is distinguished by
his extraordinary qualities and virtue, has an historical and spiritual value
in itself, and the study of that life can be a guide in a discerning analysis
of human nature.[28]

The development of the book logically follows from this theory. Michelangelo is viewed in a painstakingly created context

of individuals and events in Renaissance Italy. The method
is not so simple as it appears, for behind the erudition lies the
vitalism of Papini's view of existence. Michelangelo, not some
abstract theory, is allowed to appear amid the clutter of hu-
manists, popes, wars, murders, and general horror.

The weakness of the book, as critics noted, is that, like
the study of Augustine, the works themselves of the hero are
not sufficiently analyzed. In the immense mosaic of facts of
Michelangelo, the lack of such analysis does indeed take direction from the glittering existential ferment surrounding
the Titan. Especially one feels this loss in the short chapters
that mark the movement of the book. Their splendid inge-
nuity in evoking a life in which the great artist naturally
emerges is finally dissipated by the authorial failure to summarize, to direct the reader to abstractions from which he
can return, with relief, to the vivid picture of developing
heroism by which Michelangelo created art in his period.

This picture, however, is considerably enhanced by the
larger themes that do appear—as, for example, the neo-Pla-
tonism of Renaissance Florence and its influence on Michelangelo or the religious influence of Savonarola, who is viewed
as a prophet amid papal lust, adultery, sodomy, and greed.
Similarly, when the art works are seen in terms of paradox,
a paradox at the root of Michelangelo's being, the details
gain momentum. The incredible multitude of sharply etched
vignettes—often as bitter as the early personal essays—approach a kind of unity by virtue of their relevance to the central paradox, Michelangelo himself, the artist-hero whose human action moves into the idealization of art, towards a
greater transcendence.

Dante's influence on Michelangelo is a major part of this
biography, and the logical relationship of the three Tuscans
is focused by Papini in his concept of prophecy. The Sistine
Chapel, the *Divine Comedy,* and his own volumes are works,
in Papini's eyes, fraught with the Hebraic vision of God's
voice in history. This concept of prophecy in Italy is remarkable and is proof of Papini's originality, once converted. That
is, prophecy in Italy was hardly new; Papini superbly demon-

strates the effect of Joachim of Flora on Dante in *Dante Vivo,* and in *Michelangelo* the tragic attempts of Savonarola to reform a papacy gone mad (consider the scene where the anguished cardinals try to persuade Pope Julius not to destroy the ancient basilica of Constantine).[29] But it was Protestantism that brought back the vision of the prophetic to modern Europe, with accompanying neo-Platonic overtones. Only in Vatican Council II did the role of individual prophecy receive a restated validity; and here, therefore, years before, Papini is certainly pioneering, especially in Italy.

This insight into Dante the prophet is one of the richest sections of the popular *Dante Vivo* (1933). Dante is, of course, the great egoist-hero for Papini whose poetry most nearly approaches transcendence. To create before the modern reader all the living individualism of Dante, Papini again used the method of short chapters organized here with the loosest unity under the general headings of "Life," "Soul," "Work," and "Destiny" so that themes could be inductively developed or simply presented.

But Dante is no saint. In a staccato series of chapters on Dante's "Soul" and in a later chapter "The *Commedia* as Revenge," Papini cuts almost cruelly into the weaknesses of the poet. His use of the negative here does give insight into the failure of Dante as a person, but this valuable insight is blurred by a bad critical method: he commits too often the critical mistake of "the intentional fallacy." It is a real mistake here, for we are reduced to a level not above the art but below it, for the simple reason that the poet's consequent idealizations are seen not as art but as personal action. Such analysis will not work with Dante, and, therefore, when Papini turns to an analysis of the language and its form, he is gratuitous and falls back on the worst kind of Platonic analysis. Poetry, says Papini pompously, "is also, to speak plainly, a craft; nor is it thereby degraded"[30] but "if the soul is lifeless, what it produces is also lifeless."[31] In his reaction against Thomism, Papini seems never to have read the *Poetics*.

But this same Platonism which fails him in criticism of form deepens that analysis of Dante the prophet. The section on

Dante's image of the greyhound, the Veltro, allows Papini
to state here what will be repeated in the later works and
was first stated in *Storia di Cristo* : the imminent descent of the
Holy Spirit. Like Dante, Papini expects a renewal before the
final judgment, and, aware of Dante's own false dreams of
emperor and purified church, he nevertheless will preach as
Pope Celestine VI the necessity of the Veltro in the modern
world. This analysis of the Veltro's symbolic context in the
Divine Comedy is a concrete instance of the larger purpose :
Dante Vivo.

IV

Giovanni Papini tells us that he wrote his life of Christ under
the impulsive stimulus of something like the Veltro. It was
the first important work after his conversion, and he turned
from another work to write it. He also wrote it in the country,[32] most likely in the isolated Tuscan landscape of Bulciano,
his wife's home. This fact is important for it is obvious that
the simplicity of the Gospels converted Papini as much as
anything else. Papini had always sought a kind of primitivism
—vigorous and medieval and not Rousseau's, if we judge only
by the agnostic essays. Here, in the narratives of the life of
the God-man, the completest expression of human action as
transcendence, Papini found a synthesis of never-ending complexity and immediate simplicity : a paradox, in short, that gave
life. The beauty of the rural Tuscan landscape (and there
are many sensual echoes in Papini's narrative) is the physical
expression of the humility that lies at the root of this greatest
of his biographies. The egoist, the searcher, the Nietzschean
(there is an attack on Nietzsche in the first pages)[33] are here
balanced by the humility of the Incarnation in which paradoxically transcendence seeks human action. Christ therefore becomes, for Papini, the human actor *par excellence,* the only
one whose mask was simply His naked face, it alone masking
divinity. The great Egoist who drew all to Him, who was
the Way, has at the source of His Titanic program the irony

of humiliation or death or the utter giving away of human action for complete transcendence. Needless to say, Papini in this work demonstrates the depth of his conversion, for the whole book is suffused with the wonder of discovery.

Most of Papini's themes as a literary artist either culminate or are discovered in this work. The same is true of his concept of form. His method of the short chapters, of the vignette instead of the detailed analysis, of the image instead of the abstraction, of the method of the loose unity, originates in this book; and clearly it is the Gospels which have provided the pattern. His introduction is extremely important, for it gives us the kind of vision the reader must bring. It is a vision of personality, a focus of temperament; and this introduction immediately tells us how different the life will be from those great studies of Christ in the twentieth century by Guardini and Daniel-Rops. Unlike the others, Papini is consciously the apologist, consciously the Augustinian convert (unlike Guardini and Daniel-Rops), and consciously answering the world of *Un Uomo Finito*. "We live in the Christian era, and it is not yet finished," [34] says Papini in his introduction. A new Gospel must be written, therefore, and he has attempted such "for the Gospel's sake." [35]

Holding loyally to the words of the orthodox Gospels and to the dogmas of the Catholic Church, he has tried to represent those dogmas and those words in unusual ways, in a style violent with contrasts and with foreshortening, colored with crude and vividly felt words, to see if he could startle modern souls used to highly colored error, into seeing the truth.[36]

Fortunately, the personally perceived Jesus of this narrative was not that of an illiterate or a Rousseau primitive but of a Florentine. The result is a pictorial marvel; and the details show what Auden says of the old masters, an awareness of the human position of suffering. In the section "Four Nails" the impersonal spring morning is described; in "Perfumes in the Rock" the job of taking Jesus from the cross and burying Him is precisely described with Flaubertian realism; in "Return by the Sea" the lake is "rendered," to use Henry James's phrase, in its various appearances and serves as a kind of symbol for that metamorphosed Jesus who will soon appear to the disciples. But while certain scenes have the tightness and yet bold treatment of Sienese primitives, other scenes, the trial of Jesus and the descriptions of those ruined by wealth and materialism,[37] have the piercing caricature of a Rouault or Daumier. Similarly, in his satiric attacks on money (verbally echoing Sir Thomas More's attack on money, in the *Utopia*), his vignettes of corruption seem like chapters of Mauriac.[38]

But it is the human realism that is the center of the book. The actors of that momentous narrative become modern—literally, when Pilate is seen as an English governor of Asia or Africa but more subtly in the depiction of the disciples:

Fate knows no better way to punish the great for their greatness than by sending them disciples. . . . Here is one of the most tragic elements in all greatness: disciples are repugnant and dangerous, but disciples, even false ones, cannot be dispensed with. Prophets suffer if they do not find them; they suffer, perhaps more, when they have found them.[39]

As a result, his portrayal of these disciples, notably Matthew, is superb in its ability to draw their human dimensions. Peter especially fits the Papini love of paradox:

His surname "Cephas," stone, piece of rock, was not given him only for the firmness of his faith, but for the hardness of his head. . . . And yet he was the first to recognize Jesus as the Christ; and this primacy is so great that nothing has been able to cancel it.[40]

But it is in the long analysis of Judas' torment and anguish that Papini evokes the kind of psychological realism that, as in the great novels, finally cannot be defined:

The mystery of Judas is doubly tied to the mystery of the Redemption and we lesser ones shall never solve it.[41]

Each of Papini's commentaries on the parables also illustrates this quintessentially human—one might even say Italian—

concern. The relationships in Papini's "The Prodigal Son"
have the sorrow, affection, and warmth of *The Bicycle Thief*;
the story of the wise virgins, the clarity of Vittorini's "In
Sicily," and the story of the woman who poured perfume over
Jesus' head is full of the weeping that Papini loved in all his
work and is so very difficult to understand outside of Italy.
There are also the inevitable baroque scenes, and, with a
writer prone to excess, the simplicities that really seem simple-
mindedness.

But Christ as hero is best found, in Papini's version, not
on the Cross or Resurrected, but on the Mount of Transfig-
uration and in the Sermon on the Mount. Throughout the
work, although subdued and properly placed in relation to
the personal emphasis of the book, the reader finds Papini's
erudition. At times it is combined with exegesis for a maxi-
mum effect as in Papini's explication of Jesus' prophecy in
"Judea Overcome" and "The Parousia." But in these two
crucial scenes of the hero on the mountain, where the Greatest
Actor is as exalted as Zarathustra, knowledge and critical intelligence are used and subsumed. In these scenes Papini
shows, with the skill of an old master himself, the personality
of the God-man literally transfigured and transcendent in one
scene and, in the other, the personality of God transfiguring
human action.

V

In two works of his last period, Giovanni Papini seems almost
obsessed with the figure of the grand egoist. *Lettere agli
uomini di Papa Celestino Sesto* (1946) is a work of fiction
devised, like his novel *Gog* fifteen years earlier, as a series of
confessions. In *Gog* Papini satirizes the modern world
through an American super-millionaire, Goggins; and his
method is a series of miscellaneous papers in which the millionaire records his searching for novelty, strange adventures,
the great and near-great, and his cynicism on such searching
in the modern world. The fictional Pope Celestine also ex-

presses his observations on an insane world, and the essay-
letters are the same series of chapters first explored as method
in the early essays and *Storia di Cristo*.

In many ways the old man Pope Celestine is the most force-
ful of all Papini's masks. Papini obviously wrote this work
during the Second World War, and his work is a voice from
the apocalypse. The immediate effects of the war are seen in
the references to the bombing:

Already we have seen the erosive, consuming fire descend upon us from
the skies—now we await the sublime and healing fire of the Holy
Ghost.[42]

Also, one letter is directed "To the Hebrews" and is a change
from Papini's earlier attitude toward the Jews. It is also a
sad book in which the author has clearly seen a world vanish
before his eyes. The simplicity that he once sought in the
world of Bulciano is lost. The poor today are still poor but
their greed is as terrible as the modern rich: "no one sings
any longer nor knows poetry." [43]

It was in response to Pope Celestine's remarks about poetry
and its purpose in the chaos of the modern world that Wallace
Stevens wrote "Reply to Papini." This poem answers the Papini–Celestine attack on modern poetry with the kind of defense found in other late poems of Stevens'. What is significant
is Stevens' own response to the personal questioning of Papini
and to the depth of his fictional hero, the martyred pope:

> Celestin, the generous, the civilized,
> Will understand what it is to understand [lines 19–20].

How else could Papini the egoist respond to a technological
leveling—literally and spiritually—of the world except to
choose, for him, the supreme individual whose mask as hero
was given by God? In his essay on Pius XI, Papini had admired the papal encyclicals. Therefore, in his fiction, Papini
invents a pope who "lived in a terrible era of storm and
blood" and who "died a martyr during the last days of the
Great Persecution." [44] Clearly Papini is again in the realm
of the Veltro, and prophecy now becomes history through a

series of letters to Christians, priests, monks, theologians, the rich, the poor, the rulers, the subjects, the women, the poets, the historians, the scientists, the separated Christians, the Hebrews, those without Christ, those without God, and finally to all men. The prayer to God that ends the work is a formal rhapsody that merely reflects the rhapsodic tone of the whole work.

What is significant about the work is that it attacks not only the modern world—Papini's task since the *Leonardo*— but the mechanism of the Church itself. It is a prophetic call for renewal (and, a few years after Papini's death, Pope John XXIII in a mysterious, sudden impulse called the Vatican Council for just that purpose of renewal). Old Pope Celestine's revolutionary theology would de-emphasize Mariology[45] and would lead to new inventiveness, as illustrated in an old monk's theory of the redemption of the Devil.[46] It would emphasize the Holy Spirit[47] and would fully condemn all wealth and all capitalism.[48] It would be an eschatological theology that realizes that there are "only two types of men today: economic man, with all his appetites; and the man of God, with all his certainties"; that "we have arrived at the ultimate dilemma: Love or Death." [49] Papini has, in short, compiled the theology of all his heroes, Francis of Assisi, Joachim of Flora, Savonarola, and even of artists like Dante and the Michelangelo of the "Last Judgment."

The Devil, in Christian theology, is *the* destructive egoist —the greatest actor who must always wear a mask to cover his hideousness. In his *Il Diavolo* (1953) Papini will not accept this loss of supreme action, this colossal failure of transcendence, that is the traditional Christian Devil. The thesis of his book, therefore, is that the Devil and all the fallen will be forgiven by a God who if He "is really the Father cannot torture his children into eternity" or, if Satan is not redeemed, "we should have to think that the Father of Christ himself were not a perfect Christian." [50] Papini's arguments turn to the past as well as to the present and future. Furthermore, adding a note that does not appear in the arguments of Origen and other theologians (which Papini minutely but not always carefully examines), man must be the instrument of Satan's salvation. In one of those aphoristic paradoxes that abound in the book, Papini sees the ultimate liberation of man in this possibility: "If Satan can be freed from the hatred of Christians, men would be forever freed from Satan." [51]

The organization of the book provides a veritable encyclopedia of diabology, but the whole still remains a series of notes, another kind of biography in which the real force of Satan can be seen in literature, in art, in history, in theology, and in France, Satan's "promised land"![52] Unfortunately, this sort of study demanded the tight thesis and the controlled level of argument. Fascinated by the aesthetic and, in his mind, prophetic possibilities of paradox and a dualism that he had admired in Augustine, Papini moves from sublime mystical defenses to trivial fallacies and plain stupidity. Nowhere is there the precision of image that dominates the earlier work, and clearly, without a human subject, Papini does not succeed.

It is precisely the vitalism of his concept of action, however, that seems to betray him. Anyone as *alive* as Satan must *necessarily* be redeemed by Complete Life or God. From his early Pragmatic origins through his visions of saints and artists, the heroes who imitate the God-man Hero (a Hero vitally and completely masculine, one might add, with the role of the Father strongly centered and the role of the Virgin barely perceptible), Papini was predestined to deal with the mysterious negative presence called Satan, a vital presence felt so acutely during the Second World War and in the decade before when, if we can judge by Pope Celestine's remarks, these meditations on the Devil began.

It is easy to attack Papini's thesis. But the shock that it gave the Catholic world (to the delight of Italian Communists) was anticipated by Papini himself when he clearly pointed out that the Church of Rome did not hold such teachings[53] and, furthermore, that his book had as subtitle: "Notes for a Future Diabology." [54] Papini, like Pope Celestine in the same instance, was merely calling out for inventiveness in discussing dogma in an era when practically no dogma is deemed worthy of serious discussion.[55] Similarly, Papini was calling for that universal charity which he held to be the one source of that vitalism at the heart of all action and which, in fact, gave human action its very transcendence. The great individualist Papini, essentially inheriting a Romantic Devil (and certainly creating one in his book as well), could not bear to keep that transcendence sustaining all action from the greatest of egoists. For Papini to do so would be to deny that living transcendence within himself, himself as egoist.

VI

The world of Giovanni Papini is clearly gone. Hitler has given way to the Central Committee, and lonely hero-egoists are largely "camp." That impulse of individualism begun by the Renaissance and Reformation died in this century, and Papini's Pope Celestine (like his Devil) seems a sad relic. But what about his egoism? No matter what the historical context of Papini's personalism, there remains the seemingly enduring fact that the moment one rises above the ant society —that is, to a conception of vitalism as opposed to sheer motion—personality enters in. Or, if human action follows its own tendency as either human or action, it will end up transcending itself through a mask of personality. Transcendence is always personal, says this seemingly inexorable law of human society (whether cavemen or moon-emigrés) ; and it is a law tiresome at times and capable of wild excesses of egoism. But as Papini's biographies tell us, societies seldom transcend themselves—only the heroic human being or, in Papini's terms, the egoist like Pope Celestine who "hurled his words like arrows of light into the hearts of all men." [56]

Notes

1. Ruth Shephard Phelps, *Italian Silhouettes* (New York: Knopf, 1924), p. 79.
2. William James, "Giovanni Papini and the Pragmatist Movement in Italy,"

The Journal of Philosophy, Psychology, and Scientific Method, III, 13 (1906), 339.

3. Carlo L. Golino, "Giovanni Papini and American Pragmatism," *Italica,* XXXII, 1 (March 1955), 45.

4. James, p. 340.

5. Giovanni Papini, *Michelangelo, His Life and His Era,* trans. Loretta Murnane (New York: Dutton, 1952), pp. 5–6.

6. Giovanni Papini, *Dante Vivo,* trans. Eleanor Hammond Broadus and Anna Benedetti (New York: Macmillan, 1935), p. 3.

7. Giovanni Papini, *Laborers in the Vineyard,* trans. Alice Curtayne (New York: Longmans, Green, 1930), p. 121.

8. *Ibid.,* p. 126.

9. *Ibid.,* p. 5.

10. *Ibid.,* p. 9.

11. *Ibid.,* p. 3.

12. Papini, *Dante Vivo,* p. 3.

13. Papini, *Michelangelo,* p. 532.

14. Giovanni Papini, *Life of Christ,* trans. Dorothy Canfield Fisher (New York: Blue Ribbon Books, 1923), p. 20.

15. Giovanni Papini, *Saint Augustine,* trans. Mary Prichard Agnetti (New York: Harcourt, Brace, 1930), p. viii.

16. Quoted in Carlo L. Golino, "Giovanni Papini and American Pragmatism," *Italica,* XXXII, 1 (March 1955), 39.

17. *Columbia Dictionary of Modern European Literature,* ed. Horatio Smith (New York: Columbia University Press, 1947), p. 411.

18. Papini, *Laborers in the Vineyard,* p. 91.

19. Papini, *Saint Augustine,* p. 160.

20. Papini, *Laborers in the Vineyard,* p. v.

21. Papini, *Saint Augustine,* p. ix.

22. *Ibid.,* p. 21.

23. *Ibid.,* p. x.

24. *Ibid.,* p. 184.

25. *Ibid.,* p. 185.

26. *Ibid.,* pp. 189–190.

27. Papini, *Michelangelo,* p. 6.

28. *Ibid.*

29. *Ibid.,* p. 119.

30. Papini, *Dante Vivo,* p. 305.

31. *Ibid.,* p. 306.

32. Papini, *Life of Christ,* p. 11.

33. *Ibid.,* p. 5.

34. *Ibid.,* p. 6.

35. *Ibid.,* p. 13. Quoted from St. Paul.

36. *Ibid.,* p. 12.

37. *Ibid.,* p. 193 passim.

38. *Ibid.*, p. 176.
39. *Ibid.*, p. 177.
40. *Ibid.*, p. 181.
41. *Ibid.*, p. 286.
42. Giovanni Papini, *The Letters of Pope Celestine VI to All Mankind,* trans. Loretta Murnane (New York: Dutton, 1948), p. 17.
43. *Ibid.*, p. 33.
44. *Ibid.*, p. vi.
45. *Ibid.*, p. 39.
46. *Ibid.*, p. 64.
47. *Ibid.*, p. 65.
48. *Ibid.*, p. 75.
49. *Ibid.*, p. 209.
50. Giovanni Papini, *The Devil: Notes for a Future Diabology,* trans. Adrienne Foulke (London: Smithers and Bonellie, 1954), p. 159.
51. *Ibid.*, p. 15.
52. *Ibid.*, p. 113.
53. *Ibid.*, p. 158.
54. *Ibid.*, p. 21.
55. A balanced discussion of *The Devil* and its notoriety can be found in Giovanni Gullace, "Giovanni Papini e il diavolo," *Italica,* XXXIII, 3 (September 1956), 193–204.
56. Papini, *The Letters of Pope Celestine,* p. 12.

The Modern Catholic Novel: A Selected Checklist of Criticism

JACKSON R. BRYER · NANNESKA N. MAGEE ·
University of Maryland

This checklist includes a selection of material on the modern Catholic novel, as a supplement to the essays in this volume. The checklist is divided into two basic sections, one devoted to general studies of the modern Catholic novel and/or two or more specific modern Catholic novelists, the other to studies of the individual writers covered in the essays for this book.

Within the general section, we have been highly selective, listing only those items which we felt were particularly relevant to the essays in this book and to the type of Catholic novelists covered therein. Brief annotations are provided as indications of which specific writers are covered in many of the items. In Part II, before the listings for each specific writer, cross-references are provided to items in Part I which concern that writer.

Within the second section, the selectivity and criteria for selection vary from writer to writer. For writers about whom there is relatively little critical and biographical comment, like J. F. Powers, we have listed virtually everything which we could find. On the other hand, when we were presented with an abundance of comment, we listed only items which were most relevant to that writer as a Catholic. In most cases, however, we listed books totally about the individual author, where we could locate such books. These titles are presented in small-capital letters.

Finally, it must be noted that the difficulty of locating foreign books and articles in this country have severely limited the coverage and completeness of this listing. But whatever completeness it does have could not have been achieved without the assistance of Mrs. Loretta D'Eustachio and Miss Susan Robinson.

I. GENERAL

A. Books

Alexander, Calvert, s.j. "The Novel." In his *The Catholic Literary Revival: Three Phases in Its Development from 1845 to the Present.* Port Washington, N.Y.: Kennikat Press, 1968. Pp. 332–353. [Compton Mackenzie, Sheila Kaye-Smith, Maurice Baring, *et al.*]

Braybrooke, Patrick. *Some Catholic Novelists: Their Art and Outlook.* Freeport, N.Y.: Books for Libraries Press, 1966. [Essays on Chesterton, Belloc, John Ayscough, Robert Hugh Benson, Sir Philip Gibbs, Sheila Kaye-Smith, Katherine Tynan.]

Brée, Germaine, and Margaret Guiton. "Private Worlds." In their *The French Novel from Gide to Camus.* New York: Harcourt, Brace & World, 1957. Pp. 98–131. [Green, Mauriac, Bernanos.]

Brown, Stephen J., s.j. *Libraries and Literature from a Catholic Standpoint.* Dublin: Browne & Nolan, 1937. [See especially "Why Catholic Novels and Novelists," pp. 167–181, and "The Themes of the Catholic Novelist," pp. 182–197.]

Cruise O'Brien, Conor. *Maria Cross: Imaginative Patterns in a Group of Modern Catholic Writers.* London: Chatto & Windus, 1954; 2nd edition, Fresno, Calif.: Academy Guild Press, 1963. [Mauriac, Bernanos, Greene, O'Faolain, Waugh, Péguy, Claudel, Bloy.]

Dillistone, F. W. *The Novelist and the Passion Story.* New York: Sheed & Ward, 1960.

Dommard, Jean-Hervé. *Trois écrivains devant Dieu: Claudel, Mauriac, Bernanos.* Paris: c.d.u. et s.e.d.e.s. réunis, 1966.

DuBos, Charles. *What Is Literature?* New York: Sheed & Ward, 1960.

Espian de la Maistre, André. *Der Katholizismus als Existenz- und Kulturwert in der französischen Literatur der Gegenwart.* Würzburg: Echter Verlag, 1965.

Fowlie, Wallace. "Catholic Orientation in Contemporary French Literature." In Stanley Romaine Hopper, ed. *Spiritual Problems in Contemporary Literature.* New York: Harper, 1952. Pp. 225–241. [Bernanos, Mauriac, *et al.*]

———. *Clowns and Angels: Studies in Modern French Literature.* New York: Sheed & Ward, 1943. [Mauriac, Romains, Claudel, *et al.*]

———. *Jacob's Night: The Religious Renascence in France.* New York: Sheed & Ward, 1943. [Péguy, Maritain, *et al.*]

Gable, Sister Mariella. *This Is Catholic Fiction.* New York: Sheed & Ward, 1948.

Gregor, Ian, and Brian Nicholas. *The Moral and the Story.* London: Faber & Faber, 1962. [See especially "Grace and Morality: *Thérèse Desqueyroux* and *The End of the Affair*," pp. 185–216.]

Hallen, Oskar van der. *Epick-Beschouwinger over den katholieken Roman 1920–1940.* Brussels: U.N.U. Standaard, 1944. [Mauriac, Bernanos, Undset, *et al.*]

Las Vergnas, Raymond. *Chesterton, Belloc, Baring.* Tr. C. C. Martindale, s.j. London: Sheed & Ward, 1938.

Levaux, Léopold. *Romanciers.* Paris: Desclée, de Brouwer, 1929. [Bernanos, Mauriac, *et al.*]

Moeller, Charles. *Littérature du XXᵉ siècle et christianisme.* Vol. I: *Le silence de Dieu.* Paris: Casterman, 1953. [Bernanos, Greene, Green, *et al.*]

Mooney, Harry J., Jr., and Thomas F. Staley, eds. *The Shapeless God: Essays on Modern Fiction.* Pittsburgh: University of Pittsburgh Press, 1968. [Includes essays on Greene (by A. A. DeVitis), on Waugh (by Herbert Howarth), on Powers (by Robert Boyle, s.j.), on Flannery O'Connor (by Harry J. Mooney, Jr.), and a bibliography on "Religion and the Modern Novel" (by Maralee Frampton).]

Mueller, William R. *The Prophetic Voice in Modern Fiction.* New York: Association Press, 1959. [Chapters on Joyce, Camus, Kafka, Faulkner, Greene, Silone.]

O'Faolain, Sean. *The Vanishing Hero.* Boston: Atlantic–Little, Brown, 1956. [Sections on Greene, Mauriac, and Bernanos.]

O'Malley, Frank. "The Renascence of the Novelist and the Poet." In Norman Weyand, s.j., ed. *The Catholic Renascence.* Chicago: Loyola

University Press, 1951. Pp. 25–88. [Bernanos, Mauriac, Greene, *et al.*]

Panichas, George A., ed. *Mansions of the Spirit: Essays in Literature and Religion.* New York: Hawthorn Books, 1967.

Scott, Nathan A., Jr., ed. *Adversity and Grace: Studies in Recent American Literature.* Chicago: University of Chicago Press, 1968. [Includes essays on Flannery O'Connor (by Preston M. Browning, Jr.) and on Powers (by Maynard Kaufman).]

———. *The Broken Center: Studies in the Theological Horizon of Modern Literature.* New Haven, Conn.: Yale University Press, 1966.

———. *Craters of the Spirit.* Washington, D.C.: Corpus Books, 1968. [Chapters on Greene and Flannery O'Connor, *inter alia.*]

———. *Modern Literature and the Religious Frontier.* New York: Harper, 1958.

———. *Negative Capability: Studies in the New Literature and the Religious Situation.* New Haven, Conn.: Yale University Press, 1969.

———, ed. *The New Orpheus: Essays Toward a Christian Poetic.* New York: Sheed & Ward, 1964.

Simon, Pierre-Henri. *La Littérature du péché et de la grâce—Essai sur la constitution d'une littérature chrétienne depuis 1880.* Paris: Librairie Arthème Fayard, 1957. [Mauriac, Bernanos, *et al.*]

Stratford, Philip. *Faith and Fiction—Creative Process in Greene and Mauriac.* Notre Dame, Ind.: University of Notre Dame Press, 1964.

Turnell, Martin. *Modern Literature and Christian Faith.* Westminster, Md.: The Newman Press, 1961.

Zamarriego, Tomas. *Tipología sacerdotal en la novela contemporanea: Bernanos, Mauriac, Gironella.* Madrid: Editorial Razón y Fe, 1959.

B. *Articles*

Antush, John V., s.j. "Realism in the Catholic Novel," *Catholic World,* 185 (July 1957), 276–279. [Powers, Kathryn Hulme, Edwin O'Connor.]

Bayley, John. "Two Catholic Novelists," *National Review* (London), 132 (February 1949), 232–235. [Greene and Waugh.]

Beary, Thomas John. "Religion and the Modern Novel," *Catholic World,* 166 (December 1947), 203–211. [Greene, Waugh, Huxley, Harry Sylvester.]

Belvedere, Joseph. "Catholic Fiction: 1. Achilles' Heel," *America,* 65 (August 23, 1941), 550–551.

Boland, Allen, o.m.c. "Catholic English Literature in America," *Franciscan Educational Conference—Reports,* 22 (December 1940), 123–169.

Borne, Etienne. "Y a-t-il une littérature catholique?" *Vie Intellectuelle,* 25 (May 1954), 6–18.

Brady, Charles A. "A Brief Survey of Catholic Fiction," *Books on Trial,* 12 (January–February 1954), 159–160, 190–191.

———. "Catholic Fiction: 2. Lifting Fog?" *America,* 65 (August 30, 1941), 579–580.

Brady, Ignatius, O.F.M., M.A. "Catholic English Literature in the British Isles in the Twentieth Century," *Franciscan Educational Conference—Report,* 22 (December 1940), 103–120.

Braybrooke, Neville. "Catholics and the Novel," *Renascence,* 5 (Autumn 1952), 22–32.

———. "The Continuity of Catholic Literature," *Clergy Review,* 41 (May 1956), 257–274.

Broderick, Robert C. "The Position of the Catholic Fictionist," *Ave Maria,* 49 (February 4, 1939), 129–133.

Brown, Stephen J., S.J. "The Catholic Novelist and His Themes," *Irish Monthly,* 63 (July 1935), 432–444.

Carey, Charles M. "Catholic Novel Writing," *Ave Maria,* 47 (March 5, 1938), 298–300.

"The Catholic Novel," *Commonweal,* 19 (January 19, 1934), 312.

Connolly, Francis X. "Catholic Fiction: 4. Two Reactions," *America,* 65 (September 13, 1941), 634–635.

———. "The Catholic Theme," *America,* 50 (December 9, 1933), 233–235.

———. "The Catholic Writer and Contemporary Culture," *Thought,* 14 (September 1939), 373–383.

Dooley, D. J. "The Strategy of the Catholic Novelist," *Catholic World,* 189 (July 1959), 300–304.

Doyle, Brian. "Morals and Novels," *Ave Maria,* 77 (April 25, 1953), 532–533. [Greene and Mauriac, *inter alia.*]

English, Jack. "Can a Catholic Write a Novel?" *American Mercury,* 31 (January 1934), 90–95.

Estang, Luc. "Of Note—Art and Morality—Excerpt," *Commonweal,* 53 (March 9, 1951), 545. [Translated excerpt from *Terre Humaine.*]

Fecher, Charles A. "Literary Freedom and the Catholic Novelist," *Catholic World,* 184 (February 1957), 340–344.

Fitzmorris, Thomas J. "Formula For the Great American Catholic Novel," *America,* 53 (August 19, 1935), 425–426.

Flood, Ethelbert, O.F.M. "Christian Language in Modern Literature," *Culture,* 22 (March 1961), 28–42. [Greene, *inter alia.*]

Folk, Barbara Naver. "Fiction: A Problem For the Catholic Writer," *Catholic World,* 188 (November 1958), 105–109.

Gable, Sister Mariella, o.s.b. "'Catholic' Fiction," *Catholic World,* 152 (December 1940), 296–302.

———. "Prose Satire and the Modern Christian Temper," *American Benedictine Review,* 11 (March–June 1960), 21–34.

Graef, Hilda. "Marriage and Our Catholic Novelists," *Catholic World,* 189 (June 1959), 185–190. [Emphasis on Mauriac and Greene.]

Hazo, Samuel J. "Belief and the [Catholic] Critic," *Renascence,* 13 (Summer 1961), 187–199.

Hebblethwaite, Peter. "How Catholic Is the Catholic Novel?" *Times Literary Supplement,* July 27, 1967, pp. 678–679.

Hope, Felix. "Modern Catholic Literature," *Blackfriars,* 16 (August 1935), 600–611.

de Hornedo, Rafael Maria, s.j. "La novela católica española en 1956," *Razón y Fe,* 156 (September–October 1957), 161–166.

Hurley, Doran. "Catholic Fiction: 5. For the Defense," *America,* 65 (September 20, 1941), 662–663.

Immaculate, Sister Joseph. "The Catholic Novelist as Apostle," *Catholic Library World,* 23 (May 1952), 247–251.

"Is There a Catholic Novel?" *Commonweal,* 19 (March 30, 1934), 593–594.

Jacobsen, Josephine. "A Catholic Quartet," *Christian Scholar,* 47 (Summer 1964), 139–154. [Flannery O'Connor, Muriel Spark, Greene, Powers.]

Kennedy, John S. "Catholic Novel," *Sign,* 22 (April 1943), 551–553.

Kerrigan, W. J. "Opposed Modalities—Pitfalls For Catholic Writers," *Renascence,* 5 (Autumn 1952), 15–21.

von Kühnelt-Leddihn, Eric. "The Failure of Catholic Literature," *Catholic World,* 165 (May 1947), 116–122.

Kunkel, Francis L. "Priest as Scapegoat in the Modern Catholic Novel," *Ramparts,* 1 (May 1962), 72–78. [Bernanos, Greene, Mauriac, etc.]

Larnen, Brendan, o.p. "Novels of Catholicism," *Dominicana,* 20 (September 1935), 159–162.

McNamara, Eugene. "Prospects of the Catholic Novel," *America,* 97 (August 17, 1957), 505–506, 508. [Greene, *inter alia.*]

Marshall, Bruce. "The Responsibilities of the Catholic Novelist," *Commonweal,* 50 (May 27, 1949), 169–171.

Mason, Herbert. "Two Catholic Traditions: France and America," *Commonweal,* 74 (September 22, 1961), 516–518.

Meath, Gerard, O.P. "Catholic Writing," *Blackfriars,* 32 (December 1951), 602–609.

Monroe, N. E. "The New Man in Fiction," *Renascence,* 6 (Autumn 1953), 9–17. [Greene, Mauriac.]

Murchland, Bernard G. "Theology and Literature," *Commonweal,* 71 (October 16, 1959), 63–66.

Murphy, J. Hanley. "Not on All Fours," *America,* 68 (February 27, 1943), 577–578. [Greene, *inter alia.*]

Neame, A. J. "Black and Blue—A Study in the Catholic Novel," *The European,* No. 2 (April 1953), 26–36.

Nicholl, Donald. "La littérature catholique en Angleterre depuis la guerre," *La Vie Intellectuelle,* 25 (June 1954), 58–73. [Greene, Waugh, *et al.*]

O'Connor, Flannery. "The Church and the Fiction Writer," *America,* 96 (March 30, 1957), 733–735.

———. "The Role of the Catholic Novelist," *Greyfriar* (Siena College, Loudonville, N.Y.), 7 (1964), 5–12.

O'Connor, John J. "Catholic Writing Today," *Catholic Action,* 31 (February 1949), 8–9.

Portier, Lucienne. "Aspects du Catholicisme dans la littérature italienne d'aujourd'hui," *La Vie Intellectuelle,* 26 (May 1955), 60–77.

Quinn, K. "Notes on the Catholic Novel," *Irish Monthly,* 79 (January 1951), 8–14.

Quinn, Sister M. Bernetta. "View From a Rock: The Fiction of Flannery O'Connor and J. F. Powers," *Critique,* 2 (Fall 1958), 19–27.

Ribalow, Harold U. "Catholic Literature to an Outsider," *Catholic World,* 181 (May 1955), 120–124.

Ryan, John Julian. "Catholic Romanticism—A Diagnosis of the Aches and Pains of Catholic Fiction Writers," *Books on Trial,* 9 (October 1950), 121–122, 153.

Ryan, Stephen P. "The Catholic Novelist in the U.S.A.," *Catholic World,* 188 (February 1959), 388–393.

Sandra, Sister Mary, S.S.A. "The Priest-Hero in Modern Fiction," *Personalist,* 46 (Autumn 1965), 527–542. [Powers, Bernanos, Greene, etc.]

Sheed, Wilfrid. "The Catholic as Writer: I. Enemies of Catholic Promise," *Commonweal,* 77 (February 22, 1963), 560–563. [Emphasis on Greene.]

Sheerin, John B. "Catholic Novels and Reprobates," *Catholic World,* 168 (March 1949), 417–421.

Sonnenfeld, Albert. "The Catholic Novelist and the Supernatural," *French Studies,* 22 (October 1968), 307–319. [Bernanos, Greene, Mauriac.]

———. "Twentieth Century Gothic: Reflections on the Catholic Novel," *Southern Review,* n.s. 1 (April 1965), 388–405. [Greene, Waugh, Chesterton, Bernanos.]

Stopp, Frederick J. "Der katholische Roman im heutigen England: Graham Greene und Evelyn Waugh," *Stimmen der Zeit,* 153 (March 1954), 428–443.

Sullivan, Richard. "A Definition of Catholic Fiction," *Books on Trial,* 12 (January–February 1954), 157–181.

Sylvester, Harry. "Problems of the Catholic Writer," *Atlantic Monthly,* 181 (January 1948), 109–113.

Turnell, Martin. "Belief and the Writer," *Commonweal,* 62 (May 13, 1955), 143–146.

———. "The Religious Novel," *Commonweal,* 55 (October 26, 1951), 55–57. [Mauriac and Greene.]

II. INDIVIDUAL WRITERS

J. F. Powers

(Under General, see Mooney and Staley; Scott, *Adversity and Grace;* Antush; Jacobsen; Quinn, M. B.; Sandra.)

Bates, Barclay W. "Flares of Special Grace: The Orthodoxy of J. F. Powers," *Midwest Quarterly,* 11 (October 1969), 91–106.

Bloomfield, C. "Religion and Alienation in James Baldwin, Bernard Malamud, and James F. Powers," *Religious Education,* 57 (April 1962), 97–102, 158.

Collignon, Joseph P. "Powers' *Morte D'Urban:* A Layman's Indictment," *Renascence,* 16 (Fall 1963), 20–21, 51–52.

Dolan, Paul J. "God's Crooked Lines: Powers' *Morte D'Urban,*" *Renascence,* 21 (Winter 1969), 95–102.

Green, Martin. "J. F. Powers and Catholic Writing." In his *Yeats's Blessing on Von Hügel.* London: Longmans, Green, 1967. Pp. 97–127.

Hagopian, John V. "Irony and Involution in J. F. Powers' 'Morte D'Urban,'" *Contemporary Literature,* 9 (Spring 1968), 151–171.

———. J. F. POWERS. New York: Twayne, 1968.

Hamill, Pete. "The Art of J. F. Powers," New York *Post,* March 24, 1963, Sunday Magazine, p. 10. [Interview.]

Hertzel, Leo J. "Brother Juniper, Father Urban and the Unworldly Tradition," *Renascence,* 17 (Summer 1965), 207–210, 215.

Hinchcliffe, Arnold P. "Nightmare of Grace," *Blackfriars,* 45 (February 1964), 61–69.

Holton, Mary Louise. "J. F. Powers," *Wilson Library Bulletin,* 38 (September 1963), 80.

Hughes, Riley. "Three Americans," *Renascence,* 1 (Spring 1949), 4–12. [Powers, Harry Sylvester, Richard Sullivan.]

Hutchinson, Tom. "Talk With J. F. Powers," *Catholic Messenger,* April 16, 1959, p. 2. Reprinted in *The Critic,* 17 (June–July 1959), 50.

Hynes, Joseph. "Father Urban's Renewal: J. F. Powers' Difficult Precision," *Modern Language Quarterly,* 29 (December 1968), 450–466.

Lebowitz, Naomi. "The Stories of J. F. Powers: The Sign of the Contradiction," *Kenyon Review,* 20 (Summer 1958), 494–499.

Lundegaard, Bob. "Author: 'Writing Is Sweaty Job,' " Minneapolis *Sunday Tribune,* April 7, 1963, Feature Section, pp. 1, 6. [Interview.]

McDonald, Donald. "Interview With J. F. Powers," *The Critic,* 19 (October–November 1960), 20–21, 88–90.

Malloy, Sister M. Kristin, o.s.b. "The Catholic and Creativity: J. F. Powers," *American Benedictine Review,* 15 (March 1964), 63–80. [Interview.]

Merton, Thomas. "*Morte D'Urban*: Two Celebrations," *Worship,* 36 (November 1962), 645–650.

O'Brien, Charles F. " 'Morte D'Urban' and the Catholic Church in America," *Discourse,* 12 (Summer 1969), 324–328.

Padilla, [Brother] Carlos Villalobos. THE ART OF SHORT FICTION IN JAMES FARL POWERS. Mexico City: Universidad Autonoma de Mexico, 1963.

Phelps, Donald. "Reasonable, Holy and Living," *Minnesota Review,* 9 (No. 1, 1969), 57–62.

Powers, James F. "The Catholic and Creativity—Interview," *American Benedictine Review,* 15 (March 1964), 63–80.

Scouffas, George. "J. F. Powers: On the Vitality of Disorder," *Critique,* 2 (Fall 1958), 41–58.

Shannon, James P. "J. F. Powers and the Priesthood," *Catholic World,* 175 (September 1952), 432–437.

Sisk, John P. "The Complex Moral Vision of J. F. Powers," *Critique,* 2 (Fall 1958), 28–40.

Wedge, George F. "J. F. Powers," *Critique,* 2 (Fall 1958), 63–70. [Bibliography.]

Flannery O'Connor

(Under General, see Mooney and Staley; Panichas; Scott, *Adversity and Grace*; Scott, *Craters of the Spirit*; Jacobsen; O'Connor, F., "The Church and the Fiction Writer"; O'Connor, F., "The Role of the Catholic Novelist"; Quinn, M. B.)

Bassan, Maurice. "Flannery O'Connor's Way: Shock, With Moral Intent," *Renascence,* 15 (Summer 1963), 195–199, 211.

Baumbach, Jonathan. "The Acid of God's Grace: The Fiction of Flannery O'Connor," *Georgia Review,* 17 (Fall 1963), 334–346. Reprinted, revised, in Baumbach's *The Landscape of Nightmare.*

Brittain, Joan T., and Leon V. Driskell. "O'Connor and the Eternal Crossroads," *Renascence,* 22 (Autumn 1969), 49–55.

Browning, Preston, Jr. " 'Parker's Back': Flannery O'Connor's Iconography of Salvation by Profanity," *Studies in Short Fiction,* 6 (Fall 1969), 525–535.

Cheney, Brainard. "Miss O'Connor Creates Unusual Humor Out of Ordinary Sin," *Sewanee Review,* 71 (Autumn 1963), 644–652.

Davis, Barnabas. "Flannery O'Connor: Christian Belief in Recent Fiction," *Listening,* 1 (Autumn 1965), 5–21.

Detweiler, Robert. "The Curse of Christ in Flannery O'Connor's Fiction," *Comparative Literature Studies,* 3 (No. 2, 1966), 235–245.

Drake, Robert. FLANNERY O'CONNOR. Grand Rapids, Mich.: William B. Eerdmans, 1966.

Driskell, Leon. " 'Parker's Back' vs. 'The Partridge Festival': Flannery O'Connor's Critical Choice," *Georgia Review,* 21 (Winter 1967), 476–490.

Eggenschwiler, David. "Flannery O'Connor's True and False Prophets," *Renascence,* 21 (Spring 1969), 151–161, 167.

Friedman, Melvin J. "Flannery O'Connor: Another Legend in Southern Fiction," *English Journal,* 51 (April 1962), 233–243.

——, and Lewis A. Lawson, eds. THE ADDED DIMENSION: THE ART AND MIND OF FLANNERY O'CONNOR. New York: Fordham University Press, 1966. [Original essays by Frederick J. Hoffman, Louis D. Rubin, Jr., C. Hugh Holman, P. Albert Duhamel, Irving Malin, Caroline Gordon, Nathan A. Scott, Jr., Sister M. Bernetta Quinn, O.S.F., Harold C. Gardiner, S.J., Melvin J. Friedman, and Bibliography by Lewis A. Lawson.]

Gable, Sister Mariella, o.s.b. "The Ecumenic Core in the Fiction of Flannery O'Connor," *American Benedictine Review,* 15 (June 1964), 127–143.

Griffith, Albert. "Flannery O'Connor," *America,* 113 (November 27, 1965), 674–675.

——. "Flannery O'Connor's Salvation Road," *Studies in Short Fiction,* 3 (Spring 1966), 329–333.

Hyman, Stanley Edgar. FLANNERY O'CONNOR. Minneapolis: University of Minnesota Press, 1966.

McCarthy, John F. "Human Intelligence versus Divine Truth: The Intellectual in Flannery O'Connor's Works," *English Journal,* 55 (December 1966), 1143–1148.

McCown, Robert, s.j. "Flannery O'Connor and the Reality of Sin," *Catholic World,* 188 (January 1959), 285–291.

Marks, W. S., III. "Advertisements for Grace: Flannery O'Connor's 'A Good Man Is Hard to Find,'" *Studies in Short Fiction,* 4 (Fall 1966), 19–27.

Martin, Carter W. THE TRUE COUNTRY: THEMES IN THE FICTION OF FLANNERY O'CONNOR. Nashville, Tenn.: Vanderbilt University Press, 1969.

Merton, Thomas. "Flannery O'Connor," *Jubilee,* 12 (November 1964), 49–53. Reprinted in *Catholic Mind,* 63 (March 1965), 43–45.

Montgomery, Marion. "Miss O'Connor and the Christ-Haunted," *Southern Review,* n.s. 4 (July 1968), 665–672.

——. "O'Connor and Teilhard de Chardin: The Problem of Evil," *Renascence,* 22 (Autumn 1969), 34–42.

Muller, Gilbert H. "Flannery O'Connor and the Catholic Grotesque," *Dissertation Abstracts,* 28 (February 1968), 3193A.

Powers, J. F. "Flannery O'Connor—a Tribute," *Esprit,* 8 (Winter 1964), 40.

Praz, Mario. "Racconti del Sud," *Studi Americani,* No. 2 (1956), 212–218.

Rechnitz, Robert M. "Passionate Pilgrim: Flannery O'Connor's *Wise Blood,*" *Georgia Review,* 19 (Fall 1965), 310–316.

Reiter, Robert E., ed. FLANNERY O'CONNOR. St. Louis: B. Herder, 1968. [Reprinted essays.]

Rubin, Louis D., Jr. "Flannery O'Connor: A Note on Literary Fashions," *Critique,* 2 (Fall 1958), 11–18.

Smith, J. Oates. "Ritual and Violence in Flannery O'Connor," *Thought,* 41 (Winter 1966), 545–560.

Spivey, Ted R. "Flannery O'Connor's View of God and Man," *Studies in Short Fiction,* 1 (Spring 1964), 200–206.

Stelzmann, Rainulf. "Shock and Orthodoxy: An Interpretation of Flannery O'Connor's Novels and Short Stories," *Xavier University Studies,* 2 (March 1963), 4–21.

Sullivan, Walter. "Flannery O'Connor, Sin, and Grace: *Everything That Rises Must Converge,*" *Hollins Critic,* 2 (September 1965), 1–8, 10.

Voss, Victor. "A Study in Sin," *Esprit,* 8 (Winter 1964), 60–63.

Wells, Joel. "Misfits in a Hung-over Biblical Land," *U. S. Catholic,* 31 (July 1965), 62–63.

Evelyn Waugh

(Under General, see Mooney and Staley; Cruise O'Brien; Bayley; Beary; Nicholl; Sonnenfeld, "Twentieth Century Gothic"; Stopp.)

Bradbury, Malcolm. EVELYN WAUGH. Edinburgh and London: Oliver and Boyd, 1964.

Brady, Charles A. "Evelyn Waugh: Shrove Tuesday Motley and Lenten Sackcloth," *Catholic Library World,* 16 (March 1945), 163–177, 189.

Carens, James Francis. THE SATIRIC ART OF EVELYN WAUGH. Seattle: University of Washington Press, 1966.

Cogley, John. "Revisiting Brideshead," *Commonweal,* 80 (April 17, 1964), 103–106.

Corr, Patricia. "Evelyn Waugh: Sanity and Catholicism," *Studies: An Irish Quarterly Review,* 51 (Autumn 1962), 388–399. Reprinted in *Catholic Mind,* 61 (March 1963), 17–22.

De Vitis, A. A. ROMAN HOLIDAY—THE CATHOLIC NOVELS OF EVELYN WAUGH. New York: Bookman Associates, 1956.

Donaldson, Frances. EVELYN WAUGH: PORTRAIT OF A COUNTRY NEIGHBOR. Philadelphia: Chilton, 1968.

Doyle, Paul A. "The Church, History, and Evelyn Waugh," *American Benedictine Review,* 9 (Winter 1958), 202–208.

———. EVELYN WAUGH. Grand Rapids, Mich.: William B. Eerdmans, 1969.

———. "Evelyn Waugh's Attitude Toward Ecumenism," *Twin Circle* (Culver City, Calif.), July 27, 1969, pp. 11–12.

Hardy, John Edward. "*Brideshead Revisited*: God, Man, and Others." In his *Man in the Modern Novel.* Seattle: University of Washington Press, 1964. Pp. 159–174.

Hines, Leo. "Waugh and His Critics," *Commonweal,* 76 (April 13, 1962), 60–63.

Hollis, Christopher. EVELYN WAUGH. London: Longmans, Green, 1954.

Isaacs, Neil D. "Evelyn Waugh's Restoration Jesuit," *Satire Newsletter,* 2 (Spring 1965), 91–94. [Father Rothschild, in *Vile Bodies.*]

James, S. B. "Evelyn Waugh's Apologia," *Missionary,* 44 (December 1930), 415–417.

Jebb, Julian. "Evelyn Waugh: An Interview," *Paris Review,* 30 (Summer–Fall 1963), 73–85. Reprinted in *Writers at Work: The Paris Review Interviews,* 3rd Series. New York: Viking Press, 1967. Pp. 103–114.

Kosok, Heinz. "Evelyn Waugh: A Checklist of Criticism," *Twentieth Century Literature,* 12 (January 1966), 211–215.

———. "Evelyn Waugh: A Supplementary Checklist of Criticism," *Evelyn Waugh Newsletter,* 2 (Spring 1968), 1–3.

O'Donnell, Donat [Conor Cruise O'Brien]. "The Pieties of Evelyn Waugh," *The Bell,* 13 (December 1946), 38–49. [See also T. J. Bannington, "Mr. Waugh's Pieties," *The Bell,* February 1947, pp. 58–63; and Donat O'Donnell, *The Bell,* March 1947, pp. 57–62.]

Ryan, Thomas C. "A Talk With Evelyn Waugh," *The Sign,* 37 (August 1957), 41–43.

Semple, H. E. "Evelyn Waugh's Modern Crusade," *English Studies in Africa,* 11 (March 1968), 47–59.

Spiel, Hilde. "Enfant terrible des Katholizismus." In her *Der Park und die Wildnis: Zur Situation der neueren englischen Literatur.* Munich: C. H. Beck, 1953. Pp. 81–87.

Stopp, Frederick J. EVELYN WAUGH: PORTRAIT OF AN ARTIST. London: Chapman & Hall, 1958.

Wilson, Edmund. " 'Never Apologize, Never Explain': The Art of Evelyn Waugh," *New Yorker,* 20 (March 4, 1944), 75–76, 78, 81. Reprinted in his *Classics and Commercials.* New York: Farrar, Straus, 1950. Pp. 140–146.

Muriel Spark

(Under General, see Jacobsen.)

Baldanza, Frank. "Muriel Spark and the Occult," *Wisconsin Studies in Contemporary Literature,* 6 (Summer 1965), 190–203.

Enright, D. J. "Public Doctrine and Private Judging," *New Statesman,* 70 (October 15, 1965), 563, 566. [Review of *The Mandelbaum Gate.*]

Fay, Bernard. "Muriel Spark en sa fleur," *Nouvelle Revue Française,* 14 (February 1966), 307–315.

Hoyt, Charles Alva. "Muriel Spark: The Surrealist Jane Austen." In Charles Shapiro, ed. *Contemporary British Novelists.* Carbondale: Southern Illinois University Press, 1965. Pp. 125–143.

Hughes, Catharine. Review of *The Bachelors, Catholic World,* 193 (August 1961), 332–333.

Hynes, Samuel. "In the Great Tradition: The Prime of Muriel Spark," *Commonweal,* 75 (February 23, 1962), 562–563, 567–568.

Kermode, Frank. "The Novel as Jerusalem," *Atlantic Monthly,* 216 (October 1965), 92–94, 97–98.

——. "The Prime of Miss Muriel Spark," *New Statesman,* 66 (September 27, 1963), 397–398.

McConkey, James. Review of *The Bachelors, Epoch,* 11 (Spring 1961), 124–125.

Malkoff, Karl. MURIEL SPARK. New York: Columbia University Press, 1968.

Ohmann, Carol B. "Muriel Spark's *Robinson,*" *Critique,* 8 (Fall 1965), 70–84.

Potter, Nancy A. J. "Muriel Spark: Transformer of the Commonplace," *Renascence,* 17 (Spring 1965), 115–120.

Pryce-Jones, Alan. "Doubts About the Human Race," New York *Herald Tribune,* October 5, 1963, p. 7. [Review of *The Girls of Slender Means.*]

Schneider, Harold W. "A Writer in Her Prime: The Fiction of Muriel Spark," *Critique,* 5 (Fall 1962), 28–45.

Stanford, Derek. "The Early Days of Miss Muriel Spark," *The Critic,* 20 (May 1962), 48–53.

——. Letter to the Editor, *Times Literary Supplement,* November 1, 1963, p. 887.

——. MURIEL SPARK—A BIOGRAPHICAL AND CRITICAL STUDY. Fontwell: Centaur Press. 1963.

——. "The Work of Muriel Spark: An Essay on Her Fictional Method," *The Month,* 28 (July 1962), 92–99.

Sullivan, Oona. Review of *The Bachelors, Jubilee,* 8 (March 1961), 47.

Weatherby, W. J. "My Conversion," *Twentieth Century,* 170 (Autumn 1961), 58–63. [Interview.]

Welcher, Jeanne K. "Muriel Spark: Five Joyful Mysteries," *Catholic Book Reporter,* 1 (November/December 1961), 6–7.

Wildman, John Hazard. "Translated by Muriel Spark." In Donald

E. Stanford, ed. *Nine Essays in Modern Literature*. Baton Rouge: Louisiana State University Press, 1965. Pp. 129–144.

Graham Greene

(Under General, see Cruise O'Brien; Gregor and Nicholas; Moeller; Mooney and Staley; Mueller; O'Faolain; O'Malley; Scott, *Craters of the Spirit*; Stratford; Bayley; Beary; Doyle; Flood; Graef; Jacobsen; Kunkel; McNamara; Monroe; Murphy; Nicholl; Sandra; Sheed; Sonnenfeld, "The Catholic Novelist"; Sonnenfeld, "Twentieth Century Gothic"; Stopp; Turnell, "The Religious Novel.")

Allott, Kenneth, and Miriam Farris. THE ART OF GRAHAM GREENE. New York: Russell & Russell, 1963.

Atkins, John. GRAHAM GREENE, rev. ed. London: Calder & Boyars, 1966.

Auden, W. H. "Heresy of Our Time," *Renascence,* 1 (Spring 1949), 23–24.

Barnes, R. J. "Two Modes of Fiction: Hemingway and Greene," *Renascence,* 14 (Summer 1962), 193–198.

Beebe, Maurice. "Criticism of Graham Greene: A Selected Checklist with an Index to Studies of Separate Works," *Modern Fiction Studies,* 3 (Autumn 1957), 281–288.

Bouscaren, Anthony T. "France and Graham Greene versus America and Diem," *Catholic World,* 181 (September 1955), 414–417.

Boyle, Alexander. "Graham Greene," *Irish Monthly,* 77 (November 1949), 519–525.

Cassidy, J. "America and Innocence: Henry James and Graham Greene," *Blackfriars,* 38 (June 1957), 261–267.

Chapman, Raymond. "The Vision of Graham Greene." In Nathan A. Scott, Jr., ed. *Forms of Extremity in the Modern Novel*. Richmond, Va.: John Knox Press, 1965. Pp. 75–94.

Connolly, Francis X. "Inside Modern Man: The Spiritual Adventures of Graham Greene," *Renascence,* 1 (Spring 1949), 16–24.

Currie, John Sheldon. "Supernaturalism in Graham Greene: A Comparison of Orthodox Catholicism with the Religious Vision in the Major Novels," *Dissertation Abstracts,* 28 (February 1968), 3176A–3177A.

De Vitis, A. A. "The Church and Major Scobie," *Renascence,* 10 (Spring 1958), 115–120.

——. GRAHAM GREENE. New York: Twayne, 1964.

Duffy, Joseph M., Jr. "The Lost World of Graham Greene," *Thought,* 33 (Summer 1958), 229–247.

Engel, Claire Eliane. *Esquisses anglaises: Charles Morgan, Graham Greene, T. S. Eliot.* Paris: Éditions Je Sers, 1949.

Evans, Robert O., ed. GRAHAM GREENE—SOME CRITICAL CONSIDERATIONS. Lexington: University of Kentucky Press, 1963. [Reprinted essays by Harvey Curtis Webster, Nathan A. Scott, Jr., Francis L. Kunkel, Dominick P. Consolo, David H. Hesla, A. A. De Vitis, Herbert R. Haber, Robert O. Evans, Kai Laitinen, John Atkins, Miriam Allott, Jacob H. Adler, and Carolyn D. Scott; and Greene Bibliography by Neil Brennan.]

Fowler, Alastair. "Novelist of Damnation," *Theology,* July 1953, pp. 259–264.

Gardiner, Harold C. "Graham Greene, Catholic Shocker," *Renascence,* 1 (Spring 1949), 12–15.

Haber, Herbert R. "The Two Worlds of Graham Greene," *Modern Fiction Studies,* 3 (Autumn 1957), 256–268.

Harmer, Ruth M. "Greene World of Mexico: The Birth of a Novelist," *Renascence,* 15 (Summer 1963), 171–182, 194.

Jonsson, Thorsten. TVA ESSAYER ON GRAHAM GREENE. Stockholm: Norstedt, 1961.

Kenny, Herbert A. "Graham Greene," *Catholic World,* 185 (August 1957), 326–329.

Kohn, Lynette. GRAHAM GREENE—THE MAJOR NOVELS, Stanford Honors Essays in Humanities, No. 4. Stanford, Cal.: Stanford Junior University, 1961. [*Brighton Rock, The Heart of the Matter, The End of the Affair, The Power and the Glory.*]

Kunkel, Francis L. THE LABYRINTHINE WAYS OF GRAHAM GREENE. New York: Sheed & Ward, 1960.

Langlois, José Miguel Ibañez. EL MUNDO PECADOR DE GRAHAM GREENE. Santiago de Chile: Empresa Editora Zig-Zag, 1967.

Lewis, R. W. B. "The Fiction of Graham Greene: Between the Horror and the Glory," *Kenyon Review,* 19 (Winter 1957), 56–75.

——. "Graham Greene: The Religious Affair." In his *The Picaresque Saint.* Philadelphia: J. B. Lippincott, 1959. Pp. 220–274.

Lodge, David. GRAHAM GREENE. New York: Columbia University Press, 1966.

——. "Graham Greene's Comedians," *Commonweal,* 83 (February 18, 1966), 604–606.

Lohf, Kenneth. "Graham Greene and the Problem of Evil," *Catholic World,* 173 (June 1951), 196–199.

Madaule, Jacques. GRAHAM GREENE. Paris: Éditions du temps présent, 1949.

Marian, Sister. "Graham Greene's People: Being and Becoming," *Renascence,* 18 (Autumn 1965), 16–22.

Marković, Vida E. "Graham Greene in Search of God," *Texas Studies in Literature and Language,* 5 (Summer 1963), 271–282.

Matthews, Ronald. MON AMI GRAHAM GREENE. Paris: Desclée de Brouwer, 1957.

Mauriac, François. "La Puissance et la Gloire," *Renascence,* 1 (Spring 1949), 25–27.

Mesnet, Marie-Beatrice. GRAHAM GREENE AND THE HEART OF THE MATTER. London: Cresset Press, 1954.

de Pange, Victor. GRAHAM GREENE. Paris: Éditions Universitaires, 1953.

Prescott, Orville. "Comrade of the Coterie." In his *In My Opinion.* Indianapolis, Ind.: Bobbs-Merrill, 1952. Pp. 92–109.

Pryce-Jones, David. GRAHAM GREENE. New York: Barnes & Noble, 1967.

Rischik, Josef. GRAHAM GREENE UND SEIN WERK. Bern: Verlag A. Francke, 1951.

Rostenne, Paul. GRAHAM GREENE: TÉMOIN DES TEMPS TRAGIQUES. Paris: Juillard, 1949.

Sturzl, Erwin. VON SATAN ZU GOTT: RELIGIÖSE PROBLEME BEI GRAHAM GREENE. Vienna: Graphische Lehr- und Versuchs-Anstalt, 1954.

Traversi, Derek. "Graham Greene," *Twentieth Century,* 149 (March, April 1951), 231–240, 318–328.

Turnell, Martin. GRAHAM GREENE. Grand Rapids, Mich.: William B. Eerdmans, 1967.

Vann, J. Don. GRAHAM GREENE: A CHECKLIST OF CRITICISM. Kent, Ohio: Kent State University Press, 1970.

Wassmer, Thomas A. "Faith and Reason in Graham Greene," *Studies,* 48 (Summer 1959), 163–167.

——. "Graham Greene: A Look at His Sinners," *The Critic,* 18 (January 1960), 16, 72.

——. "The Problem and Mystery of Sin in the Works of Graham Greene," *Christian Scholar,* 43 (Winter 1960), 309–315.

Wichert, Robert A. "The Quality of Graham Greene's Mercy," *College English,* 25 (November 1963), 99–103.

Wyndham, Francis. GRAHAM GREENE. London: Longmans, Green, 1955.

Zabel, Morton Dauwen. "Graham Greene—The Best and the Worst." In his *Craft and Character in Modern Fiction*. New York: Viking Press, 1957. Pp. 276-296.

Georges Bernanos

(Under General, see Brée and Guiton; Cruise O'Brien; Fowlie; Hallen; Levaux; Moeller; O'Faolain; O'Malley; Simon; Zamarriego; Kunkel; Sandra; Sonnenfeld, "The Catholic Novelist"; Sonnenfeld, "Twentieth Century Gothic.")

Aaraas, Hans. À PROPOS DU "JOURNAL D'UN CURÉ DE CAMPAGNE": ESSAI SUR L'ÉCRIVAIN ET LE PRÊTRE DANS L'OEUVRE ROMANESQUE DE BERNANOS. Paris: Lettres Modernes, 1966.

——. GEORGES BERNANOS. Oslo: Gyldendal, 1959.

Albérès, René Marill. "Bernanos ou l'homme déchiré." In his *La Révolte des écrivains d'aujourd'hui*. Paris: Corrêa, 1949. Pp. 86–121.

von Balthasar, Hans Urs. LE CHRÉTIEN BERNANOS. Tr. Maurice de Gandillac. Paris: Éditions du Seuil, 1956.

——. "L'Oeuvre de Bernanos et l'église dans ce temps," *La Table Ronde*, No. 100 (April 1956), 58–71.

Beaumont, E. "The Vision of Georges Bernanos," *The Month,* 16 (August 1956), 92–99.

Béguin, Albert. BERNANOS PAR LUI-MÊME. Paris: Éditions du Seuil, 1954.

Bernian, Daniel, F.S.C. "The Mystery of Charity and the Novelist Georges Bernanos," *Four Quarters,* 9 (January 1960), 6–12.

Blumenthal, Gerda. THE POETIC IMAGINATION OF GEORGES BERNANOS. Baltimore, Md.: Johns Hopkins Press, 1965.

Bridel, Yves. L'ESPRIT D'ENFANCE DANS L'OEUVRE ROMANESQUE DE GEORGES BERNANOS. Paris: M. J. Minard, 1966.

Brodin, Pierre. "Georges Bernanos." In his *Maîtres et témoins de l'entre-deux guerres*. Montreal: Éditions Valiquette, 1943. Pp. 185–199.

Burkhard, Willy. LA GENÈSE DE L'IDÉE DU MAL DANS L'OEUVRE ROMANESQUE DE GEORGES BERNANOS. Zürich: Juris Verlag, 1967.

Bush, William. L'ANGOISSE DU MYSTÈRE: ESSAI SUR BERNANOS ET MONSIEUR OUINE. Paris: M. J. Minard, 1966.

——. SOUFFRANCE ET EXPIATION DANS LA PENSÉE DE BERNANOS. Paris: M. J. Minard, 1962.

Chaigne, Louis. GEORGES BERNANOS, 3rd ed. Paris: Éditions Universitaires, 1960.

Debluë, Henri. LES ROMANS DE GEORGES BERNANOS OU LE DÉFI DU RÊVE. Neuchâtel: La Baconnière, 1965.

Demorest, Jean-Jacques. "Le Roman surnaturaliste de Bernanos," *Symposium,* 10 (Spring 1956), 75–83.

Dreyfus, Dina. "Imposture et authenticité dans l'oeuvre de Bernanos," *Mercure de France,* 316 (September 1, 1952), 30–51.

Estang, Luc. PRÉSENCE DE BERNANOS. Paris: Plon, 1947.

Estève, Michel. BERNANOS. Paris: Gallimard, 1965.

de Fabrìgues, Jean. BERNANOS TEL QU'IL ÉTAIT. Tours: Mame, 1963.

Fabretti, Nazareno. "Bernanos e il mistero della salvezza," *Humanitas,* 19 (January 1964), 58–73.

Falk, Eugene H. "The Leap to Faith: Two Paths to the Scaffold," *Symposium,* 21 (Fall 1967), 241–254. [Bernanos and Gertrud von Le Fort.]

Fay, Bernard. "Georges Bernanos, ou l'indignation créatrice." In his *L'École de l'imprécation ou les prophètes Catholiques du dernier siècle (1850–1950).* Paris: E. Vitte, 1961. Pp. 145–218.

Fragnière, Marie Agnès. BERNANOS FIDÈLE À L'ENFANT. Fribourg: Éditions Universitaires, 1963.

Fraigneux, Maurice. "Il y a dix ans mourait Georges Bernanos," *Revue Générale Belge,* 6 (June 1958), 46–64.

Frohock, W. M. "Georges Bernanos and His Priest-Hero," *Yale French Studies,* No. 12 (1953), 54–61.

Gaucher, Guy. GEORGES BERNANOS OU L'INVINCIBLE ESPÉRANCE. Paris: Librairie Plon, 1962.

———. LE THÈME DE LA MORT DANS LES ROMANS DE GEORGES BERNANOS, rev. ed. Paris: M. J. Minard, 1967.

Gillespie, Jessie Lynn. LE TRAGIQUE DANS L'OEUVRE DE GEORGES BERNANOS. Paris: M. J. Minard, 1960.

Grégor, Paul. LA CONSCIENCE DU TEMPS CHEZ GEORGES BERNANOS. Zürich: Juris Verlag, 1966.

Halda, Bernard. BERNANOS—LE SCANDALE DE CROIRE. Paris: Éditions du Centurion, 1965.

Hatzfeld, Helmut. "Georges Bernanos, 1888–1948," *Thought,* 23 (September 1948), 405–424.

Hebblethwaite, Peter. BERNANOS: AN INTRODUCTION. New York: Hillary House, 1965.

Hofer, Hermann. "Georges Bernanos: Der Dichter einer neuen Welt," *Schweizer Rundschau,* 60 (January 1961), 565–575.

von Holthusen, Hans Egon. "Bernanos als Dichter der Kirche," *Hochland,* 48 (February 1956), 267–278.

Jennings, E. "Vision of Joy: A Study of Georges Bernanos," *Blackfriars*, 40 (August 1959), 291–298.

Judrin, Roger. "Georges Bernanos et le dragon," *Nouvelle Revue Française*, 10 (March 1962), 503–506.

Lefèvre, Frédéric. GEORGES BERNANOS. Paris: Édition de la Tour d'Ivoire, 1926.

———. "Georges Bernanos." In his *Une heure avec . . .* , 4th series. Paris: Gallimard, 1927. Pp. 157–177.

Macchi, Pasquale. BERNANOS E IL PROBLEMA DEL MALE. Varese: La Lucciola, 1959.

Marie Céleste, Sister. BERNANOS ET SON OPTIQUE DE LA VIE CHRÉTIENNE. Paris: Nizet, 1967.

———. "Bernanos: A Man of Spirit," *Culture*, 21 (December 1960), 413–418.

———. LE SENS DE L'AGONIE DANS L'OEUVRE DE GEORGES BERNANOS: ESSAI D'ANALYSE PHÉNOMÉNOLOGIQUE SUR L'AGONIE DU MONDE MODERNE. Paris: P. Lethielleux, 1962.

Milner, Max. GEORGES BERNANOS. Paris: Desclée de Brouwer, 1967.

Moch, Léa Rosalie. LA SAINTETÉ DANS LES ROMANS DE GEORGES BERNANOS. Paris: Société d'édition "Les belles lettres," 1962.

Müggler, Rosemarie. DIE MENSCHLICHEN BEZIEHUNGEN IM WERKE VON GEORGES BERNANOS. Winterthur: P. G. Keller, 1960.

Noth, Ernst Erich. "The Prophetism of Georges Bernanos," *Yale French Studies*, No. 2 (1949), 105–119.

O'Sharkey, Eithne M. "Bernanos and the Carmelite Martyrs," *Dublin Review*, 240 (Summer 1966), 181–189.

———. "Portraits of the Clergy in Bernanos' *Diary of a Country Priest*," *Dublin Review*, 239 (Summer 1965), 183–191.

Padberg, Magdalena. DAS ROMANWERK VON GEORGES BERNANOS ALS VISION DES UNTERGANGS. Hamburg: Cram, de Gruyter, 1963.

Pézéril, Daniel. "Bernanos a-t-il copié Gertrud von le Fort?" *Figaro Littéraire*, 25 (April 1959), 6.

Picon, Gaëtan. GEORGES BERNANOS. Paris: R. Marin, 1948.

———. "Sur Bernanos romancier," *Mercure de France*, 343 (November 1961), 385–404.

Raymond Marie, Sister. "La Simplicité des humbles et des petits," *Culture*, 20 (September 1959), 315–336.

Reck, Rima Drell. "Georges Bernanos: A Novelist and His Art," *French Review*, 38 (April 1965), 619–629.

Rousseaux, André. "Georges Bernanos, ou l'homme vrai." In his *Âmes* *et visages du XXe siècle.* Paris: Éditions Bernard Grasset, 1932. Pp. 298–312.

Scheidegger, Jean. GEORGES BERNANOS, ROMANCIER. Neuchâtel: V. Attinger, 1956.

Schultheiss, Reinhold. DIE FREUDE IM WERK VON GEORGES BERNANOS. Tübingen: Präzis, 1966.

Simon, Pierre-Henri. "Bernanos et le saint." In his *Les Témoins de l'homme—La Condition humaine dans la littérature du XXe siècle.* Paris: Petite Bibliothèque Payot, 1966. Pp. 137–160.

Thérive, André. "Bernanos ou le flagellant." In his *Moralistes de ce temps.* Paris: Amiot-Dumont, 1948. Pp. 251–276.

Tilliette, Xavier. "Bernanos et Gertrud von le Fort," *Études,* 300 (March 1959), 353–360.

Ulanov, Barry. "Our Church Is the Church of the Saints," *Today,* 11 (January 1956), 30–32.

Vier, Jacques. "*Sous le soleil de Satan,* de Georges Bernanos." In his *Littérature à l'emporte-pièce.* Paris: Éditions du Cèdre, 1958. Pp. 170–182.

François Mauriac

(Under General, see Brée and Guiton; Cruise O'Brien; Fowlie, "Catholic Orientation . . ."; Fowlie, *Clowns and Angels*; Gregor and Nicholas; Hallen; Levaux; O'Faolain; O'Malley; Simon; Stratford; Zamarriego; Doyle; Graef; Kunkel; Monroe; Sonnenfeld, "The Catholic Novelist"; Turnell, "The Religious Novel.")

Beltrán de Heredia, Benito, O.F.M. FRANÇOIS MAURIAC—O TRAS LAS HUELLAS DEL INFINITO. Madrid: Editorial Cisneros, 1959.

Blanchet, A. "À François Mauriac," *Études,* 311 (October 1961), 61–64.

Brown, J. L. "François Mauriac and the Catholic Novel," *Catholic World,* 149 (April 1939), 36–41.

Cormeau, Nelly. L'ART DE FRANÇOIS MAURIAC. Paris: Grasset, 1951.

D'Souza, Jerome. "What Constitutes a Catholic Novelist? A Study of François Mauriac," *The Month,* 158 (October 1931), 315–326.

Du Bos, Charles. FRANÇOIS MAURIAC ET LE PROBLÈME DU ROMANCIER CATHOLIQUE. Paris: R.- A. Corrêa, 1933.

Fillon, Amelie. FRANÇOIS MAURIAC. Paris: Société française d'éditions littéraires et techniques, 1936.

Fincato, Giovanni. "Umanità di Mauriac," *Humanitas,* 13 (March 1958), 227–229.

Finn, James. "Mauriac," *Jubilee,* 11 (February 1964), 45–51.

——. "Under the Eye of God—Reflections of Mauriac," *Commonweal,* 73 (March 17, 1960), 633–635.

Flower, J. E. "François Mauriac and Social Catholicism: An Episode in *L'enfant chargé de chaînes,*" *French Studies,* 21 (April 1967), 125–138.

Gallant, Clifford J. "La mère dans l'oeuvre de François Mauriac," *Kentucky Foreign Language Quarterly,* 11 (Number 2, 1964), 79–85.

Granfield, D. "François Mauriac and Theology," *American Ecclesiastical Review,* 140 (March 1959), 182–187.

Hourdin, Georges. MAURIAC, ROMANCIER CHRÉTIEN, 2nd ed. Paris: Éditions du temps présent, 1945.

Jarrett-Kerr, Martin. FRANÇOIS MAURIAC. New Haven, Conn.: Yale University Press, 1954.

Jenkins, Cecil. MAURIAC. New York: Barnes & Noble, 1965.

Jerome, Sister M. "Human and Divine Love in Dante and Mauriac," *Renascence,* 18 (Summer 1966), 176–184.

Krug, Justine, "François Mauriac and the Drama of the Catholic Novelist," *Catholic World,* 181 (July 1955), 262–267.

Landry, Sister Anne Gertrude. REPRESENTED DISCOURSE IN THE NOVELS OF FRANÇOIS MAURIAC. Washington, D.C.: Catholic University of America Press, 1953.

Majault, Joseph. MAURIAC ET L'ART DU ROMAN. Paris: R. Laffont, 1946.

Moloney, Michael F. FRANÇOIS MAURIAC—A CRITICAL STUDY. Denver: Alan Swallow, 1958.

——. "François Mauriac: The Way of Pascal," *Thought,* 32 (Autumn 1957), 389–408.

——. "Time and François Mauriac," *Blackfriars,* 38 (April 1957), 171–177.

North, Robert J. LE CATHOLICISME DANS L'ŒUVRE DE FRANÇOIS MAURIAC. Paris: Éditions du Conquistador, 1950. [Includes also, pp. ix–xlvi, "Quelques réflexions sur l'état présent de la littérature catholique," by Gaétan Bernoville.]

Palante, Alain. MAURIAC, LE ROMAN ET LA VIE. Paris: Le Portulan, 1946.

Pell, Elsie Estelle. FRANÇOIS MAURIAC—IN SEARCH OF THE INFINITE. New York: Philosophical Library, 1947.

Rideau, Émile. COMMENT LIRE FRANÇOIS MAURIAC. Paris: Éditions "Aux étudiants de France," 1945.

Robichon, Jacques. FRANÇOIS MAURIAC. Paris: Éditions Universitaires, 1953.

de Sacy, Samuel Silvestre. L'OEUVRE DE FRANÇOIS MAURIAC. Paris: P. Hartmann, 1927.

Schwarzenbach, James. DER DICHTER ZWIESPÄLTIGEN LEBENS F. MAURIAC. Cologne: Benzinger, 1938.

Simon, Pierre-Henri. FRANÇOIS MAURIAC PAR LUI-MÊME. Paris: Éditions du Seuil, 1953.

Srinivasa, Iyengar, K.R. FRANÇOIS MAURIAC, NOVELIST AND MORALIST. Bombay: Asia Publishing House, 1963.

Stansbury, Milton H. "François Mauriac." In his *French Novelists of Today*. Philadelphia: University of Pennsylvania Press, 1935. Pp. 33–51.

Stoker, J. T. "The Question of Grace in Mauriac's Novels," *Culture,* 26 (September 1965), 288–302.

Stratford, Philip. "One Meeting With Mauriac," *Kenyon Review,* 21 (Autumn 1959), 611–622. [Interview.]

Turnell, Martin. "The Style of François Mauriac: Sin and the Novelist," *Twentieth Century,* 164 (September 1958), 242–253.

Vial, Fernand. "François Mauriac Criticism: A Bibliographical Study," *Thought,* 27 (Summer 1952), 235–260.

Vier, Jacques. FRANÇOIS MAURIAC, ROMANCIER CATHOLIQUE? Paris: Épuisé, 1935.

Julien Green

(Under General, see Brée and Guiton; Moeller.)

Bernier, Fernand. "Le Sentiment religieux chez Julien Green (d'après ses ouvrages)," *Revue de l'Université Laval,* 17 (January 1963), 420–444; 17 (February 1963), 520–538; 17 (March 1963), 611–633; 17 (April 1963), 716–730.

Brisville, Jean-Claude. À LA RECONTRE DE JULIEN GREEN. Brussels: La Sixaine, 1947.

Brock, Ignatius W. "Julien Green: A Biographical and Literary Sketch," *French Review,* 23 (March 1950), 347–359.

——. "Julien Green: A French Novelist With a Southern Background," *Emory University Quarterly,* 1 (March 1945), 31–43.

——. "Julien Green: The Mood and Style of His Novels," *Emory University Quarterly,* 1 (December 1945), 259–264.

Brodin, Pierre. JULIEN GREEN. Paris: Éditions Universitaires, 1957.

Cabanis, José. "Julien Green et le Royaume de Dieu," *La Table Ronde,* 172 (May 1962), 53–59.

Carrel, Janine. L'EXPÉRIENCE DU SEUIL DANS L'OEUVRE DE JULIEN GREEN. Zürich: Juris Verlag, 1967.

Eigeldinger, Marc. JULIEN GREEN ET LA TENTATION DE L'IRRÉEL. Paris: Éditions des Portes de France, 1947.

Fongaro, Antoine. L'EXISTENCE DANS LES ROMANS DE JULIEN GREEN. Rome: Signorelli, 1955.

Fowlie, Wallace. "Julien Green," *Ramparts,* 1 (March 1963), 82–90.

Gorkine, Michel. JULIEN GREEN—ESSAI. Paris: Nouvelles Éditions Debresse, 1956.

de Gruson-Karplus, Anne. "Esthétique de l'imaginaire dans les romans de Julien Green," *French Review,* 35 (May 1962), 539–545.

van Itterbeek, Eugène. "Het dagboek van Julien Green," *Dietsche Warande en Belfort,* 107 (January 1962), 56–64.

——. "Julien Greens geheim," *Dietsche Warande en Belfort,* 111 (December 1966), 770–782.

Kanters, Robert. "Julien Green," *Revue de Paris,* 71 (August–September 1964), 129–136.

Keating, L. Clark. "Julien Green and Nathaniel Hawthorne," *French Review,* 28 (May 1955), 485–492.

Koella, Charles E. "La Puissance du rêve chez Julien Green," *PMLA,* 54 (June 1939), 597–607.

Kohler, Dayton. "Julian [*sic*] Green: Modern Gothic," *Sewanee Review,* 40 (April 1932), 139–148.

Lauresne, Henri. *Deux romanciers de la solitude morale: George Eliot et Julien Green.* Paris: Le Rouge et le Noir, 1928.

Ottensmeyer, Hilary. "Julien Green and His Search for Truth," *American Benedictine Review,* 18 (September 1967), 325–337.

Poulet, Georges. "L'univers double de Julien Green," *Preuves,* 200 (October 1967), 18–33.

Prévost, Jean-Laurent. JULIEN GREEN OU L'ÂME ENGAGÉE. Paris: Éditions E. Vitte, 1960.

Rose, Marilyn Gaddis. "The Production of Julien Green: Microcosm of Mid-Century Writing," *French Review,* 34 (December 1960), 164–169.

Sémolué, Jean. JULIEN GREEN OU L'OBSESSION DU MAL. Paris: Éditions du Centurion, 1964.

Stokes, Samuel Emlen. JULIEN GREEN AND THE THORN OF PURITANISM. New York: King's Crown Press, 1955.

Elisabeth Langgässer

Augsberger, Eva. ELISABETH LANGGÄSSER: ASSOZIATIVE REIHUNG, LEITMOTIV UND SYMBOL IN IHREN PROSAWERKEN. Nuremberg: Carl, 1962.

Behrsing, Gert. ERZÄHLFORM UND WELTSCHAU DER ELISABETH LANGGÄSSER. Zürich & Munich: Montana, 1957.

Blume, Bernhard. "Kreatur und Element: Zur Metaphorik in Elisabeth Langgässers Roman *Das unauslöschliche Siegel*," *Euphorion*, 48 (Heft 1, 1954), 71–89.

Broch, Hermann. " 'The Indelible Seal': A German Novel of the Pilgrimage of Faith," *Commentary*, 10 (August 1950), 170–174.

De Nichiló, Maria. "Letteratura e vita: Elisabeth Langgässer," *Humanitas*, 13 (June 1958), 478–483.

Grenzmann, Wilhelm. "Elisabeth Langgässer—Die Element und der Logos." In his *Dichtung und Glaube*. Bonn: Athenäum Verlag, 1950. Pp. 193–216.

Hardenbruch, Ilse. DER ROMAN 'DAS UNAUSLÖSCHLICHE SIEGEL' IM DICHTERISCHEN WERK ELISABETH LANGGÄSSERS: EIN BEITRAG ZUR FORM DES MODERNEN RELIGIÖSEN ROMANS. Düsseldorf: Triltsch, 1962.

Menck, S. "Elisabeth Langgässer," *Commonweal*, 52 (September 22, 1950), 579–580.

Politzer, Heinz. "*The Indelible Seal* of Elisabeth Langgässer," *Germanic Review*, 27 (October 1952), 200–209.

Reid, J. C. "The Novels of Elisabeth Langgässer," *Downside Review*, 78 (Spring 1960), 117–127.

Riley, Anthony W. "Elisabeth Langgässer and Juan Donoso Cortés: A Source of the 'Turm-Kapitel' in *Das unauslöschliche Siegel*," *PMLA*, 83 (May 1968), 357–367.

Rinser, Luise. "In Memory of Elisabeth Langgässer," tr. John Michalski, *Renascence*, 13 (Spring 1961), 139–142.

Storz, Gerhard. "Elisabeth Langgässer." In Hermann Friedman and Otto Mann, eds. *Deutsche Literatur im 20. Jahrhundert*, Vol. II. Heidelberg: Wolfgang Rothe Verlag, 1961. Pp. 245–259.

Carmen Laforet

Alborg, Juan Luis. "Carmen Laforet." In his *Hora actual de la novela española*. Madrid: Taurus, 1958. Vol. I, pp. 131–141.

Ayala, Francisco. "Testimonio de la nada," *Realidad,* 1 (January–February 1947), 129–132.

Cano, José Luis. Review of *La isla y los demonios, Insula,* 7, No. 77 (May 15, 1952), 6–7.

——. Review of *La llamada, Insula,* 9, No. 108 (December 15, 1954), 6–7.

"Carmen Laforet," *Insula,* 116 (August 1955), 2.

Castillo Puche, J. " 'La isla y los demonios,' segunda novela y segundo éxito de Carmen Laforet," *Cuadernos Hispanoamericanos,* 30 (June 1952), 384–386.

DeCoster, Cyrus C. "Carmen Laforet: A Tentative Evaluation," *Hispania,* 40 (May 1957), 187–191.

Eoff, Sherman. "*Nada,* by Carmen Laforet: A Venture in Mechanistic Dynamics," *Hispania,* 35 (May 1952), 207–211.

Foster, David William. "*Nada,* de Carmen Laforet," *Revista Hispánica Moderna,* 32 (January–April 1966), 43–55.

García-López, J. "Carmen Laforet." In his *Historia de la Literatura Española.* New York: Las Americas, 1964. P. 677.

García-Viñó, M. "Carmen Laforet: La mujer antigua y la mujer nueva." In his *Novela española actual.* Madrid: Guadarrama, 1967. Pp. 75–95.

Hornedo, Rafael M.ª de. "*La mujer nueva* [de Carmen Laforet]," *Razón y Fe,* 156 (September–October 1957), 166–176.

Horrent, J. "L'Oeuvre romanesque de Carmen Laforet," *Revue des Langues Vivantes,* 25 (May–June 1959), 179–187.

Hoyos, Antonio de. "El arte literario de Carmen Laforet." In his *Ocho escritores actuales.* Murcia: Aula de Cultura, 1954. Pp. 21–56.

Micó Buchón, José Luis, s.j. "El hombre viejo y la mujer nueva," *Cristianidad,* No. 13 (November 1956), 303–304.

Murillo Rubiera, Jaime. "Al margen de un libro de Carmen Laforet: *Paulina o la sinceridad,*" *Cuadernos Hispanoamericanos,* No. 76 (April 1956), 114–117.

Nora, Eugenio G. de. *La novela española contemporánea (1927–1960).* Madrid: Gredos, 1962. Vol. II, pp. 147–155.

Roig, Rosendo, s.j. "El primer 'Premio Menorca': Leyendo *La mujer nueva* de Carmen Laforet," *Razón y Fe,* 153 (May 1956), 699–703.

Torrente Ballester, Gonzalo. *Panorama de la literatura española contemporánea.* Madrid: Guadarrama, 1956. Vol. I, pp. 423–424.

Vásquez Zamora, Rafael. "The Appearance of Carmen Laforet on the Spanish Literary Scene," *Books Abroad,* 30 (Summer 1956), 394–395.

Vázquez Dodero, J. L. "Lo humano y lo divino en *La mujer nueva*," *Nuestro Tiempo*, No. 20 (February 1956), 101–104.

Giovanni Papini

Allodoli, Ettore. "Giovanni Papini," *Italia che Scrive*, 40 (September 1957), 157–160.

Apollonio, Mario. PAPINI. Padua: Adam, 1944.

Bargellini, Piero. GIOVANNI PAPINI. Verona: M. Bettinelli, 1956.

Basane, Agustin. "Giovanni Papini," *La Nuova Democrazia*, 40 (October 1960), 34–37.

Brophy, L. "The Violence of Giovanni Papini," *Friar*, 7 (May 1957), 6–10.

Casnati, Francesco. PAPINI OPERAIO DELLA VIGNA. Como: Sagsa, 1956.

Cossio del Pomar, Felipe. "Papini." In his *Con los luiscadores del camino*. Madrid: Ediciones ulises, 1932. Pp. 135–150.

De Mattei, Rodolfo. "La 'catilinaria' di Giovanni Papini," *Capitolium*, 38 (November 1963), 554–557.

Deidda, Antonio. "Note sul Lessico di Giovanni Papini," *Lingua Nostra*, 18 (June 1957), 42–48.

Fatone, Vicente. "El Hombre: Papini." In his *Misticismo Épico*. Mexico: Ediciones Especiales, 1928. Pp. 15–49.

Fondi, Renato. UN COSTRUTTORE: GIOVANNI PAPINI. Florence: Vallecchi Editore, 1922.

di Franca, N. Mario. GIOVANNI PAPINI—PANORAMA BIOGRAFICO E CRITICO. Modena: Edizioni Paoline, 1958.

Franchini, Vittorio. PAPINI INTIMO. Bologna: Cappelli, 1957.

Frigessi, Delia. "Per un giudizio sul Papini," *Il Ponte*, 12 (August–September 1956), 1405–1413.

Gallo, Ugo. "Giovanni Papini," *Cuadernos Hispanoamericanos*, 30 (January 1957), 123–128.

Girardi, Enzo N. " 'Giudizio Universale' di Papini," *Vita e Pensiero*, 41 (January 1958), 53–56.

Golino, Carlo L. "Giovanni Papini and American Pragmatism," *Italica*, 32 (March 1955), 38–47.

Gozzini, Mario. "Il sogno ultimo di Papini," *L'Ultima*, 9 (Nos. 81–83, 1956), 252–256.

Grana, Gianni. "Papini dopo il *Giudizio*," *Letterature Moderne*, 11 (March–April 1961), 220–231.

Gullace, Giovanni. "Giovanni Papini and the Redemption of the Devil," *The Personalist*, 43 (Spring 1962), 233–252.

——. "Giovanni Papini e il diavolo," *Italica,* 33 (No. 3, 1956), 193–204.

Horia, Vintila. GIOVANNI PAPINI. Paris: Wesmael-Charlier, 1963.

Iriarte, Joaquín. "Papini y sus modos de intelectual florentino," *Razón y Fe,* 155 (February 1957), 111–122.

James, William. "Giovanni Papini and the Pragmatist Movement in Italy," *The Journal of Philosophy, Psychology and Scientific Method,* 3 (June 21, 1906), 337–341.

Lisi, Nicola. "Spiritualità di Giovanni Papini," *Fiera Letteraria,* 11 (November 25, 1956), 5.

Lovreglio, Janvier. "Giovanni Papini," *Revue des Études Italiennes,* n.s. 3 (October–December 1956), 315–338.

——. "Umanità di Papini," *Fiera Letteraria,* 11 (November 25, 1956), 6.

Maranzana, Mother Clelia. "Papini: Warrior at Rest," *Catholic World,* 186 (October 1957), 45–49.

Mignon, Maurice. "Giovanni Papini," *La Table Ronde,* Nos. 117–120 (September 1957), 171–179.

Mondrone, Domenico. "Diario di Papini," *Civiltà Cattolica,* 114 (May 18, 1963), 354–362.

Montagna, Gianni. "Papini: L'Homme, son oeuvre, son évolution spirituelle," *Les Lettres Romanes,* 12 (February 1, 1958), 19–34.

Palmieri, Enzo. INTERPRETAZIONI DEL MIO TEMPO: I. GIOVANNI PAPINI. Florence: Vallecchi Editore, 1927.

Passerone, Maurizio. GIOVANNI PAPINI: METODO DI UNA SCRITTURA E DI UN'ANIMA: APPUNTI. Genoa: Arti grafiche San Giorgio, 1966.

Prezzolini, Giuseppe. GIOVANNI PAPINI. Turin: Piero Gobetti, 1924.

Ridolfi, Roberto. VITA DI GIOVANNI PAPINI. Milan: A. Mondadori, 1957.

Ruschioni, Ada. "Nell' anniversario della Morte di Papini–Gianfalco–Frate Lupo–Fra Bonaventura," *Vita e Pensiero,* 60 (August 1957), 546–559.

Santucci, Luigi. "Papini maestro," *L'Ultima,* 9 (Nos. 81–83, 1956), 257–264.

Vettori, Vittorio. GIOVANNI PAPINI. Turin: Borla, 1967.

Viviani, Alberto. LA MASCHERA DELL' ORCO: L'INTIMA VITA DI GIOVANNI PAPINI. Milan: Bietti, 1955.

Wilson, Lawrence A. "A Possible Original of Papini's Dottor Alberto Rego," *Italica,* 38 (December 1961), 296–301.

Index

269